PRAISE FOR
THE SCIENCE WRITERS' HANDBOOK:

"At its best, science writing weaves together quests for knowledge, personal struggles, rivalry and conflicts, and moments of great insight to reveal how science works and why it matters. This book shows you how to write science stories that count." —**Siri Carpenter, senior editor,** *Discover Magazine,* **and cofounder of** *The Open Notebook*

"In a world growing ever more complex, people with a talent to explain are in demand. Nowhere is this truer than in science writing—a field that is entering a vibrant new age. Whether you're a beginner or a veteran, these reports from the frontline provide an invaluable guide." —**George Johnson, author of** *The Cancer Chronicles: Unlocking Medicine's Deepest Mystery* **and cofounder and director of the Santa Fe Science Writing Workshop**

"What happens when more than 30 freelance writers come together to build something? You get a smart, compelling, and, most of all, helpful book filled with tips, ideas, and insights that only 300+ years of combined experience could make possible. It doesn't get much better than freelancers helping freelancers." —**Sara Horowitz, founder of the Freelancers Union and author of** *The Freelancer's Bible*

"Science is replete with moving, profound and important stories. But the art and craft of telling those stories is complex: it takes more than desire to become a science writer. *The Science Writers' Handbook* is a fabulous book: it uses real writers' experiences to show those who want to tell science stories how to do so." —**Jay Ingram, cofounder and chair of the Banff Centre Science Communications Program and author of** *Fatal Flaws: How a Misfolded Protein Baffled Scientists and Changed the Way We Look at the Brain*

• JILL U ADAMS • MONYA BAKER • JENNIFER CUTRARO • HELEN FIELDS • DOUGLAS FOX • ROBERT FREDERICK • ALISON FROMME • EMILY GERTZ • VIRGINIA GEWIN • LIZA GROSS • THOMAS HAYDEN • ADAM HINTERTHUER • HANNAH HOAG • EMMA MARRIS • JESSICA MARSHALL • AMANDA MASCARELLI • ROBIN MEJIA • SUSAN MORAN • BRYN NELSON • MICHELLE NIJHUIS • STEPHEN ORNES • KENDALL POWELL • HILLARY ROSNER • ANNE SASSO • MARK SCHROPE • EMILY SOHN • GISELA TELIS • BRIAN VASTAG • ANDREAS VON BUBNOFF • CAMERON WALKER • SARAH WEBB •

THE
SCIENCE
WRITERS'
HANDBOOK

Everything
You Need to Know
to Pitch, Publish,
and Prosper in
the Digital Age

The
Writers *of* SciLance
Edited by
Thomas Hayden
and Michelle Nijhuis

Da Capo
LIFE
LONG

DA CAPO LIFELONG BOOKS
A Member of the Perseus Books Group

Designed by Cynthia Young

Library of Congress Cataloging-in-Publication Data
    The science writers' handbook : everything you need to know to pitch, publish, and prosper in the digital age / the writers of SciLance, edited by Thomas Hayden, Michelle Nijhuis.—First Da Capo Press edition.
        pages cm
    Includes bibliographical references and index.
    ISBN 978-0-7382-1656-0 (pbk.)—ISBN 978-0-7382-1657-7 (e-book)
    1. Technical writing.   I. Hayden, Thomas C., editor of compilation.
II. Nijhuis, Michelle, editor of compilation. III. SciLance (Firm)
T11.S35 2013
808.06'65—dc23
                                                    2013000128

Published by Da Capo Press
A Member of the Perseus Books Group
www.dacapopress.com

This project was funded in part by a grant from the National Association of Science Writers. Reference to any specific commercial product, process, or service does not necessarily constitute or imply its endorsement of or recommendation by the National Association of Science Writers, and any views and opinions expressed herein do not necessarily reflect those of the National Association of Science Writers.

Da Capo Press books are available at special discounts for bulk purchases in the U.S. by corporations, institutions, and other organizations. For more information, please contact the Special Markets Department at the Perseus Books Group, 2300 Chestnut Street, Suite 200, Philadelphia, PA, 19103, or call (800) 810-4145, ext. 5000, or e-mail special.markets@perseusbooks.com.

10 9 8 7 6 5 4 3 2 1

CONTENTS

Foreword by Kendall Powell, ix

PART I
THE SKILLED SCIENCE WRITER

1 What Makes a Science Writer? *by Alison Fromme,* 3

2 Finding Ideas *by Emily Sohn,* 9

3 Making the Pitch *by Thomas Hayden,* 23
   Box: Classic Mistakes We Can All Avoid *by Monya Baker,* 32
   Box: Pitching Endurance *by Douglas Fox,* 33
   Box: A Tale of Two Query Letters *by Thomas Hayden,* 36

4 Getting the Story, and Getting It Right
   by Andreas von Bubnoff, 40
   Box: Making a Reporting Plan, 48
   Box: A Science Writer's Emergency Question List, 49
   Box: On and Off the Record, 50
   Box: "So When Can I Read Your Draft?" 51

5 By the Numbers: Essential Statistics for Science Writers
   by Stephen Ornes, 53

6 Excavating the Evidence: Reporting for Narrative
   by Douglas Fox, 59
   Box: Who Pays for Travel? 71

7 Sculpting the Story *by Michelle Nijhuis,* 75
Box: Story Anatomy, 84

8 Working with Editors—and Their Edits *by Monya Baker and Jessica Marshall,* 87

9 Going Long: How to Sell a Book *by Emma Marris,* 99
Box: Sample Query Letter, 112
Box: The Six Steps to Authorship, 114

10 Multilancing *by Robert Frederick,* 116

11 Just Write the Friggin' Thing Already! *by Anne Sasso,* 123
Box: Thirty Books in Thirty Days *by Emily Sohn,* 130

PART II
THE SANE SCIENCE WRITER

12 The Loneliness of the Science Writer *by Stephen Ornes,* 137

13 Good Luck Placing This Elsewhere: How to Cope with Rejection *by Hillary Rosner,* 142

14 Beyond Compare *by Michelle Nijhuis,* 149
Box: Measuring Success in a World Without Performance Reviews *by Alison Fromme,* 154

15 An Experimental Guide to Achieving Balance *by Virginia Gewin,* 157
Box: How the &%@ Do I Take a Real Vacation? 163
Box: Balance, Schmalance *by Liza Gross,* 165

16 Creating Creative Spaces *by Hannah Hoag,* 167

17 Avoiding Domestic Disasters *by Bryn Nelson,* 175

18 Children and Deadlines: A Messy Rodeo *by Amanda Mascarelli,* 183

PART III
THE SOLVENT SCIENCE WRITER

19   Minding the Business *by Anne Sasso and Emily Gertz*, 195

20   Networking for the Nervous *by Cameron Walker*, 215
Box: The Introvert's Survival Guide for Conference
Cocktail Parties, 221

21   Paid to Grow *by Robin Mejia*, 223

22   Contract Literacy *by Mark Schrope*, 230
Box: Time and Money: Can I Afford This Project?
by Stephen Ornes, 244

23   The Ethical Science Writer *by Brian Vastag*, 246
Box: The Journalism-Promotion Divide *by Helen Fields*, 256

24   Social Networks and the Reputation Economy
by Emily Gertz, 259
Box: Blogging: My Digital Calling Card *by Sarah Webb*, 265

25   The Diversity of Science Writing *by Sarah Webb*, 267

26   Sustainable Science Writing *by Jill U Adams*, 273

Afterword: Finding, or Founding, Your Own Tribe
by Kendall Powell, 279
Box: I Started My Own Group and So Can You
by Helen Fields, 281

Acknowledgments, 283

Contributors, 285

Selected Resources, 289

Index, 301

FOREWORD

By Kendall Powell

Ten years ago, I was finishing up an internship at *Nature* in Washington, D.C., and preparing to begin a career as an independent science writer. I was terrified. How would I find assignments? Would I be able to make any money at all? As a freelancer working from home, how would I stay motivated—and stay away from daytime TV?

Two of my *Nature* editors gave me sage and calming advice. Colin Macilwain began: "If you can turn in copy on time and to length, and know how to form even a decently written paragraph, then you'll be . . . " He paused, and Paul Smaglik finished his thought: "Golden."

I thought they were just being polite, but they were right. After a couple of years, I had a stream of assignments from a half dozen steady clients, and my science writing career was humming along nicely.

But my inner social butterfly suffered. When I left *Nature,* I had moved in with my then-boyfriend in Colorado, a state where I knew exactly one individual: him. As a freelancer, it wasn't easy to make connections in a new place, and I found myself dashing outside to greet the mailman for small talk and befriending baristas at my local Starbucks.

Then, like a home-birthed baby, SciLance was born in a bathtub. Okay, it wasn't that messy or dramatic, but still, it's a moment I'm not likely to forget.

The idea for an online community of writers first came to me at the 2005 National Association of Science Writers meeting in Pittsburgh. I was soaking my conference-sore feet with three other writers in a huge jet-tub in the hotel's honeymoon suite (someone's reservation had been lost, and the suite was the hotel's apology). We sat around the edge, pants rolled up, chatting over the pizza and wine we had brought upstairs from the bar.

I complained that while I met so many interesting colleagues at conferences, and always loved talking shop with them, it was difficult to keep up that camaraderie once we headed home. Online groups were too impersonal, or too public, or too prone to internal conflict. But what about a smaller, more intimate group, I wondered? Could that serve as a virtual jet-tub?

A month later I created an online group known as SciLance and invited about ten colleagues to join me in an experiment. I wanted to create a reasonably confidential group where members could share advice on the business and craft of science writing. One e-mail at a time, we began to troubleshoot one another's problems, suggesting sources, editors, and solutions to late paychecks.

Eight years later, the group has grown to a stable thirty-five members, located across the US and Canada, and the conversation is still lively. We now share not only practical advice from our combined three hundred years of experience, but also support and inspiration, encouraging one another to finish that pitch, apply for that fellowship, or take that long-overdue vacation. We're proud that members of SciLance have published in the *New York Times, National Geographic,* and dozens of other print, web, and broadcast outlets. We've also won bundles of journalism awards; contributed to *The Best of Technology Writing* and *The Best American Science and Nature Writing* anthologies; taught science writing at Johns Hopkins, Stanford, and elsewhere; and been awarded Scripps, MIT-Knight, and Alicia Patterson Foundation journalism fellowships.

With this book, we hope to share what we've learned from one another and inspire you to start a conversation of your own. Part I is a primer in the skills of science writing. Part II contains our advice on remaining sane and (mostly) balanced as a science writer, and Part III sums up our hard-earned guidance on best business practices.

You'll discover that there's no one right way to shape your career: we've gotten to the middles of ours on at least thirty-five different roads, and expect our futures to be even more divergent. But we hope that the stories of our successful paths, and not-so-successful detours, will give you a sense of the available routes.

Almost every member of our group has written a chapter of this book, but this is more than an anthology: each chapter also includes perspectives from other members of the community, identified by name throughout the book. (SciLancers are referred to by first and last names in their first mentions within a chapter, and first names thereafter.) You'll find that many of the chapters deal with "soft" skills—handling rejection, dealing with financial uncertainty, grappling with envy—because those are the skills we've all found to be the most valuable in the long haul. As my editors at *Nature* told me, the ability to report, write, and file on time will get you assignments. But to construct a sustainable career on the shifting sands of modern journalism, you need to know how to survive both financially and emotionally, and with or without the support of a traditional employer. Most of the members of SciLance currently work as freelance science writers, and much of our advice comes from that perspective. In uncertain times, we think the resilience, flexibility, and drive needed for freelancing are just as important for staff writers: in a sense, we're all freelancers now.

Each chapter also serves as an introduction to an issue relevant to science writers. If you want to dig deeper, we recommend places to start in the Resources section at the end of the book. After you finish reading, we hope you'll still want to pursue science writing—but please don't attempt it alone. At the end, I'll give you pointers for creating your own science-writing hive.

A foreword is supposed to give you a glimpse of where a book will take you, but no writer knows exactly where he or she is headed—that's part of the beauty and frustration of the work. If you're a curious person who appreciates words and intellectual freedom, though, I can promise you'll enjoy the quirky, nerdy, fascinating job of explaining how the world works—regardless of where you end up.

Onward,

Kendall Powell

PART I

THE SKILLED
SCIENCE WRITER

Chapter 1

What Makes a Science Writer?

By Alison Fromme

You know what science writing is. If you're like us, you might have dodged deadly viruses with Richard Preston in *The Hot Zone,* or admired Rachel Carson's ability to turn science into the tragic poetry of *Silent Spring.* Maybe you followed Mary Roach as she documented the colorful afterlives of cadavers in *Stiff,* or voyaged with Charles Darwin, perhaps the most famous science writer of all, in *The Origin of Species.* Or maybe you've listened to the work of science writers on radio shows and in documentary films.

Despite the impression most of us got in our high school chemistry classes, science—and science writing—is inherently dramatic. It's about struggling to find answers, persevering despite setbacks, arguing with colleagues, fighting failure, and celebrating successes. It's about the world around us—what's in our bones, how stars are born, and why drought scars the landscape—and how new knowledge fits into our society. When done right, science writing can inform, inspire, and even change the course of history. When done wrong . . . well, let's not go there. This book is about doing it right.

We science writers, the wordsmiths behind the scenes, are as varied as the subjects we cover. We work for magazines, newspapers, radio and television programs, universities, federal laboratories, educational publishers, museums, and increasingly for ourselves. We research stories over the phone, in libraries and museums, at laboratory benches, and—when we're lucky—on far-flung expeditions around the world. We write articles, books, and blog posts. We help create movies, podcasts, websites, and television shows.

Our common mission is to explain very complicated things with both maximum simplicity and maximum accuracy. It's a puzzle with infinite variations and infinite solutions, and we science writers rarely tire of the challenge. After all, there's always more to learn about the subject at hand, and there's always a better, clearer, more graceful, or more charming way to communicate it to others.

While not all science writers are journalists, the writers of this book believe that all science writers can and should approach their subjects journalistically, with curiosity, an open mind, a healthy sense of skepticism about the material, and transparency about our methods, biases, and sources. Whether we're writing for the general public or for scientists themselves, our primary responsibility is to our readers, and we owe it to them to look at all aspects of the work at hand.

At the time of this book's printing, science-writing positions at many newspapers and magazines have been cut. Grim projections have been made about the future of traditional print publications and journalism itself. But we're not sulking. Our personal experiences and those of many other science writers show that while the field is full of uncertainty, it's also full of exciting opportunities.

Most of the writers of this book work as freelance science writers, and many of us find that the number, reach, and potential of new outlets are growing. Photos, videos, audio, and animation are all enriching the storytelling experience and making our work more collaborative. At the same time, scientists are continuing to make new discoveries, many of them useful (how to avoid heart disease), important (how poor neighborhoods are targeted by toxic industries), or wondrous (the physics of gecko feet). We believe that there will always be fantastically interesting science stories to discover, media to convey them—and a way to make a living telling them.

One warning: science writing, freelance or otherwise, is very, very seldom a path to riches. (In fact, for many people who try it, it's not even a path to middle-class respectability—you should see the cars some of us drive.) But with luck, hard work, and talent, you can make a decent living at it, and much of the advice in this book is shaped to help you do just that. In this chapter, we'll look at how to get started.

Where Science Writers Come From

Perhaps you earned a journalism degree, landed a newspaper job, and found yourself drawn to the science desk, curious to learn more. Perhaps you toiled in a graduate-school lab but found yourself wanting to explain your research—rather than actually complete it. Or perhaps you're happily working as a researcher and want to do your part to share science with the world. There are many paths into the science-writing world, but aspiring science writers often have similar questions. Here are the ones we encounter most often:

Do I Need to Finish My Graduate Degree in Science?

A lot of science writers have a eureka moment during their undergraduate or graduate science courses: they realize that while they love science, their wide interests make them better suited to be science writers than scientists. The AAAS Mass Media fellowship and short-term science-writing workshops (such as the annual events in Banff, Alberta, Canada, and Santa Fe, New Mexico) offer opportunities to check out the science-writing profession before committing to it full-time. Whether to finish your science degree is a personal decision and might depend on how close you are to completion. But don't finish your degree because you think that those letters after your name will help you in journalism: editors know that while a PhD in physics might help you recognize great stories in the subject, it might also make it difficult for you to explain the field to outsiders. Your clips and your connections matter most.

Do I Need to Go to Graduate School in Journalism or Science Writing?

Not necessarily, but doing so offers many advantages: you'll learn solid reporting skills, boost your résumé, have access to internships that might otherwise be unavailable, and meet professors and alumni who are well-connected, established, and successful writers. However, programs can be expensive and may saddle you with debt that limits your options after graduation.

Do I Need to Do an Internship?

If you don't have any journalism or formal writing experience, probably yes. An internship offers a behind-the-scenes look at the way a publication operates: how editors plan content, how pitches are evaluated, the ins and outs of the editing and fact-checking process, and more. Plus, an internship will connect you with the staffers at the organization, who might become valuable contacts later on in your career.

What About Alternative Paths?

While some writers have broken into the profession through blogging alone, it's not easy to do, and it almost always takes months or years of unpaid labor. For most beginning science writers, blogging is not a stand-alone strategy but a tool for leveraging the experience they've gained from a graduate program, an internship, or a staff position. Regular, accurate, interesting posts can help writers of all levels build credibility, define their beat, and hone their skills. (See "Blogging: My Digital Calling Card" on p. 265.) More than a few members of the Science Online community (www.scienceonline.com) have taken blogging further, establishing stellar reputations and wide audiences: among the notable examples are Ed Yong of *Not Exactly Rocket Science*, Maggie Koerth-Baker of *BoingBoing*, David Dobbs of *Neuron Culture*, Maryn McKenna of *Superbug*, and Bora Zivkovic of *A Blog Around the Clock*. (While you're in the blogosphere, also check out *The Last Word on Nothing*, an independent group science blog that counts several SciLancers among its members.)

Am I Crazy to Consider This Career?

No. Even though academia likes to divide the humanities and the sciences, a lot of people are interested in both. Storytelling and science define us as humans, and it's natural to be attracted to both of them.

Joining the Independents

At some point in your career, whether out of choice or necessity, you may decide to strike out as a freelance writer. Parts II and III of this book cover many of the practical and emotional concerns of all writers working in the digital age, including freelancers. But how and when should your freelance adventure begin?

If You Can, Ease Your Transition

Some people are forced into freelancing by a layoff or a family move. But if you're entering the freelance world by choice, experiment with freelancing before you leave your full-time job, or hang on to a part-time job while you establish your freelance clientele. SciLancer Susan Moran juggled part-time adjunct teaching at a university journalism school while starting her freelancing career. "It was a steady—if small—paycheck, and it kept me connected to budding journalists and academia, and to the world beyond the little package called 'me and my stories,'" she says.

Plan for Your Financial and Health Care Needs

Will you burn through savings? Lean on a spouse or partner? Buy an individual health plan? For me, security and flexibility were key: I had some savings, no mortgage, no kids, and a spouse to lean on. (Read more about financial considerations in Chapter 19, "Minding the Business.")

"I've come to think that the best way to start freelancing is to save up about six months' worth of living expenses before launching, do nothing else but pitch and write for three months, and then take stock to see if it's working," says SciLancer Stephen Ornes, who started freelancing after completing MIT's graduate program in science writing. And keep in mind, that's six months' expenses *on top* of whatever financial cushion you need to feel secure.

Consider Your Existing Connections

New freelancers with staff experience can draw on relationships forged during years of casual conversations and editorial meetings. "It's great to have one solid client when you start freelancing—an editor or a group of editors who know you and trust your work," says SciLancer Michelle Nijhuis. "Whether that's a contact from an internship or a staff job, that kind of relationship can really protect you financially *and* emotionally—especially during the first few months of freelancing, when you realize no one cares about you or your career all that much!"

But even without staff experience, you can mine the depths of your résumé and get valuable help from past employers, colleagues, college professors, friends, and relatives. Tell everyone you know that you are starting your freelance career and ask (politely, of course) if they know of anyone who can help you. I started freelancing right out of grad school without many contacts in publishing, but the editor of my graduate school alumni magazine offered to send me a few assignments while I found my footing—a small gesture that mattered in those first uncertain weeks. Read more about networking strategies in Chapter 20, "Networking for the Nervous."

Read, Read, Read Publications You Admire—Then Start Pitching

Analyze your favorite media outlets to get a sense of their typical stories. Then target your pitch to the appropriate editor and department. Get much more advice on pitching in Chapter 3.

Foster Relationships with Editors and Other Writers

Groups such as the National Association of Science Writers—and their regional chapters, such as the Northern California Science Writers' Association—offer advice and resources that will help you get started. I set an early goal to meet two or three new people at networking events every month, which meant I endured some awkward conversations. But those connections led to both assignments and professional friendships. If a formal group doesn't exist in your region, you can attend a national conference and reach out to local writers there.

Act Like a Businessperson

A professional attitude and a structured schedule can help you navigate the confusing first months of freelancing. I budgeted for professional development and planned the number of pitches I'd send each week, the networking events I'd attend regularly, and the magazines I'd approach. I kept a regular daily schedule and tracked administrative tasks with spreadsheets. Chapter 19 includes many more tips on business management.

Gobble Up Opportunities, and Keep Your Sense of Humor

As SciLancer Douglas Fox says, "I always think of Ernest Shackleton and his men trekking across the Antarctic sea ice in the Southern Ocean. They were in this incredibly harsh environment, but the universe kept sending things their way—penguins and seals and other animals that they shot and cooked and ate, yum, yum. Freelancing feels a little like that. Opportunities just kind of show up, and you cook and eat them. It's important not to get overconfident and to remember that the opportunities can disappear at any time. But really, it's incredibly exciting."

So, dear reader, off we go across the ice. Yum, yum.

Chapter 2

Finding Ideas

By Emily Sohn

For my first real job as a science writer, I joined a crew of eight multimedia professionals on expeditions to remote and exotic international locations. Nearly every day during these weeks-long "Quests," our team used a portable satellite device to send educational reports, videos, and images to a website, where hundreds of thousands of students in classrooms around the world followed our every move.

In the months before my first Quest, a six-week expedition to the Peruvian Amazon, my coworkers and I created a schedule, mapped out a route, and conducted a lot of background research to figure out what kinds of stories we might tell along the way. But none of that research prepared me for what we encountered one day during the second half of the trip.

We had already survived a treacherous week on inflatable rafts in a tiny Amazonian tributary. Now, we had upgraded to a larger river, the Ucayali, and a live-aboard boat that was patrolled twenty-four hours a day by armed guards keeping an eye out for Amazonian pirates. (Yes, pirates.)

It was early afternoon when our sun-scorched, bug-bitten crew stepped off the boat into a dusty, off-the-grid town called Roaboya. There, families live in thatched-roof huts that sit on low stilts for protection against floods, and kids spend the day in a one-room schoolhouse. In fluent Spanish, our team leader and our team anthropologist greeted the village leader. It was an unusual day, the leader told us. A hunter had gone missing in the jungle three days earlier. The village shaman had been enlisted to help.

As the sweltering afternoon wore on, we interviewed, photographed, and filmed the man's family and neighbors, asking not just about him, but also about their daily lives, their oral traditions, and the turtles they caught and cooked for dinner. As the sun sank toward the horizon, we watched in amazement and, by this point, joy and relief as the search crew returned with the missing hunter. They had found him exactly where the shaman had predicted he would be. When darkness fell, we sat cross-legged and witnessed an ayahuasca ceremony, during which participants drank a plant-based brew that induced wild hallucinations, and the shaman thanked the spirits for returning the man safely.

The stories we produced that day were among the most vivid and gripping of the entire trip—even the ones that had nothing to do with the main drama. While waiting for the search party to return, for example, I watched some men chop down a tree near the village. They needed the wood and, having already gained an intimate view of these people's lives, I was able to reflect on deforestation in the Amazon in a more nuanced way. Before the trip, I'd thought cutting down trees in the rain forest was a universally bad thing. By the end of my day in Roaboya, I was conflicted, and I explored my uncertainty with my online audience of kids.

My brief time in that tiny community, along with experiences in other Amazonian villages, had a profound influence on the way I look for story ideas today. No matter where you are, I've learned, the key to finding a man lost in the jungle—or any great story that no one else has—is to get yourself into positions where you are likely to bump into a story telling itself. When you do stumble across a scoop, all you need is the ability to take furious notes and the willingness to forget everything you thought you came for.

This smart luck—or planned serendipity—can serve any writer well. And you don't have to go to the Amazon to find ideas that will wow editors. Once you learn how to look for them, you will find a never-ending supply of science stories.

Anatomy of an Idea

No matter the publication you work for or the kind of stories you write, it's essential to distinguish between topics and stories. During a summer internship at a newspaper science section more than a decade ago, I suggested an article about the origins of oil. I still remember listening with a twinge of embarrassment as my editor explained that while it was an interesting *topic,* it was not a newspaper *story*—at least, not until it was important to understanding current events. I make this mistake far less often than I used to, but I still catch myself doing it.

After all, for a person who makes a living off of curiosity, it's easy to get excited about a cool natural phenomenon, an endangered animal, or a breathtaking place without having a clear idea of what the story is. A story, in its most basic form, contains characters engaged in some kind of journey or conflict. It follows those characters toward a discovery or resolution through a series of linked events, progressing through a clear beginning, middle, and end. Journalists' stories must also have a news "hook"—a reason to tell the story *now*—and a connection to a larger idea. In other words, it's usually not enough for your story to be really cool. It has to be important, too.

Robert Irion, director of the science communication program at the University of California, Santa Cruz, says he uses some form of the following dialogue to help his science-writing students turn topics into stories:

STUDENT: So, Rob, I want to write about elephant seals.

IRION: Okay, that's a topic, not a story. What about them?

STUDENT: Well, they are charismatic megafauna, and they have big brown eyes.

IRION: That might help attract readers, but what will make them read the story?

STUDENT: Researchers are studying how deep they dive and where they go to eat.

IRION: Yes, but those studies have been going on for twenty-five years. What's new?

STUDENT: The scientists attach GPS devices to the elephant seals and track where they go in the ocean in real time, and how deep they dive along the way.

IRION: Okay, that's a cool technique, and it could be part of your story. But what have they found?

STUDENT: Elephant seals go to this one place out in the middle of the Pacific Ocean every year to bulk up for the winter. It's a feeding frenzy—other GPS tags show that sharks and albatross go to this same place. It's a new picture of how marine animals make a living.

IRION: There you go. Now find some characters, and I think you've got a story.

Reading lots of top-level nonfiction is one of the first and easiest things you can do to refine your sense of story. And even if you want to write solely about science, you can learn valuable lessons from stories about other subjects. "Sometimes it's harder to see the story elements in science than in music, or sports or politics or whatever," says Thomas Hayden, a SciLancer who teaches science communication at Stanford University. That might be because scientists are trained not to express the hope, frustration, jealousy, and other emotions they feel in the course of their work, he says. "But once you get the knack of it," says Thomas, "you see that the world is full of pitchable, executable science stories."

When you think you've hit on an awesome new idea, make sure it's interesting to other people, too. To gauge whether readers, and in turn editors, are going to bite, try telling friends about it. If you can get the essence of the story across in just a few sentences, you're on the right track. Even better, suggests SciLancer Robert Frederick, try out your idea on strangers at a bar. "If your audience has no follow-up questions, that's a warning sign that the story isn't worth your time," he says.

The Chase

Most people encounter science and scientists through the work of science writers. That means we have a responsibility to understand how science works, and when science is ready to be written about. For better or worse, the academic journal system is the major driver of daily and weekly science news for general audiences.

Here's how it works: After toiling for months or years on their work, researchers write up their results and submit papers to one journal at a time. After a period of review by other experts in the field—referred to as "peer review"—acceptance leads to eventual publication. (Rejection leads to edits and resubmission to another, usually smaller and more specialized journal.) In some ways, it's not unlike the process we writers go through when pitching an article idea.

Major journals, such as *Science, Nature,* and the *Proceedings of the National Academy of Sciences* (*PNAS*), publish studies on a wide range of subjects. Specialty journals, such as *Nature Neuroscience, Molecular Ecology,* or *BMJ* (formerly the *British Medical Journal*), focus on narrower themes. Many journals also use embargoes, which set a day and time before which journalists are not allowed to publish news of the work. These journals often send out abstracts and press releases about upcoming studies a few days before the publication ban lifts, however, giving writers a chance to conduct interviews and write stories that will be ready to run when the embargoes expire. Publishing even an hour before an embargo expires can result in major repercussions for you and the publication you are writing for, including public embarrassment and being shut out of future embargoed material.

Once you understand the journal system and embargo schedules, you will begin to notice recurring patterns in news coverage. Stories based on *Science* articles begin to appear in news outlets every Thursday at 2 p.m. Eastern time. The same happens when *Nature* embargoes lift on Wednesday at 1 p.m. and when *PNAS* allows press coverage to begin on Monday at 3 p.m.

Pitching news stories on these studies can be tough. Editors get the study summaries from major journals, too, and they're likely to assign the stories they're interested in to staff writers, or to freelancers already associated with their publication. But even if you're a new freelancer, or one looking to break into new markets, these press releases can be useful.

If you already have connections with news editors and can work fast, you may be able to turn press releases into rapid turnaround stories that pay relatively quickly. For the past few years, I've been a contributing writer on contract with *Discovery News,* and these "me-too stories"—stories based on papers from major journals—account for at least half of the dozen or so articles I write for the site every month. Writing these stories generally requires two basic interviews: one with the lead author of the new study and one with an expert who wasn't involved in the work but can comment on why it's important or what its limitations are. And since news story structures tend to be fairly formulaic, incorporating these quickie articles into my work mix helps boost my bottom line.

To get in on the receiving end of the press release feed, start with on-line news services, such as EurekAlert! and Newswise, which require you to request password access but are free once you're deemed a legitimate reporter. Daily e-mails from both services include press releases from a wide variety of journals, universities, and research institutions. I highly recommend sorting this stream of news alerts into an e-mail folder to avoid being totally overwhelmed by them. Regularly dipping into this folder when you have time can help you stay up-to-date with research fields that interest you, and help you learn to recognize news when you see it. (A carefully sorted social-media stream can work the same way. See Chapter 24 for more on the uses of social media in science writing.)

Press releases can yield more than just daily news stories. As you read through study summaries and the coverage that follows them each week, you might also start to notice trends and patterns. Then it's just a matter of finding the right spin to distinguish your idea.

For example, press releases on several related studies may lead you to a story about a larger issue. Maybe a researcher mentioned in a press release has an interesting backstory that would make him or her a good profile subject. Maybe a national story has local angles—or vice versa. Next time you get a press release or promotional e-mail, imagine that it contains hidden pictures: look at it from a different angle, and you might see a great story hiding beneath the predictable one being sold to you.

That's what SciLancer Mark Schrope did in 2007, when he received an e-newsletter from a local design group announcing some advertising awards it had won. The winning project involved graphics and animations created for another local company, which was planning to build multiple offshore cargo-monitoring bases. Instead of covering the design group, he decided to write about the new bases: how they worked, who was building them, and why. The resulting story filled a two-page spread in *Popular Science* and also ran on CNN.com.

To meet the insatiable editorial desire for fresh stories, it can help to cast a wide net. A few e-mails and phone calls will get you on mailing lists for overlooked journals, universities, research institutions, and even private companies. Most lesser-known journals receive very little press attention and do not use embargoes.

When SciLancer Douglas Fox first started freelancing, he trolled through journals at a medical library, where he focused on second- and third-tier publications, such as the *Journal of Experimental Biology* and *Biochemical and Biophysical Research Communications*. He found that these journals were filled with quirky, surprising studies that crossed disciplinary boundaries. His first feature for *New Scientist* came from a paper he saw in the journal *Biopolymers* describing attempts to make synthetic spider silk.

It's also useful to look abroad. European journals and research institutions churn out a lot of fascinating work that US reporters often miss. I recently signed up for a daily e-mail about Scandinavian research, and I've already written several news stories about studies not covered by other US publications.

As you find your own rhythm in the news cycle, a few short pieces can quickly add up to more in-depth story possibilities. SciLancer Virginia

Gewin, who writes a short news story every month for the journal *Frontiers in Ecology and the Environment,* says the gig forces her to stay up-to-date on the ecology beat, giving her an insider's view into broader trends in the field. More than once, she has uncovered feature ideas that she has sold to other publications.

Going Deeper

Press releases, tables of contents, and study abstracts are standard sources of inspiration for science writers, but they aren't the only types of reading material that can feed you ideas. Local newspapers and regional magazines are often full of characters and anecdotes that speak to bigger issues.

A few years ago, SciLancer Jill Adams noticed an article in the *Albany Times Union* about scientists at a nearby museum who had unearthed a fossil that earned them a paper in *Nature.* Since the museum was just fifteen minutes away from her house, Jill followed up and found that non-degreed scientists had done the bulk of the work. Her story about them turned into a short narrative for *The Scientist.* She wrote about the same work for *Discover*'s top-science-stories-of-the-year issue.

Everything in the paper is fair game. After noticing an obscure ad for isolation tanks in *New York* magazine, SciLancer Bryn Nelson sold a story about them to the business news website Portfolio.com. "I dug a little deeper and found that isolation tanks were not only a business and health trend, but had a fascinating history," Bryn says. "And the session was so relaxing that I fell asleep in the tank."

Get Out!

To find the freshest story ideas, you need to talk to real people, and one of the best places to find them is on the conference circuit.

As a reporter, you can get free admission to major scientific conferences, such as those hosted by the American Association for the Advancement of Science, the Society for Neuroscience, the American Geophysical Union, the American Chemical Society, the American Astronomical Society, and so on. You can also gain access to much more specialized gatherings of scientists—small meetings where you may well be the only reporter. Unlike some journal articles, posters and presentations at meetings are not embargoed and are fair game for all reporters.

Getting into these conferences often requires signing up through a press liaison, and if you are a freelancer, you may have to explain why they should let you in. Usually, mentioning a publication or two that you've written for does the trick, but simply using the word "freelancer" often is enough. Whichever kind of meeting you choose, start by sitting in on sessions that sound interesting to you. Listen for "by the way" comments—passing mentions of upcoming studies or emerging trends. Look at posters. Talk to researchers and public-relations contacts—not just in lecture rooms, but also at wine-and-cheese receptions. And ask lots of questions.

At one AAAS conference a few years ago, Robert attended a dermatologist's presentation on the use of lasers to treat skin cancer. During his talk, the skin doctor mentioned his work with a quarter-mile-long tunable laser at Jefferson National Lab in Newport News, Virginia. When the session was over, Robert asked the researcher more about the technology, and ended up with a story for National Public Radio about the use of advanced laser technology to remove tattoos.

Conferences may be intimidating at first. But they are full of uncovered ideas that anyone can snatch up, including beginners. Early in her freelance career, SciLancer Robin Mejia heard a conference presentation about forensics that led to a story for *New Scientist,* another for the *Los Angeles Times,* and eventually to a documentary she worked on for CNN. (She tells the story in more detail in Chapter 21.)

A single conference often fuels story ideas for months. So, no matter which lecture rooms you choose to sit in, don't forget your notebook. (For more on networking at conferences, see Chapter 20.)

Talk to Anyone, Talk to Everyone

One holiday season, SciLancer Michelle Nijhuis opened a Christmas letter from a friend who is an avid caver. The letter mentioned another spelunker, a microbiologist named Hazel Barton, and Michelle wrote down Barton's name as a potential future source or profile subject. Eventually Michelle called Barton and learned that she was frantically busy trying to understand white-nose syndrome, a fungus that had been killing bats with alarming speed.

White-nose syndrome was something Michelle had wanted to write about for a while, but felt she needed a character to make the story accessible. Barton was that character, and the cold call turned into an award-winning story for *Smithsonian.* Her experience points to the value of taking the time to dig during the development of an idea—before the pitch—to find the right combination of characters and action that will make a story sell. "Editors rarely bite on a sliver of a story," Michelle says. "So those few calls and the extra work of developing the pitch can give a good idea a fighting chance."

Even talking to people at home can yield great ideas. SciLancer Sarah Webb's husband, who religiously reads the *New York Times* Arts section, pointed her to an article about musician Yo-Yo Ma, who was scheduled to play the cello for Barack Obama's 2009 inauguration. Since the forecast called for cold weather, Ma was debating whether to play his multi-million-dollar wooden cello or a carbon-fiber instrument. Sarah turned that nugget into a fun-to-report story for *Scientific American* about synthetic-material cellos.

Strangers can be excellent resources, too. After SciLance member Jessica Marshall met someone at a friend's wedding who told her that earthworms were an invasive species in most of the United States, she wrote a short feature about the problem for *New Scientist*.

One caveat: when people learn you are a journalist, they may throw ideas at you like sand bags at a carnival dunking game. Do not feel you have to follow up on everything. Your mother-in-law wants you to write about a great new recipe she got at a church picnic? Nod politely and blame your editors for saying no if she brings it up again.

Play First, Write Later

I firmly believe that one of the best ways to drum up interesting story ideas is to prioritize playtime. By getting out in the world and doing what excites you, you may find that ideas come along and grab you.

Mark's first paid feature idea came out of a group kayaking lesson off the coast of Santa Cruz, California, where he met a paddling chemistry professor whose research—on the development of a new molecule that allowed for the precision formation of plastics—sounded interesting. More recently, he noticed massive numbers of jellyfish on the beaches near his Florida home following major ocean swells. The observation turned into a feature for *Nature*.

These success stories also serve as cautionary tales: as a science writer, a trip to the beach is never just a trip to the beach. But as long as your traveling companions are equally enthusiastic about learning new things, your professional status can open all sorts of unusual doors.

On a vacation to India in 2004, I visited a camel research center. In Costa Rica with my husband and then two-year-old son, I met with two jaguar researchers. I love the way traveling makes my writing more interesting, and I love how the stories make the traveling more fulfilling. I also enjoy ending up in places I never would have seen—and meeting people I never would have known—if I were just an ordinary tourist.

If you're willing to give up on the idea of true leisure (but gain the ability to count many of your travel expenses as tax deductions), you'll need to dedicate some hours to research before setting off on your next trip. My usual strategy is to surf the Web and look through guidebooks for mentions of conservation organizations located near my destination. Then I send out a blitz of e-mails and phone calls asking about ongoing projects and researchers who might be working in the field while I'm there. It may take a dozen or more messages to yield one or two on-site interviews. But it takes only one good contact to lead to a great story.

Douglas has funded extensive trips around the world with what he calls the "brute force approach" to story scouting. His first step is to plant himself in front of a computer, where he begins a massive search through study abstracts. Before a trip to Australia in 2001, he looked through every paper with an Australian author published in *Science* and *Nature* over the previous five years. Next he scoured a wider array of journals by searching for Australian institutions in combination with dozens of location-specific or tantalizing words, such as "kangaroo," "wallaby," "stromatolite," "crystal," and "fractal." From a scan of about 5,000 abstracts, he found twenty or so studies worth further investigation. Eventually he netted seven feature ideas.

This strategy can work for local adventures, too. SciLancer Alison Fromme had high hopes for a cold call she made to a salamander expert, but the interview didn't yield a story. Still, she figured it couldn't hurt to take him up on his offer to give her a tour of his university's vertebrate biology museum. There, he casually introduced her to another researcher, who was poring over maps of the Sierra Nevada in an attempt to retrace the steps of a biologist who had studied animals in the area eighty years earlier. Eventually that work became the basis of a story for *Backpacker*.

You can even find story ideas in your very own behavior. When Jessica sat down in front of the TV for another episode of *Buffy the Vampire Slayer*—even though she had work to do and small children who would

I want to stress the importance of just thinking when you're looking for good ideas. Seriously, when you have a nagging feeling about something, just listen to your gut and look deeper. This habit is tough to develop when we're constantly reading other people's ideas, but they can pay off in great stories. Give yourself permission to think deeply about the topics important to you.

—ALISON FROMME

wake up before dawn—she wondered why good stories are so addictive. The thought eventually turned into a feature for *New Scientist* about the neuroscience of storytelling.

Follow Your Nose and Dive into Holes

As you read, travel, and follow up on random conversations, you may find your interests leading you down rabbit holes. Do not fear. The trail may lead you into dead ends, but occasionally you will find yourself in very interesting places.

Alison was browsing articles online when she stumbled on an article about attempts to prevent light pollution in the national parks. She called the person in charge of the program, identified herself as a reporter, and asked him what he was up to. He invited her to join him as he collected data, and she wrote about his work for *Backpacker*.

Stories often beget stories, so while reporting one piece, keep an eye out for details that fascinate you but don't quite fit into the story at hand. Those errant thoughts might lead to their own assignments. Jessica wrote a series of three stories for *New Scientist* that began with a feature about the genetics of skin color. A comment by one interviewee led to a separate feature about sunscreen and UVA rays. And a reader comment on that story sparked a third feature about cancer and the hygiene hypothesis.

Using an assignment as an excuse to do some extra legwork can also help turn a story thread into a web of ideas. When SciLance member Hillary Rosner was looking for a character or project to anchor a feature assignment, she started by scanning websites of related departments at two universities near her. She picked out a handful of researchers who might have useful information and contacted them all. None became the focus of her original assignment, but she turned two of her conversations into separate projects. "Conversations lead in interesting directions—you never know what you're going to learn," Hillary says.

Many science writers on the hunt for ideas have found that they can avoid dry spells by periodically calling sources from projects they worked on months or even years ago. You might hit the jackpot with a quick "What are you up to now?"

Another favorite—and simple—technique is to end every interview with a basic question: "What else are you working on?" That's what SciLancer Stephen Ornes did while fact-checking another writer's story for *CR* magazine (now *Cancer Today*), a cancer research publication.

Stephen listened as the public-health official he was interviewing started lamenting the lack of public standards for tissue storage and the potential problems for tumor biology research. Stephen looked into the issue and eventually followed the path of a donated tumor through the corridors of Yale–New Haven Hospital—a journey he wrote about for *CR*.

No assignment is too small to serve as a gateway, adds Douglas. He once spun a feature out of something he noticed while writing a two hundred–word sidebar on, he says, "the then wacky-sounding idea that life might have originated in ice, rather than in some hydrothermal vent." A paper he read while conducting research mentioned an experiment that had been running for twenty-seven years at –78 degrees Celsius. That seemed unusual, and Douglas followed up—only to find a fascinating and surprisingly extensive backstory. His *Discover* feature about the experiment won a spot in *The Best American Science and Nature Writing* anthology.

And don't throw out your notes: interesting topics can yield successive stories, sometimes for years. During an internship at *Nature* in 2004, SciLancer Amanda Mascarelli wrote a news story about a new worm species that was discovered growing on decaying whale skeletons, which had sunk to the seafloor. Months later, she sold *Nature* a feature story about the extreme lengths researchers go to in order to reach sunken whale carcasses. Three years later, an editor at *Audubon* who had seen the *Nature* piece asked her to write a story about these "whale falls," which involved a full day of reporting on board a research boat. The story went over well and led to another feature assignment for the magazine.

The Daily Grind

It's true that ideas are everywhere. But don't assume that they will always fall in your lap. Digging up ideas is part of any science writer's job, and it takes constant vigilance to keep new ideas rolling in.

Some writers find that they fall into boom-and-bust patterns. A frenzy of ideas may keep things busy for a while, only to be followed by a long drought. Learning how to turn these spurts into a steady stream can be a never-ending work in progress.

But droughts can offer important lessons about how to get the ideas rolling again. Thomas has noticed that his idea well is fullest when he's busy going to lectures, making phone calls, and having drinks with scientists at conferences. Just engaging in the act of talking and thinking allows the ideas to flow. "The best way to find ideas is to be actively reporting on something, anything," he says.

And don't expect too much of yourself. Very few writers make a living solely by writing groundbreaking, long-form, one-of-a-kind stories on topics that nobody has read about before. More common is a mix of occasional passion projects with steadier, less glamorous work. As you sustain yourself with interesting-enough writing that pays the bills, keep your eyes and ears open for the winning elements that will turn an ordinary idea into something that you can't help but talk about at every party you go to.

The Long View

Even when times are tough or stories get rejected, persistence often pays off. Any idea that doesn't pan out today might find a life a year—or a decade—from now.

In 1999, a graduate-level course drew Virginia's attention to the debate over marine reserves along the Oregon coast. Ten years later, proposals for the large-scale use of wave energy sparked an unprecedented coastal planning effort that brought together fishers, surfers, wave energy developers, and marine reserve advocates. Virginia followed every development. When the time seemed right, she made a few key calls and put together a feature for *Portland Monthly* about plans for the first wave buoy park in the continental United States.

Likewise, SciLancer Andreas von Bubnoff learned about John Ioannidis—a scientist who analyzes the accuracy of biomedical studies—while working at the *Chicago Tribune* in 2004. After he did some initial reporting on the work, Andreas's story fell through, but the topic remained in the back of his mind. About a year later, he unsuccessfully pitched another story about Ioannidis's work, but he refused to let go of the idea. More than another year later, after seeing Ioannidis talk at a scientific meeting, he finally found the right focus for the story; the piece ran in the *Los Angeles Times* and appeared in the 2008 edition of *The Best American Science and Nature Writing*. "It takes time for some ideas to mature," Andreas says. "It turns out that sometimes rejection can be a good thing."

SciLance says . . .

- The **elements of a good story** include: characters, a journey, conflict, linked events, a news hook, and a big-picture idea. These elements distinguish a *story* from a *topic*.

- One of the best ways to learn how to identify good story ideas is to **read top-level nonfiction**, including non-science articles.

- Test your ideas on strangers and friends at bars or cocktail parties. If you **hook them in a few sentences** or less, you're on the right track.

- Understand the news cycle, including the journal system and embargo schedules. **Never break an embargo**.

- To find stories everyone doesn't already have, look to **obscure and international journals**. They are often filled with quirky and interesting studies.

- **Conferences and meetings** can be excellent sources of story nuggets. Follow your interests and follow up on offhand comments.

- **Local newspapers** can offer local angles that might lead to stories with broader appeal.

- **Talk to anyone and everyone**, everywhere you go.

- Playtime is an often-overlooked source of observations and conversations that can spark sellable ideas. **Pursuing hobbies and interests** can lead to interesting work projects.

- With a little legwork before your next trip, you can **turn your travels into fountains of feature ideas**—as long as you're willing to give up on the idea of a work-free vacation.

- If at first your idea is rejected, **don't give up**. Many writers have tales of stories that were years in the making.

Chapter 3

Making the Pitch

By Thomas Hayden

Online or on paper, written, spoken, or acted out with puppets: If you've got a story you want to tell, you're first going to have to convince an editor to give you the space and resources to produce and publish it. The traditional way to approach an editor is with a brief written proposal, or pitch, called a query letter. And if that letter isn't good, no one but the readers of your personal blog will find out whether your story could have been, too.

There are a hundred variations on the standard query letter, ranging from laboriously researched documents to hallway conversations between colleagues. (Yes, staffers have to pitch, too.) News stories—direct, to the point, and focused on a specific study or event—are fundamentally different from magazine-style features, which tend to play out as narratives with characters, plotlines, and maybe even a moral or two. The pitch for each story type is correspondingly different. (See "A Tale of Two Query Letters" on p. 36 for an example of each.) And there are as many individual preferences as there are editors. But the fundamental elements are the same, and no matter how you put them together, they are essential to the success of any pitch:

The story idea: What are you proposing to write, specifically? (See Chapter 2 for the difference between topics and stories.)

Relevance: Why does this story matter, and why is it a good fit for the specific publication? (Sometimes "because it's cool" is reason enough. But you usually need more.)

Timeliness: Why should this story be assigned now, rather than, say, a year ago, or in six months? Is there breaking news, an upcoming anniversary, or some other "news peg" to hang the story on?

Execution: Are you proposing a 350-word news brief or a 3,000-word feature? A profile, an investigation, an essay? Will the story require travel, or hard-to-get interviews, or Freedom of Information Act requests?

Extras: Are there photo opportunities, or data for graphics or interactive maps, or other possible adornments to the primary story?

Author: Why are you the writer for the job? Reasons might include your writing experience or knowledge of the field, access to the key sites or sources, or a unique perspective on the issue.

Some editors prefer very brief query letters—a paragraph or two of plainly stated facts and figures. Others respond well to a more comprehensive approach, showing detailed research and analysis of the story idea and its context. And many publications post submission guidelines online, sometimes in considerable detail—read them carefully. With experience, you'll find your own approach to pitching, and learn to shape it for different stories, publications, and editors. But as a general rule, an initial query letter should be a single page (about five hundred words) or less, even for longer stories.

There are two reasons. First, editors are universally busy, and thus tend to value clarity and brevity. The second reason is even simpler: in some ways, the best outcome of a query letter is an editor's desire to know more.

That doesn't mean you can just dash off a few lines, though. For anything more than a short news piece, a good pitch should be reported and written. That is to say, you should make a couple of preliminary phone calls, reaching out to key sources to confirm that they'll speak with you and that your idea has a solid basis in reality. And the query letter should demonstrate both the strength of your idea and the strength of your writing. Some writers draft an opening paragraph or two that could work for the final story, and use them to open the query letter. It shows they've thought through the idea as a story and that they can capture the tone and style of the outlet they're pitching.

"I rely a lot on the writing that I'm already reading: the writing in the e-mails, the writing in the pitch," says Adam Rogers, senior editor at *Wired*. "Those e-mails to me are auditions all on their own. So are the interactions I have on the phone. I want to feel like this is a professional that I'm going to be in good hands with."

You want to build your queries around good story ideas. But you also want to send another message: that working with you will be a low-risk proposition. When an editor assigns a story, he or she is making a bet—that a new writer will be able to deliver the goods, or that an expensive reporting trip will pay off. A clear, well-thought-out, and polished query can help an editor feel more secure in taking a chance on your proposal. "Quite often I think there's a good story behind the pitch, but the pitch is not well written," says Helen Pearson, lead features editor at *Nature*. "That tells me it's too much of a gamble" to make the assignment.

The newer you are to science writing, or to the specific editor you're pitching, the more formal and complete your query letter should be. For short news articles, which tend to be less complicated to report, write, and edit, a short, crisp memo is your best bet. For features, which tend to be longer, more complicated, and higher-risk for editors, you'll need to research and write a more comprehensive but still succinct query letter. (See "A Tale of Two Query Letters" on p. 36 for examples.)

How much research should you do before drafting your query? There's no hard-and-fast rule, but as a general guideline you should start by reading any scientific papers or other background material the story will be based on. Next, you should check to make sure the publication you plan to pitch hasn't run similar stories in the recent past. If you're pitching a news story, that may be plenty. But if you're pitching a longer feature, you've got more work to do. You won't always know the ending of the feature story you're pitching, but you do need to know enough to show that it *is* a story, not just a hunch.

When I first started working as a science reporter, I was amazed by how quickly people returned my phone calls requesting interviews—I had an easier time getting leading scientists on the phone than I did scheduling a meeting with my own PhD adviser. By and large, most scientists respond well to a polite, enthusiastic request, by phone or by e-mail, to discuss their research with a reporter—even if you don't have an assignment yet. It's easier if you have a staff job and can say you're calling from publication X or research foundation Y. For freelancers, transparency is best: simply explain that you're a science journalist looking into a story you plan to propose to publication X, and ask for ten minutes to make sure you understand the key points.

Sure, sometimes a potential source will say no. But more often than not, she'll say yes. And when she does, be brief, polite, and focused. Don't subject your source to a fishing expedition. (For more on interviewing, see Chapter 4.)

The Art of Conversation

I learned almost everything I needed to know about pitching from my very first query: a comically bad, justifiably unsuccessful pitch that happened to find a generous editor. I never did write the story I proposed, but I probably became a professional science writer because of it.

I was in graduate school at the time, studying biological oceanography at the University of Southern California. I had very little media experience, but I was a magazine junkie, and I had become the default reviewer of manuscripts in my department. I had never written about science for a general audience, but I had a vague sense that I would like to.

So I searched online for the e-mail address of an editor at the now-defunct Canadian magazine *Equinox* and fired off a long, meandering message about a set of experiments I was tangentially involved in. Specifically, the proposal was for a cover story on attempts to fertilize the oceans with iron, which might boost fish populations and help control global warming, or have horrific unintended consequences. It was a good story idea—and a terrible query letter. (See "A Tale of Two Query Letters" on p. 36 for two attempts at making it better.)

It didn't even deserve a response, but I got something more valuable than an assignment: an ongoing conversation. The editor explained to me, for example, that magazine cover stories are something one works up to over a professional career. He also offered me a much more modest assignment, a short roundup of geoengineering ideas. The editor offered me a tryout, essentially—a low-risk situation for him, and a great opportunity for me.

Nearly two decades later, I've pitched hundreds of science stories successfully, and taught scores of students to do the same. I've learned that while there are lots of common errors that can sink an otherwise decent pitch (see "Classic Mistakes We Can All Avoid" on p. 32), there is no golden secret that will guarantee the success of even a terrific one. It's pure black magic: a mixture of good luck, good timing, and benign cosmic interference—and that's if you already have a great story idea. But a handful of guidelines can help give your pitch its best chance:

- *Know the outlet you're pitching.* I had read *Equinox* since its first issue, so I knew the types of stories its editors ran, and that they hadn't already covered the story I was pitching. You can do the same by reading back issues and combing through archives. You don't want to propose a story an outlet has already published, or something it never would.
- *Pitch a person, not a publication.* Look at the masthead, search online, ask friends and colleagues—anything to increase the chances that your e-mail will find a living, breathing editor and not wind up in an electronic slush pile at the far end of a "submissions@" e-mail address. And if you can find someone who knows the editor and is willing to introduce you, so much the better.
- *Practice.* Journalism conferences often feature a "pitch slam," where a panel of editors hears and critiques story pitches from audience members. We've found a less harrowing way to get critical feedback in SciLance, by breaking into smaller groups online, reading and critiquing one another's pitches, and helping to brainstorm outlets for the stories.
- *Be both audacious and humble.* Have the courage to pitch ambitious stories and leading outlets—and the humility to be grateful for any response, whether or not it leads to an assignment right away.
- *Be flexible.* Be specific in your pitch, but adaptable in any follow-up conversations. It's great to be passionate about your own ideas, but especially early in your career, you'll get further, faster if you're eager to execute your editors' ideas, too.

Finding Your Target

So . . . you have a story idea. The next step? Decide where you're going to pitch it. I tell my journalism students to think about pitching stories the same way they might have thought about applying to colleges: survey many possibilities and identify "match, stretch, and safety" options. For science writers, a safety option might mean a free blog outlet hungry for content. A match is probably an outlet you've written for previously, or a close equivalent. And a stretch is that next rung of audience size, prestige, or pay—the publication you've long admired, and dream of breaking into. Knowing the full range of possible outlets for your work, and where they line up in that scheme, will be a key part of your success pitching science stories. The good news is that unlike when you had to choose a college, you can write for more than one publication at once, and you may well have different pitches out to publications at each level at any given time.

Keep in mind that for every famous national outlet, there are many smaller, less-well-known equivalents that are easier to break into. That quirky tidbit about a researcher that would make a great "Talk of the Town" item in the *New Yorker*? It might make an even better "lede" (journalism-speak for an opening paragraph or section) for a full profile in the alumni magazine of the scientist's home institution. And sure, your idea for a long feature on new solutions to a socially relevant public health problem might work great at the *Los Angeles Times*. But it could work just as well in a free weekly newspaper that isn't being bombarded with science story pitches every day.

The point is that there are more potential outlets for your work than you could ever read, and most have at least something to recommend them. They range from the news sections or websites of academic journals, to trade association newsletters, to annual reports put out by funding agencies and university departments or colleges. They include nonprofit groups' home pages, museum catalogs, United Nations reports, and public radio station news blogs.

Some are small, some are specialized, and some are overseas—pitching relevant local stories to international publications can make you a foreign correspondent without ever leaving town. Not all outlets take freelance submissions, or pay for them if they do. But make discovering and charting all the possibilities one of your professional projects, and you'll open whole new fields of opportunity. (For more, see Chapter 25, "The Diversity of Science Writing.")

Each time you publish a story, you'll be one step closer to the next rung of visibility and, hopefully, pay. No matter how obscure the outlet may be, a published "clip" always counts for more with new editors than an unpublished "writing sample." And a terrific feature clip from a small regional publication can be worth more than a generic news brief in a glossy magazine with a million subscribers.

If science writing is your career, or you hope it will be, then money will be a crucial consideration, too. You'll find more information about pay rates (and negotiating contracts) in Chapter 22, but when you're deciding where to pitch your ideas, you can't overlook the fact that some outlets simply pay more than others do. And some require a great deal more work for stories of the same length. As you build your science-writing business, you want to keep discovering new publications, and adding them to your list of potential outlets. When you do, make a note of how well they compensate you for your time.

Pulling the Trigger

The best time to pitch a story idea is shortly after you've discovered or developed it, and well before anyone else does. You're seeking the sweet spot in an editor's mind between "I've never heard a word about this, therefore it's not important," and "This is so five minutes ago." Rest assured that if you sit on a good story, someone else will discover it and beat you into print.

Initial queries should be sent by e-mail, in the body of the message, not as attachments. (Distaste for e-mail attachments just may be the one thing all editors have in common.) When you're introducing yourself to a new editor, you can link to a few samples of your best work, or to your professional website, at the bottom of the query letter. You can also offer to send electronic copies of your published clips upon request—just don't attach them, or anything, to your initial query e-mail.

As a matter of courtesy and custom, you should send your query letter to just one publication at a time. This can get ticklish quickly, especially for time-sensitive pitches. Most editors say they do try to respond to pitches, yea or nay, as soon as they can, but every writer has stories of life-shortening stress as they waited for a response to a pitch whose news peg was rapidly approaching.

If your story's freshness will expire on a particular date, make sure that's clear in your query letter and include the phrase "time-sensitive pitch" in your e-mail's subject line. And then hit send, and wait.

How long should you wait? It depends on several factors, including the shelf life of your story's relevance and the publication frequency of the outlet you've pitched. For a daily outlet and a fast-approaching news peg, you might send a follow-up e-mail the next day. For monthly magazines and more shelf-stable stories, waiting two weeks or more for a response is pretty common.

Some writers note in their query letter that they will send the pitch to other publications if they haven't heard back by a certain date. But that's a pretty aggressive move, and runs the risk of alienating your editor rather than spurring a response. Instead, if you don't hear anything within a reasonable amount of time for the story and outlet—say, a couple of days for a daily, or a couple of weeks for a monthly—follow up twice. And in the second follow-up, after about half as much time has gone by, let the editor know you're ready to move on. "I say something like 'Since this is a time-sensitive story, if I haven't heard back from you by the end of the week I'll assume you're not interested. Thanks again for your consideration, and I hope to work with you in the future,'" says SciLancer Michelle Nijhuis. That way, if the editor does pop up again after you've sold your story elsewhere, you'll have a digital trail that shows she had her chance. (Most writers stick with e-mail for their follow-ups, but some swear there's no substitute for picking up the phone: if nothing else, it tends to get you your rejection more quickly, so you can move on.)

Unfortunately, a pitch does not give you exclusive rights to a story idea. It's always possible that a publication you pitch, or a colleague you talk with too openly, will consciously or unconsciously take your idea. But in our experience, outright idea theft is rare: even moderately reputable outlets won't simply poach your story idea and assign it to someone else. More often, publications receive very similar pitches from multiple writers, and give priority first to staffers, then to freelancers who already have a working relationship with the outlet. The more original your idea is, and the more effective your query, the better chance you have of being the writer others resent. Er, admire.

But hopefully you'll get an answer quickly, and it will be either yes or no. If it's no, turn immediately to Chapter 13, on dealing with rejection. And if the answer is any variation on the word yes? Huzzah! Celebrate by reading Chapter 22, on contracts, and get ready to work.

Remember, you're pitching a story *idea,* not a finished article. If your pitch does find an interested editor, he or she will become a collaborator, helping you to shape and refine the original idea and plan out the execution. Well, the good ones do that, anyway. "You want to make sure as an editor and as a writer that the two of you are on the same page before the full scope of the reporting gets done," says Peter Aldhous, the San Francisco bureau chief for *New Scientist.*

So, if your assignment is anything more than a straightforward news story, pick up the phone and have a conversation with your editor—that will help you clarify expectations from the outset, collect answers to the editor's questions as you report, and write with confidence that your first draft will be on target. After you talk, send an e-mail to your editor noting the key points of your discussion to make sure you understand each other—and that you've got a record to refer to in case of future disagreements. (Many publications will do the same for you in an assignment letter. But it never hurts to be proactive.)

Dating Around or Settling Down

How often should you pitch? When it comes to frequency and number, there are two primary pitching strategies, each with its vocal proponents. You might think of them as the sea urchins and the sharks. Sea urchins are famously fecund, throwing off millions of eggs or sperm in the hopes that a few will bump into each other and mature into healthy adults. Most sharks are more circumspect. They mature later in life, breed rarely, and often brood their eggs internally, giving birth to just a few self-sufficient pups. Both strategies work, with sea urchins accepting steep rates of attrition while sharks invest much more to improve each offspring's chances of survival.

When it comes to pitching, you'll soon learn whether you're a natural broadcast spawner, reeling off dozens of pitches a month in the hopes that a few find their mark, or a brooder, who pours days or weeks of work into each query, relying on that effort to lead to an assignment almost every time. In practice, many science writers combine both approaches, and often metamorphose from echinoderm to elasmobranch as careers advance. The effort required to pitch also tends to change as you develop relationships with individual editors—once you're trusted, you can save time by pitching informally over the phone or in person. If the editor is interested in your informal pitch, you can follow up with a detailed written query.

One more sexual analogy: Some writers find they are happiest with solid, predictable professional relationships. They work on staff, or pitch most of their story ideas to just one or a few primary outlets. Others, literarily speaking, are downright promiscuous, preferring to match each story idea with the best potential outlet, rather than shaping their ideas for publishing partners they already know. Ultimately, it doesn't matter which strategy you use, as long as you use one.

If you're reading this book, chances are you agree with us that the world needs great science writing. But that doesn't mean that the universe owes you a career, or that editors are standing by bemoaning their empty pages and unspent budgets. Still, there is more room and appetite for quality science writing than ever before, and a near infinite variety of stories waiting to be told. Most important, there are people waiting to help you tell them, and to pay you for the pleasure. All you need is to convince them to let you do it.

Classic Mistakes We Can All Avoid

By Monya Baker

Dumb Typos

If you don't get the editor's name right, you won't get the assignment. All your hours of research, writing, and sweat—all that will count for nothing if you don't check the number of "l"s in Hillary or make sure Alex Nguyen is a man before you send an e-mail to "Mr. Nguyen." Even worse is a message addressed to someone other than the recipient. *Technology Review* is not going to accept a pitch if you leave in the "Dear Mr. Remnick" from your pitch to the *New Yorker,* or the sentence about why your story is just right for *Wired.* And believe us, pitches are one place where spelling and grammar count—a lot. Take care that a stray semicolon or three-second cut-and-paste doesn't sabotage your hard work.

Inappropriate Informality in Early E-mails

Your initial e-mails to an editor should resemble digital business letters: formal, cleanly formatted, and succinct. Even if you've met an editor in person, addressing him or her in an e-mail with "hey" or without using a name at all will make a bad impression. Once you get to know an editor, you'll soon be on a first-name basis. But in your first e-mail, play it safe with a "Dr.," "Mr.," or "Ms."

Wrong Magazine

Nature is not a wildlife magazine. If you don't take the time to know what kinds of stories a magazine runs, your ignorance will show. You won't get the assignment you pitched, and you'll lose credibility for subsequent pitches. Don't let this happen.

Pitching the Story That Just Ran, or Is Sure to Be Running

If you see a story on the EurekAlert! online news service that looks perfect for a particular magazine, you can be sure that staff writers and regular freelancers have had first crack. (See Chapter 2 for more.) Don't even try to pitch these picked-over stories unless you can bring something special to them, such as on-site reporting or an unexpected take. Similarly, if a topic is hot or timely, don't pitch an obvious explainer or roundup. If an editor wants an everything-you-need-to-know-about-composting story for the gardening season, she'll assign it to someone she knows. Be sure to offer a specific narrative or special perspective.

Forsaking the Phone

Insecure newbies often spend too much time on background research, trolling through countless articles on PubMed without actually contacting a practitioner in the field about their story idea. Sure, you need to read up a bit to know whom to call, but ultimately a reporter's job is to learn about what hasn't already been published. Writers who forsake the phone are losing the opportunity not just to find potential characters for their stories, but also to get expert guides to the literature and the latest data.

Pitching Endurance

By Douglas Fox

Pitching a story, especially a long, travel-intensive feature, usually requires patience, persistence, and luck—and sometimes megadoses of all three.

In March 2007 I secured a spot on an expedition to Antarctica, embedded with a team studying lakes hidden beneath the West Antarctic

(Continues)

Ice Sheet. I would spend seven weeks on the ice, five of them sleeping in a tent just 375 miles from the South Pole. My editor at *Discover* was interested in the story, and I was about to send her a full proposal.

The departure date was November 8, 2007. Things started falling apart in July.

Several weeks after sending a full proposal to *Discover*, I received an apologetic voice mail from my editor informing me she couldn't assign the story after all, because another Antarctic feature had already been approved at the magazine without her knowledge. From there began a flurry of pitching and repitching the story.

August 7: *Wired* said no. The editors thought the science was too incremental, and they already had an Arctic story in progress that might overlap with mine, despite being poles apart.

August 8: *National Geographic* said no. They needed more lead time and would have to send one of their photographers along, which wasn't logistically possible at this point.

August 9: *Smithsonian* said no. They had already published a photo essay on the Antarctic volcano, Mount Erebus, the year before.

August 22: *Men's Journal* was interested but needed more time to decide. Who is this scientist, they asked, and what does he *look* like? I hadn't actually met him, so I drove down to the University of California in Santa Cruz to do that.

September 20: *Men's Journal* stopped answering e-mails or phone calls. I sent them a note telling them that I planned to take the story elsewhere.

October 3: *National Geographic Adventure* was intrigued, but tired of depressing stories involving melting ice. They suggested that I call to discuss further when I got back.

My frustration grew with each passing week. I couldn't back out of an opportunity that might never happen again. And yet I couldn't spend nearly two months and thousands of dollars on a trip without having a significant outlet signed up for a story.

Things finally looked up on October 17. At 11:16 a.m., an editor at the *Christian Science Monitor* agreed to take a couple of 1,200-word pieces. And then at 2:52 that afternoon, after a month's silence, *Men's Journal* e-mailed and told me the story was a go.

And so I went to Antarctica, with noncompeting assignments from *MJ* and the *Monitor*. The trip, as I describe in Chapter 6, exceeded expectations.

But by the time I returned home and filed the story with *MJ*, new problems were already emerging. The story was fine, but the photo editor wasn't happy with the shots. Rather than having the story languish, I negotiated with *MJ* to have it killed immediately so that I could pitch it elsewhere.

I knew that I had the best story I had ever written, and no one wanted to print it. I quickly obtained a second round of rejections from *Smithsonian* and *National Geographic Adventure*. I was getting desperate, and losing credibility with the people who had so generously taken me to Antarctica in the first place, when my editor at *Discover* asked out of the blue how the Antarctica trip had gone, and suggested that I pitch her the story again. I happily did this—but yet again, there were challenges.

Discover had run its other Antarctic story, the one that bumped mine, in November 2007. That story was devoted to subglacial lakes, just as mine was. It took some doing to reposition my story around climate change and the stability of the West Antarctic Ice Sheet. I did receive some help from an unexpected source: Michael Crichton had featured the work of my Antarctic hosts in his climate-skeptic novel *State of Fear*. That touch of controversy and the shift in focus were enough for *Discover*, and the story was published with my photos.

Ultimately I published six other stories from the trip: two for the *Christian Science Monitor* and four for science-focused publications. Was it worth it? For me, it was. But I learned that when it comes to time-consuming, travel-intensive stories, the pitching process should start as early as possible—and that I should prepare for the unpredictable.

A Tale of Two Query Letters

By Thomas Hayden

My first magazine pitch was a dismal failure—a solid topic, but with no structure, story arc, or sense of relevance beyond "it's really cool." So what should I have written instead? I attempt to redeem myself here with two versions written to demonstrate the differences between a news query and a feature query. Remember that even with a perfect pitch, you still need the reporting and writing chops to deliver the story: I probably could have executed the news story back then, with lots of help from an understanding editor. But I was far too green to handle a complex feature story—not to mention too close to the primary sources for most publications. (The most important thing there is disclosure, so that interested editors can decide whether you have a potential conflict of interest.) And before you pitch, be sure to check out the archive of real query letters at The Open Notebook (www.theopennotebook.com), too.

News Pitch
Subject line: News Pitch | Making the ocean bloom

Dear Mr./Ms. Editor,

For decades, scientists have struggled to understand why some regions of the global ocean teem with life, while other vast stretches can sustain only the sparsest of ecosystems. A unique experiment currently under way in the equatorial Pacific suggests the first clear answer: these biological "deserts" are apparently starved for iron. When oceanographers added small quantities of the metal to the seawater, it caused a dramatic bloom of microscopic plants, the base of the marine food web. The scientists insist they want only to understand how the ocean works, but this kind of deliberate oceanic "fertilization" on a larger scale could ultimately combat global warming and boost fish supplies—or create unintended consequences, such as oxygen-free "dead zones" and deadly toxic algae blooms.

The scientists return to port in one week and will release a statement to the press at that time. As an oceanography graduate student and colleague of two of the researchers, I have advance notice of the preliminary results and can be ready to go with a five hundred–word news story as the research vessel docks.

I've spoken with two of the scientists already, and expect interviews this week with the chief scientist (by electronic mail) and two prominent critics of the expedition. Headshots of key researchers and photographs of the expedition's departure are available from their home institutions' press offices.

I can be reached by return e-mail, or at (310) 555-1867.

Thomas Hayden

Feature Pitch
Subject line: Feature Pitch | The friendship behind the "experiment of the decade"

Dear Mr./Ms. Editor,

Two thousand kilometers off the coast of Ecuador, the surface waters of the equatorial Pacific are all but devoid of marine life. For the scientists aboard the research ship *Melville*, more than a week into a unique, experimental expedition, the world was an uninterrupted sweep of blue sky and ocean. Until, that is, the oceanographers on board started dumping nearly five hundred kilograms of iron into the sea, over an area the size of Manhattan. After that, the ocean teemed with microscopic life, turning the water green, proving a decade-old theory, and potentially affecting everything from the global climate to the world's supply of seafood.

It's an experiment that oceanographer John Martin would have loved. There's just one problem: Martin died two years ago, as the first test of his radical "iron hypothesis" was being planned. The idea that certain

(Continues)

"high nutrient, low chlorophyll" (HNLC) areas of the ocean could be made to bloom by fertilizing them with iron was so unpopular, it might well have died with Martin. But Kenneth Coale, a young colleague of Martin's at Moss Landing Marine Laboratory, near Monterey, California, refused to let that happen.

As lead scientist for what many are calling the most audacious experiment of the decade, Coale had to fight an uphill battle against dismissive colleagues, wary funders, and alarmed critics. With vindication finally in sight, it seems clear that his persistence had as much to do with the bond between two very different scientists—the older one fiery and iconoclastic, the younger one calmly determined—as it did with the underlying science.

I'm proposing a feature story on the IronEx II experiment, told through the lens of John Martin's and Kenneth Coale's struggles to make it happen. Sidebars could include one on the potential for iron fertilization to combat global climate change and augment seafood supplies, and another on possible unintended consequences, including toxic algae blooms and oxygen-deprived "dead zones." Graphics could include a time line of related ocean research, including future iron experiments, a map of the study area and other HNLC areas, and a graphic illustrating the chemistry and biology of iron fertilization. I have access to onboard photographs taken by several of the cruise participants.

I'm a third-year PhD student in biological oceanography. I know this field well and have access to most of the researchers involved in IronEx II, including two of my lab mates. (I'm not involved in the primary experiments, but I have run some chemical analyses for a side project.) My professional writing experience is limited to music reviews and the script for an interactive digital textbook on the Amazon rain forest. I would be happy to send samples on request.

I can be reached by return e-mail, or at (310) 555-1867.

Thomas Hayden

- Each time you pitch a new editor, you're not just trying to sell a story—you're introducing yourself to a potential employer, and trying to **sell your skills** and the quality of your ideas.

- Be sure you're **pitching stories, not just topics**.

- The right time to pitch is just **after you've confirmed** your story idea is real, and **before you write**. If your editor likes the idea, he or she will help you shape it.

- Develop a **diverse list of potential outlets**, to increase your chances of finding one that fits your idea.

- **Research and report your story ideas** enough to know they're real, and that key sources will talk with you.

- **Err on the side of formality**, especially when you're pitching a new outlet or editor.

- Many outlets list **submission guidelines** online, sometimes in considerable detail. Read them carefully. If you can't find them online, e-mail the general editorial address and request a copy.

- Pitch a **person, not just a publication**. Secure an introduction to new editors if you can—or introduce yourself in person at a conference or meeting.

- Make sure **your query represents you well**—no typos or grammatical errors.

- Find a friend or group and **critique one another's query letters**.

- Send your query **in the body** of an e-mail, not as an attachment.

- You can send your query letter to only **one publication at a time**, so work quickly and choose carefully.

Chapter 4

Getting the Story, and Getting It Right
By Andreas von Bubnoff

Once you have landed that assignment and have a deadline, you may start to feel what we call "The Fear": That this time, you won't make it. That this time, "they"—your editor, your readers, your sources, your mother—will find out you're a fraud. But if you break down the research process into steps, The Fear will fade, and even complicated projects will become manageable. This chapter discusses strategies for making your reporting more effective and efficient.

Finding Sources

Often the first step in reporting is to find someone—the right someone—to talk to about your topic. If you've pitched or proposed the story to an editor, you already know the names of at least one or two of the main sources for your story. For a news brief on a research finding, an obvious place to start is with the researcher who conducted the main study. In my experience, the leader of the study—called the principal investigator, or PI, and generally the last author listed—is the best source for big-picture quotes about the meaning of the findings. Graduate students or postdocs, who often do the bulk of the work, can discuss the details of the research but may be afraid to say what they really think—or may simply be too close to the work to comment on its larger implications.

When you talk to the PI, ask her or him to recommend other researchers who can comment on the findings. Other potential sources and "sources of sources" are the authors of related papers, often cited in the original paper; scientists on relevant advisory panels; scientific societies; scientific publication databases; and even your own friends in related fields. (While journalistic ethics prevent reporters from quoting friends or colleagues in an article, friends can suggest sources and give you their unvarnished opinion on the work, which may help inform your questions.) Many scientists are happy to talk about the criticism their work has received and direct you to their critics, so don't be afraid to ask.

For a feature story, the reporting process is more complex, partly because it can lead in multiple, unexpected directions. Often my first step is to look in PubMed (for biomedical research) or Google Scholar for researchers who have recently written review articles on the topic of the story, especially for leading journals such as *Science* or *Nature*. The *Annual Reviews,* which cover more than forty disciplines, are valuable summaries of current research and contain hundreds of citations. Online "expert" databases, such as ProfNet and the Newswise directory, and expert guides published by university public-relations offices can also provide good starting points. Make sure to check nearby institutions for possible sources when you're working for local outlets. When I talk to these researchers, I ask them to suggest other people working on the topic.

Investigative stories, which reveal information that sources would rather keep secret, often involve filing Freedom of Information Act requests and using other tactics to acquire key documents. (See the Resources section for further information on investigative reporting.)

When I first contact potential sources, I generally use e-mail, or call if there isn't much time. I've found that many scientists respond to e-mail surprisingly fast, often in a few hours or less, and e-mailing to arrange a time to talk can reduce the time both you and your source spend playing phone tag.

Your initial e-mail should be short, polite, and professional, including an appropriate salutation, a signature box, and, needless to say, good spelling and grammar. I usually introduce myself as a science writer, briefly describe the publication I'm writing for and the nature of the story, and ask if there is a convenient time to talk. I also mention how much of the interviewee's time I expect to need, and make it clear if my deadline is tight. If the researcher says he or she can't do it, I ask for suggestions of people to contact instead.

If a source doesn't respond within a reasonable time, send a reminder e-mail, call, or enlist the help of the institution's public information officer, or PIO. While it's almost always worth trying to contact your source directly first, some institutions will let you interview sources only if you contact a PIO first; sometimes, if a researcher is a high-profile scientist or the story is attracting a lot of press, working with a PIO may be the only way to get your source on the phone. PIOs, especially those at government agencies and federal labs, may also want to sit in on phone or in-person interviews, which can be helpful or restrictive depending on the sensitivity of the interview topic and the attitude of the PIO.

Make sure you don't schedule more interviews in a day than you can handle: interviews of any kind can be oddly tiring, and you need time to process what you've been told. "I try to limit the number of in-person interviews in a day to two and the number of phone interviews to four," says SciLancer Robert Frederick, adding that it takes much more energy to do interviews in person than on the phone, because reporters have to be more actively attentive during in-person interviews.

Preparing for an Interview

How much research you do before an interview depends on the type of story. Your preparation for news article interviews, during which you'll need to ask specific questions about new research, will be different than your preparation for, say, a profile piece, for which you may want to ask more personal questions about the subject's life and work. In general, prepare enough so you don't waste a source's time, but not so much that you lose your own sense of the big picture. "I read as much of the paper as I can, but always the abstract and the discussion," says SciLancer Hannah Hoag. "Other news coverage of the research is useful to a point, but sometimes very dated or wrong, and I don't like to read too much because I don't want it to influence my questions or reporting."

In some cases, though, extensive preparation can pay off, as it did for SciLancer Monya Baker. After struggling through a technical paper before interviewing its author, she still didn't understand a few details. She asked the researcher; he explained. "Then he said something to the effect that he'd just gotten the most exciting results he'd seen in years," she says. "They were so preliminary that he was reluctant to talk to reporters about them, but he thought I could handle them. Those results became my story."

Make sure you compile a list of questions, even if you have just five minutes to spare before the interview. This way, if for any reason you lose your train of thought, you have something to fall back on. If you're writing about a subject that's familiar to you, don't forget to ask more general questions before delving into the details: put yourself in your reader's shoes and imagine the questions you might have if you were encountering the subject for the first time. (See "A Science Writer's Emergency Question List" on p. 49 for suggestions.)

The list of questions will also allow you to give the interview a structure, which may differ depending on the type of story. "I try to structure the interview chronologically if I'm really trying to get the story behind the work, or logically if we're talking about a particular piece of research," says Hannah.

For certain types of projects, such as question-and-answer-format (Q&A) interviews for print or audio, a structured list of questions and good preparation are especially important, because you will be less able to rearrange the material later for the finished piece.

If you record your interview, make sure you have enough space on your recorder and spare batteries on hand. Oh, and before the interview, make sure you go to the bathroom.

Conducting the Interview

There are different ways to start an interview. With sources who don't often speak with the media, it may help to begin with some brief small talk, but don't force it; other sources may find chitchat to be an annoying waste of time. It's always a good idea to briefly summarize the subject and scope of your assignment; after that, you can often get an interviewee talking by asking how he or she came to study the topic, or by asking for a summary of his or her findings and their implications.

Remember that your job as an interviewer is "not to translate the subject on behalf of your source, but to respectfully interrogate him or her for your audience," says SciLancer Thomas Hayden.

Also remember that you are in control. Think of yourself not just as a listener, but also as the director of what Thomas describes as a "weirdly focused, slightly augmented conversation." For example, it's perfectly reasonable to ask sources to repeat themselves; to ask for additional details in follow-up questions; to stop sources who give you too much information; or to ask them to speak more slowly if necessary.

Even as you direct, try to keep the conversation as natural as possible. Ask open-ended questions, as you would in casual conversation. Don't talk too much; sources often respond to a little silence with new and interesting information. As SciLancer Liza Gross discovered, "It's amazing

For news stories, I like to get at the backstory first: "I'd love some background before we get into what you did and what you found and why it's important. So, what did you know going in and what were you hoping to learn with this study?"

—EMILY SOHN

how often they end up saying something unexpected that I never would have heard if I'd butted in."

The purpose of an interview is not only to understand the material yourself, but also to get vivid, interesting quotes that will help your story come alive for your readers. So make sure you ask your interviewees to speak in lay terms so you will have to do less "translating" during the writing process. Ask them for metaphors so you won't have to find your own; for instance, you might ask a molecular biologist, "If cellular component X were big enough to hold in my hands, what would it look like?" Also ask them to put their research into context understandable to your readers, and to describe the general state of the field, including any controversies around the topic of your story. Jessica Marshall, another SciLance member, says, "I often blame my editor or the reader for my questions: 'I know my editor won't let me put (complicated word or concept) in the story. Can you say that a different way?' or 'Many of our readers won't know what X is.' That helps them remember who they're ultimately talking to."

And even for a news story, don't forget to ask about your interviewees' emotions. "Leave room for questions like 'Was this surprising?' or 'What was that like?'" says Jessica. Sometimes a personal comment—"I would have been terrified"—can get a subject talking about his or her own feelings.

Even if you've spent hours or days preparing, never assume you know everything: ask the questions you think you know the answers to as well as the ones you don't. The practice will help you not only avoid mistakes, but also get stronger quotes.

As for structuring the interview, print reporters often move from more general to specific questions. Audio and video journalists sometimes ask about specifics first and save their general questions for later, to make sure that the interviewee stays excited during the interview. If you have sensitive questions, you may want to ask them toward the end of the interview, after you've established some rapport with your source. (If you know you have extremely limited time with a high-profile or difficult-to-access source, however, ask your most important questions first.) If your source refuses to comment, you might want to point out that a mention of the refusal to comment in your article might be more damaging than any comment. You can also grant anonymity or go off the record, but make sure you carefully explain what that means beforehand, especially if you're speaking with someone who has never spoken to the media (see "On and Off the Record" on p. 50).

To save yourself work later, try to do as much fact-checking as you can during the interview. One way to do that is to paraphrase back to the source what you think he or she said and ask if your interpretation is correct. If you have a follow-up question but don't want to interrupt the flow of the conversation, make a note and ask at the end of the conversation.

The length of interviews varies widely: twenty to thirty minutes should be enough for news pieces and even most feature stories, although an hour can make sense for a feature story if the person is a major source. For certain story types, such as profiles, interviews can last several hours.

At the end of the interview, confirm how to spell the source's name, check their title, and of course ask who else you should talk to. The last minute or two of an interview are often the most important of the entire process: the source is usually comfortable with you and feeling expansive, and with a little prompting he or she may come up with unusually clear and reflective quotes. "I always ask, 'Is there anything we didn't cover that you feel is important?' Often that leads to an exceptional nugget," says SciLancer Anne Sasso.

Getting It All Down

This is where that typing class you took in high school may come in handy. Some reporters are more comfortable taking handwritten notes; the fastest way to do that is probably by learning shorthand or speed writing. Some develop their own version of speed writing or save time by dropping vowels when taking notes. "I scribble on a steno notepad, and use a kind of personal shorthand with lots of half-words and abbreviations I make up on the fly," says SciLancer Jill Adams, adding that she later types up her scribbles. Just make sure you can read your own shorthand!

Recording and transcribing an interview is one way to make sure you get everything. Turning on a small digital recorder also lets you focus on the interview and on the next question, rather than on your notebook or laptop. That can be especially important when you are in the field and moving around. Recording also allows you more time for taking notes on your own impressions—what you're seeing and hearing around you, how the source is behaving, and all the other details essential to any feature story.

If you do record, make sure you ask the source to state his or her name near the beginning (believe me, later you may have no idea who is on the recording). And it's important to ask for permission to record, since several states require two-party consent to record a phone conversation.

If you combine typing with recording, turn on the tracking function in Microsoft Word so that you can time-stamp interesting passages, or note the time when the source says something important so that you can easily find it later in the recording. It's often helpful to write a brief summary just after the interview of the most important things an interviewee said. I've also found that for news stories with few sources, I can often just write a rough draft of the article while listening to the recording—no transcribing required.

Even partial transcribing of interviews can be time-consuming, and often impossible on a tight deadline. Also, recording can be a crutch that prevents you from focusing completely on the interview and what you really need from it. So practice doing interviews without your recorder—you may find that with time, you become a more efficient, and equally accurate, reporter.

Taking notes and recording in the field has its own challenges. For more, see Chapter 6.

Structuring the Reporting Process

So how many interviews do you need? For news stories, you'll need to talk to at least one main source and one outside source not connected to the study. For a feature story, you'll likely need to interview several sources until you understand what's happening in a field of research and know who the main players are. It's also important to identify any controversies in the field you're covering, and then talk to all sides. For investigative stories, you may need to secure supporting documents or do extra interviews to confirm your findings.

In general, when you start hearing the same points made over and over again, and your sources start recommending sources you have already spoken with, you're nearing the end of the reporting process.

Robert Irion of the science communication program at the University of California, Santa Cruz, says that for any story longer than a few hundred words, reporters should interview at least one source for every 250 words. He's quick to add that the ratio varies depending on the length and complexity of the story and the style of the publication, but it is a useful rule of thumb.

After your first handful of interviews, you may want to start sketching out a draft. Many reporters find that an early draft helps them identify and focus on gaps during the rest of their reporting. "I used to do all my interviewing, then write," says SciLancer Douglas Fox. "But I find that the writing—or at least outlining—comes earlier and earlier." (For more on the process of structuring and writing your story, see Chapter 7.)

The downside of beginning to write too early, however, is to miss or not be open or prepared enough for unexpected turns and twists in the story. Sometimes it is that one last phone call that gives you the contrarian source who criticizes everything others have told you before. And that's not the only advantage of extra reporting: "I think a lot of great new story ideas come from over-reporting," says Douglas.

Fact-Checking and Follow-up Questions

Journalism, at its most basic level, is truth-telling: everything a reporter writes should be verifiable, and based on firsthand observation, robust documentation, or reliable sources. And as we've said before, while not all science writing is journalism, we believe that all science writing can and should be done journalistically. So once the article is written, you'll need to make sure that it's completely correct—especially after the editing process, which often raises unanticipated follow-up questions and sometimes introduces errors. (For more on working with editors, see Chapter 8.)

For magazine features, you may work with a staff or freelance fact-checker, who will ask you to provide an annotated draft so that he or she can confirm all the facts in your story. But even in these cases, it's best to check all your facts yourself, and rely on the fact-checker as a triple-check. With any story, short or long, go through your final edited draft line by line, noting all the facts—names, titles, institutions, numbers, dates, places, interpretations of research findings. Then, even if you think you have them right, confirm them with your sources or with reliable documents.

When you check facts, whether on the phone or by e-mail, you may want to tell the source that the process is about accuracy, not style. To help a source focus on factual accuracy, it can be helpful to break down the facts you are checking into separate statements and present them in a different order than they appear in the story. (See "So When Can I Read Your Draft?" on p. 51 for more on sharing your copy with sources.)

When I started out, I over-reported intensely, and wrote last. It worked, but it was also frustrating and inefficient. I slowly learned to report less, and in a more targeted way, but found some of the joy going out of the process, and some of the quality and richness out of the stories. I now try to match reporting intensity to the work. If it's a quick job or a rent-payer, I report less, and more briefly. If it's a "heart job"—something I'm doing for all the reasons that I started doing this stuff in the first place—I indulge myself and impose on my sources to do the kind of long, meandering, hyper-tangential reporting I really enjoy.

—THOMAS HAYDEN

Also, while all publications want you to check your facts, most will not want you to read a verbatim quote back to a source: once a source said it, it's fair game, and many sources, on hearing their original language, will want to water it down or make it less colorful. That said, you should check the facts within your quotes by paraphrasing them to your source or sources.

If all goes well, fact-checking is the last stage in your process. Soon you'll have a well-reported, accurate story in print—and another deadline on the horizon.

Making a Reporting Plan

Peter Aldhous, San Francisco bureau chief of *New Scientist* and a lecturer at the University of California, Santa Cruz, science communication program, suggests that writers use a reporting plan to organize and streamline their research.

Even for short news stories that need to be done in a day, Aldhous says, it's helpful to make an initial list of sources to contact. For longer projects, Aldhous keeps track of his reporting progress in a spreadsheet that lists sources he has spoken to and needs to speak to, their contact information, and their relationship to the story. He notes the times of scheduled interviews in his Outlook calendar.

For projects that involve data or document-driven reporting, a reporting plan might also include a list of documents (court records, for example) or data sets that need to be obtained. For long-term projects, Aldhous includes a timetable for the completion of different stages.

Of course, reporting often leads to new information that changes the direction or focus of the story, and the plan should respond. "The plan evolves as you work on the story," Aldhous says.

A Science Writer's Emergency Question List

You should always prepare for your interviews. But sometimes you'll get an unexpected opportunity to ask a source a few questions. What then?

Frank Allen, a former environment editor for the *Wall Street Journal* and founder of the Institutes for Journalism and Natural Resources (www.ijnr.org), suggests the mnemonic G-R-O-S-S to remember the essentials:

G *for Goals*—What is your source trying to accomplish?

R *for Reasons*—Why is your source trying to do what he or she is doing?

O *for Obstacles*—Who or what stands in the way of the goals?

S *for Solutions*—How can those obstacles be overcome?

S *for Start*—How will your source begin to overcome them (or, alternatively, how did your source start to be interested in the topic at hand)?

For stories about scientific research, it's also important to ask: Who pays? Who benefits? How do you know (X result)? Could you explain that again—in terms my readers will understand?

And finally, at the end of every interview, ask what's missing: Is there anything we didn't cover that you feel is important? Who else should I talk to?

On and Off the Record

Terms such as "off the record" are often used to define the degree of anonymity a reporter grants to a source. Unfortunately, these terms are very poorly defined, even among reporters. If you decide to grant anonymity to a source, make sure that the two of you agree not just on a term but on the definition of that term.

"On the record" means that everything a source says during the interview can be used and the source can be identified as the person the comments came from (i.e., "with attribution").

"Not for attribution" typically means that the information a source told the reporter can be quoted but that the source can be identified only in general terms, such as "a government official."

"On background" is sometimes used as a synonym for "not for attribution," but it can also mean that information from the interview can be used in the story, but direct quotes may not be used.

"Off the record" means that nothing a source said can be used in the story and that the source cannot be identified, even in general terms. (This does not prevent the reporter from getting the same information from another source on the record, in which case it can be used.) For a remark to be off the record, it needs to be clear *before* the remark is made that what follows will be off the record. In other words, anything said to a reporter is on the record unless specified otherwise in advance. If you're interviewing a source with little media experience about a sensitive subject, do take the time to explain this convention.

"So When Can I Read Your Draft?"

While it is good journalistic practice to check facts with sources, many of them—especially scientists accustomed to collaborative writing and the process of peer review—will ask you to run the entire article past them before publication. In academic and corporate settings, where the science writer and the major sources work together, that's standard practice. But most journalistic publications won't let you share prepublication drafts with sources, as it threatens reporters' independence from those sources. At some publications, the practice is banned outright. Others will allow sharing short passages, perhaps up to a few paragraphs, of technical material for fact-checking. Check your publication's policy with your editor, and when in doubt, don't do it.

There are different ways to explain this journalistic norm to your source. First, there's the practical matter of time: even if reporters wanted to show a draft to every source in their stories, most deadlines wouldn't leave them enough time to do so. You can also point out the general importance of journalistic independence: "I'll say something along the lines of, 'Well, city reporters don't run their stories past the mayor'—not in a snarky way, but to explain, by analogy at least, how journalism works," says SciLancer Jennifer Cutraro. Finally, you can make it clear to your sources that you are interested in accuracy and are a professional in your job just as much as they are in theirs, says SciLancer Hillary Rosner. "I usually try to make the point that I respect their work and defer to them on the science, and they need to do the same to me on the journalism," Hillary says. "And I explain to them that I've got a stake in getting it right, too, since otherwise I'll look bad and the next scientist I call might not want to talk to me."

SciLance says . . .

- Before you start reporting, **make a reporting plan** that includes names and contact information for key sources and core questions you need to answer during your interviews.

- When you approach potential sources, **provide basic information** about your publication, your assignment, how long you expect the interview to take, and your deadline.

- Do **enough interview preparation** so you don't waste a source's time with too-basic questions, but not so much that you lose your own sense of the big picture.

- Make **a list of questions**, even if you have only five minutes to spare before an interview.

- During an interview, remember that **you are in control**. Keep the conversation as natural as possible, but don't hesitate to ask for more or less information if necessary.

- Be polite, but when sources are evasive or reluctant to talk, **be persistent**.

- Even when you're thoroughly prepared for an interview, **never assume you know everything**: ask the questions you think you know the answers to as well as the ones you don't.

- When you start hearing the same points repeated during interviews, and your sources start recommending sources you have already spoken with, you're **nearing the end of your reporting process**.

- Once the article is written and edited, make sure that it's completely correct by **thoroughly double-checking all your facts**, even those within quotes.

- **Don't show unpublished drafts to sources** unless your editor or publication requires you to do so.

Chapter 5

By the Numbers

Essential Statistics for Science Writers

By Stephen Ornes

The practice of science almost always requires measurement, and measurement often means fitting precise tools to an imprecise, messy, and complex world. As a result, scientific research—and science writing—can involve an ongoing wrestling match with uncertainty: every measurement introduces the opportunity for statistical error, human error, and a misunderstanding of the data (often by the science writer). In this chapter I'll offer some general guidelines for how to think about scientific uncertainty, and then some tips on how to assess how serious the first two issues are in a given study, and to avoid being the cause of the third.

The Uncertainties of Uncertainty

During interviews, scientists often implore science writers to take note of caveats. But for a writer, that can mean using part of your precious word count to dwell on nuances that are meaningful (and comprehensible) only to experts in the field. Too many caveats can result in a highly accurate piece that no one reads.

So how much uncertainty do you include in your article? There's no easy answer, but here are some variables to consider.

Story length. If you're writing a three hundred–word story on new research, you have enough room to hit only the high points. You can nod to the inherent uncertainty of the results with a word or two—by saying, for instance, that a correlation appears "very likely." If you're writing a 3,000-word feature, you may find that describing the reasons for the uncertainty—in accessible, clear terms—adds a level of depth to your reportage.

Your audience. News articles written for the general public don't need to include every caveat and condition posited by the researcher. And the general public doesn't need a behind-the-scenes peek at every new paper. However, that doesn't mean science journalists have to be cheerleaders of the research: always consult at least one outside source, especially someone who can address the limitations of the new findings.

The implications of the uncertainty. The level of acceptable uncertainty varies wildly among fields. A clinical trial might gain notice for results that, to a particle physicist, have a laughably high level of uncertainty. Could a large degree of uncertainty undermine the study's findings? Or—as is often the case in astronomy—does uncertainty suggest an interesting new direction for research? Ask the researchers.

Seeing the Story in the Stats

Can't tell a confidence interval from a p-value? Don't know the difference between *absolute* risk and *relative* risk? It's time to do a little homework. Science writers often have to wade through papers packed with statistics, and the jargon is easy to misinterpret. Here are some tips to help make your story as accurate as possible, and a short glossary of common stats terms. (I'll often use examples from biomedical research, but the concepts apply to everything from astronomy to zoology.)

Percent vs. percentage points. Let's start off with an easy one. A **percent**, by definition, is the amount in each hundred something occurs. For example: 12 out of 50 US states start with a vowel, which means 24 **percent** of US states start with a vowel—and therefore 76 percent start with a consonant. Percentage points are totally different. Percentage points are the difference between two percentages. The difference between the percent of states that start with a consonant and those that start with a vowel is 76 – 24 = 52 **percentage points**. The difference between a 6 percent mortgage and a 4 percent mortgage is 2 **percentage points,** even though 6 is 50 **percent** more than 4.

Know that correlation does not imply causation. Large observational studies have reported an association between higher consumption of alcoholic beverages and increased risk of breast cancer. However, that doesn't mean we can use those studies to report—as many outlets do— that "drinking alcohol increases your risk of cancer." Because observational, or epidemiological, studies compare what has already happened to one group to what has happened to another in the general population, they can identify only correlations, not causes. So if the scientists use an observational study and report an "increased risk," that doesn't mean they found the cause of the increase—the drinkers could all be doing something else that contributes to cancer, for example. (Causality is remarkably difficult to establish, but there are other types of studies in which medical researchers have more control over the variables and can therefore come closer to identifying a cause.) It bears repeating: if the scientists use an observational study to report an "increased risk," that doesn't mean they found the cause of the increase.

Ask a statistician. If you're not sure whether you're accurately reporting the findings from a particular study, look at the author list. For medical studies, find the biostatistician. Call or e-mail. Ask. If you're unsure whether the statistical measurements justify the conclusions of the paper, find a disinterested statistician who did not work on the study. Ask.

Pay attention to the tools being used. Did the study report *relative risk, odds ratios,* or *hazard ratios*? Or something else? Make sure you report which populations are being compared. Do researchers claim a "reduced risk" in press releases when the study reports only odds ratios? Find out why. (And see the glossary on p. 56 for definitions of those terms.)

Look at the *confidence interval.* Peer-reviewed studies that present a conclusion based on statistics almost always include the confidence interval, which is the numerical range that *likely* (usually with 95 percent *probability*) includes the true value. Large confidence intervals indicate high uncertainty, and may mean that the finding isn't as strong as the headline you have in mind would imply.

For health studies, compare the increase or decrease in risk to the risk itself. A study that connects some genetic quirk to a 50 percent increased risk for some disease seems a lot less important if the likelihood of developing that disease is, say, 0.5 percent—in which case that genetic quirk is associated with an overall risk of 0.75 percent. See *absolute risk* below.

Find sources you trust. If you're working on a story and come across a stats expert who can explain things really well, keep that person's contact info handy. Next time you're in a bind, that person may be able to help you out. (And remember, the next time you meet that source at a conference, the beer's on you.)

Use appropriate language to describe the evidence. If you're reporting on a study that tested a human medical treatment on mice, be sure to point out that the subjects were mice, not humans. Specify how many mice, and what the next level of testing will measure.

A Science Writer's Statistical Phrasebook

Statistical Significance

What it means: Statistical significance gives researchers a way to distinguish between events that happen at random and those that may happen for a reason. Results are usually said to be "statistically significant" if there is a less than 5 percent chance that the measured outcome would have occurred at random.

What to watch for: Statisticians have pointed out that the 5 percent cutoff is arbitrary, and some researchers go so far as to say that studies that rely on *statistical significance may not themselves be reliable.* Small sample sizes and large confidence intervals may indicate that the findings have *weak support from the evidence.* Watch for follow-up studies that verify or discredit the original.

P-value

What it means: The p-value tells you the likelihood that the observed test result happened by chance. *A low p-value means the results were significant and unlikely to have occurred by chance.* "Statistical significance" usually requires a p-value of less than 0.05, which means that there is at most a 5 percent chance that the outcome occurred at random.

What to watch for: p-values larger than 0.05 suggest that the correlation is weak.

Confidence Interval

What it means: The range of values that likely includes the reported value of the measurement, within the probability determined by the p-value.

What to watch for: Does it seem like a large range of possible values? Ask the researchers why it seems so big. Do the possible values of the measurement include zero? That may be a red flag.

Odds Ratio

What it means: This is a common tool used in studies that compare people with a particular condition—such as a particular disease, or on a particular drug—to people who do not have that condition. Odds ratios compare the likelihood of an event's occurrence—such as death—in two groups in a study. Specifically, it compares the odds of the event in one group to the odds of the event in the other.

What to watch for: Be wary of reporting odds ratios as risk. If a study reports an odds ratio of 1.35, that doesn't automatically mean they found an increased risk of 35 percent. Talk to the study authors or a statistician to get a good handle on what the number means—and how to report it.

Relative Risk

What it means: Another common tool used to compare risk, or probability, in two different groups.

What to watch for: Be careful not to report relative risk as absolute risk. That can lead to overstating the importance of a result (see below). For example, studies have found an association between aspirin and significantly reduced *relative risk* of cancer, but that corresponded to only a small drop in an average person's risk.

Absolute Risk

What it means: In disease studies, this is the average lifetime risk of a person developing the disease.

What to watch for: In studies that compare risk between different groups, be sure to know how they report their results. Say the absolute risk of developing Disease X is 10 percent, and researchers find a 50 percent increase in *relative* risk associated with a rare genetic mutation compared to people without the mutation. Then the absolute risk of developing Disease X, for people with that mutation, is 10 × 1.5, or 15 percent.

SciLance says . . .

- Use **simple but scientifically appropriate language** in your reporting. Make sure what you write accurately conveys the evidence from the scientific study.

- **Get to know your stats.** Become friends with confidence intervals, p-values, relative risk, and their friends. When in doubt, don't fudge—ask a statistician.

- Determine the **sources of uncertainty in the fields you cover.** Do they arise from the tools themselves? What do the experts worry about? What do they criticize each other for?

- **Understand the implications of the study you're covering.** What does it mean if it's accurate? How will it affect people? What about if it's false?

- Find **sources you trust** to give you perspective on new research. Pamper them.

- **Think critically** about the research you're covering. Seek outside opinions on the findings to put them in perspective.

THE SCIENCE WRITERS' HANDBOOK

Chapter 6

Excavating the Evidence

Reporting for Narrative

By Douglas Fox

In 1999, I was working on the sixth story of my career: a feature on the severe epidemic of adult-onset diabetes among the Tohono O'odham people of Arizona. I had begun magazine writing because I wanted to create the sort of scene-based narratives, populated by flesh-and-blood people, that I had grown up reading. If any story I'd worked on had the potential to fulfill that expectation, I thought, this was it. I had access to important elements in the story: the backdrop of the Sonoran Desert, the Salt River Reservation, the Indian Health Service (IHS) clinic where much of the research was done and the patients were treated. I even had access to the physician who in 1963 had discovered that 50 percent of the local tribe members over thirty years of age suffered from type 2 diabetes. All of these elements lay on the outskirts of my own hometown, Phoenix. For the price of a tank of gas, I figured, I could produce an epic narrative.

Unfortunately, that's not how it went.

The story I produced was the best thing I had written at the time. It waded into a bitter debate over what ails indigenous populations around the world, and I'm still proud of it. But despite the fact that I spent half a dozen afternoons at that IHS clinic, despite the fact that I visited the gray-haired doctor who discovered the epidemic, the story conveyed no sense of character, personal history, or narrative.

The root problem wasn't my writing. It was this: by the time I sat down to write, I hadn't collected the details I needed to tell a gripping story. It's a common pitfall: great writing requires great research, and many potentially great stories are already condemned to mediocrity before the first sentence is written, simply because their dirt wasn't adequately excavated and sifted.

In this chapter I'll offer a handful of strategies for researching and envisioning narrative stories. While my specialty is print journalism, many of these strategies can be used in audio and video as well. And importantly, none of these strategies requires that you be a superhero who spends weeks in the field. These reporting tools can be used in projects of any size, even when reporting a story by phone. The goal, in any case, is to collect the best possible material.

Scribbling in the Notebook

Whether you're visiting someone's lab for sixty minutes or spending weeks with a team of researchers, on-site reporting can be intense. There you are, scribbling into your notebook as the scientist talks and the proverbial mouse runs through its maze. It's easy to get so caught up in scribbling down explanatory quotes that you're looking at the notebook rather than the person—and ignoring everything else.

Michelle Nijhuis, like many other SciLancers, spends a lot of time scribbling into her notebook. But her choice of what to scribble is important: not only quotes but also descriptions of people's clothing, sounds and smells, odd bits of dialogue—interactions that will bring the scientists and their settings to life in a way that their lecture-room personalities never do.

In Michelle's 2011 story "Crisis in the Caves" in *Smithsonian,* these elements produced a visceral impact:

> [They] pick their way through the fallen rocks on the mine floor, the beams of their headlamps cutting through the cool, misty half-dark. . . . Here and there, a dead bat lies on the ground, the bodies hardly more substantial than dried leaves.

When the researchers edged farther into the cave and found that raccoons had ruined their year-long experiment, Michelle asked about their feelings rather than asking for an explanation. "I only have that one moment to get their genuine reactions," she says. "I go for the emotions first." The scientific explanation can happen during the car ride home.

Field reporting can be exhausting. I try to schedule in some downtime, often at night. This time, usually in a tent or a shabby motel, is for regaining perspective, getting out of the mode of constantly reacting, second by second, to what is happening. It's about hovering above the story and seeing the bigger picture—the new questions and insights that have emerged.

During this downtime, I try to sketch out how I want to structure the story when I actually sit down to write it a month down the road, and especially what kind of scenes I'll need to build that structure.

This kind of planning helped guide my reporting when I spent five days with a team of geologists in the Utah desert for a story in *High Country News* in 2011 ("Omens of a Vanished Sea"). Their work was captivating, but like much of science, highly repetitive: eight hours per day searching the same mountain range for nuggets of the same minerals. These days provided a lot of classic *wow what a beautiful crystal* moments and *these layers represent 10,000 years* moments, but I had to keep an eye out for moments that expressed other elements of the story: the quirky ways in which field geology is actually done (scientist breaks open rock and smells it like a grapefruit); the personal history of the research (scientist shows me the spot deep in a cave where he made a key discovery fifteen years before); and subtle signs that an ancient lake left on the landscape (I spent several hours alone exploring mountainsides for the remains of ancient, gravelly shorelines hundreds of feet above the valley floor). Sketching out the story in advance helped me know what kind of material to look for.

While you don't want to overly stage-direct your reporting, you do want to keep an eye out for such potentially powerful scenes—not only during the reporting trip, but also during the stage of planning the trip, when you're deciding whom to visit and what to see.

A Field Journalist's Toolkit

When I'm in the field, I carry a digital recorder, a notebook, and a camera that can shoot both still shots and video. I'm not trying to produce multimedia, just get what I need to write a good print story. (For more on multimedia reporting, see Chapter 10.) Digital recorders are great for capturing rapid, complex dialogue among, say, several geologists in a cave, but when background noise is high (due to a brisk wind, or laboratory freezer fans), you'll need to rely on a notebook and pen.

I often shoot one hundred to two hundred photos in a day purely for note-taking purposes—documenting the weather, the landscape, the crystal that's just been pulled from a cave wall, even the gaudy casino signs by the road. I also shoot video clips and close-up portraits of key individuals. It's nice to have these extra resources in hand when I'm trying to capture an individual's personality, mannerisms, and essence in a few sentences.

I also produce many hours of digital recordings during field time. The value of having the recorder on is that you never know when cool stuff will happen—and it has a tendency to fly past by the time you've scribbled a couple of words in your notebook. The pitfall is the sheer amount of data (and work) that recording produces. I usually listen to and transcribe only a handful of my recordings in the end, based on notes that I scribbled down about when the good stuff happened and perhaps a few random samplings of the recordings.

A recorder can change people's behavior in negative ways. It often puts them into a stiff "talking to the press" mode. I try to strike a balance between letting people know that I'm recording and not making them overly conscious of it. When I participated in a fifty-seven-day research cruise down the Antarctic Peninsula in 2010, I made a habit of wearing my recorder in plain sight around my neck: when I introduced myself to the crew and scientists at the start of the cruise I pointed out the recorder and said that sometimes it would be on—other times not. It quickly faded into the background.

Field preparation takes on a whole new meaning if you're visiting the deep field, places where you may be hours or days from a wireless connection. "The field is totally unpredictable, and you just have to roll with the punches," says SciLancer Emily Sohn. She vividly remembers when, on a rafting expedition on a remote Amazonian tributary, her laptop fell into the river. For this and a million other reasons, it's important to back up data and ensure that backups travel separately from your computer. It's also good to safeguard electronics, whether you're in the jungle, in Antarctica, or, for that matter, in your own neighborhood. So make sure you—and your equipment—are well-prepared for the climate and conditions you'll be in.

Negotiating Access and Setting Expectations

When you're reporting on site, it's important to be transparent about your expectations ahead of time. For a daylong lab visit, this might simply mean establishing that you, the writer, want to see something *happen*—see an experiment under way, for example, or watch scientists peek for the first time at a stone core that was drilled from the floor of the Ross Sea. For a longer field visit, setting expectations often means making it clear that reporting is a full-time job. The team may want you to help out with the scientific work forty days into a cruise, at 1 a.m., when everyone's nerves are fraying—and this is entirely understandable. But whenever possible, you will need to be observing, recording, and writing instead. Before an eight-week research cruise, I tactfully told the chief scientist that his worst days would sometimes be my best days. In other words, *unless it becomes a safety issue, I need to be watching.* Whatever your boundaries are going to be during a field outing, it's worthwhile to establish this, explicitly, ahead of time.

Access and expectations are sometimes contingent on each other. SciLancer Kendall Powell recalls a feature she wrote for *Nature* on the mysterious and opaque process by which scientists' grant applications are reviewed by anonymous panels ("Making the Cut," 2010). Kendall managed to negotiate access to a daylong discussion of a panel of scientists reviewing grants for the American Cancer Society. Such intimate access was virtually unheard of—"an exercise in trust-building," she says. It involved agreeing to some ground rules: conversations wouldn't be recorded, and panel members would remain anonymous. Kendall kept her editor in the loop for all of these negotiations, and the editor agreed that the restrictions were outweighed by the important perspective that the story would provide to readers. The final story still contained plenty of revealing dialogue that Kendall captured through nimble typing.

When it comes to access, think big. In 2008 I wrote a profile for the *Christian Science Monitor* on a woman who kept six hundred cats in her home and property. As I talked to her on the phone to arrange a visit, she mentioned that the cats were so loud that it was difficult to sleep at night. I immediately thought: I have *got* to spend the night in that house! I threw a sleeping bag in the car, just in case the opportunity arose. I ended up sleeping in a motel instead; it was clear, after I spent the afternoon with her, that she wouldn't take to the idea. But the key is to look for these opportunities. Four out of five times they won't work out. When they do, you'll have a great story.

Reconstructing the Story

Constructing a story based on scenes that you've witnessed is, of course, wonderful. But often the important action has already happened by the time you take up a story. And reporting trips, no matter how well planned, sometimes fail to produce moments that scream to be included in the narrative. What's more, some stories naturally lend themselves to the approach of reconstructing what already happened days or weeks or years ago. I'm a firm believer that even if you see some amazing things when you visit a subject, it's important that your narrative focus on the action that's actually important to *the story*—even if that turns out to be action you didn't see.

One of my favorite reconstructions was published by *Wired* contributing editor Joshua Davis in "High-Tech Cowboys of the Deep Seas," a 2008 story for the magazine. Davis tells the story of seven men who salvage the *Cougar Ace,* a 55,000-ton cargo ship carrying 4,703 new Mazda automobiles that was abandoned after partially capsizing off the Aleutian Islands. He describes the salvage in stunning, cinematic detail:

> Deep within the ship, the men dangle on ropes . . . and peer through a doorway into the number-nine cargo deck. Their lights partially illuminate hundreds of cars tilted on their side, sloping down into darkness. Each is cinched to the deck by four white nylon straps. Periodically a large swell rolls the ship, straining the straps. A chorus of creaks echoes through the hold. . . . It's a cold, claustrophobic nightmare slicked with trickling engine oil and transmission fluid. [Colin] Trepte lowers a rope and eases into the darkness.

But Davis didn't witness the salvage. To write his story, he obtained a blueprint of the ship showing the decks and passages that the team traversed during the mission, the locations and capacities of the water ballast tanks that were used to bring the ship back up to level, and the positions of the heavy cargo winches that one team member hit during a fatal eighty-foot fall. Davis visited the team half a dozen times, interviewing them singly and in groups to resolve the discrepancies in their individual accounts. On top of this formal interviewing, he spent many days (and sometimes alcohol-saturated evenings) in their company, soaking up personalities and pet phrases, and scribbling the occasional war story into his notebook as it was told.

Even after this, Davis felt himself struggling as he tried to write one scene: that of deep-sea diver Colin Trepte sipping rum and listening to Led Zeppelin on his fishing boat in Trinidad just before a phone call summoned him to the Aleutians. "It didn't feel real yet," says Davis. "I didn't think I could put the reader there." So he rang his source a fifth and then a sixth time to ask which brand of rum he had been sipping and exactly which Zeppelin song he had been listening to. Davis had Trepte e-mail him a photograph of his boat, which revealed a telltale placard on its stern—THIS IS MY SHIP, AND I'LL DO AS I DAMN PLEASE—that Trepte hadn't mentioned. Most of these details made it into the scene.

Even when the story fee and deadline don't allow for this kind of epic effort, there's still plenty that can be done to dig up helpful details in shorter order, often without leaving your desk. In addition to interviews, it's crucial to find other, independent sources of information: to corroborate accounts and to glean more information from the people you do talk to, and sometimes to jog their memory with an odd detail they hadn't thought to mention.

I use Google Earth and satellite imagery to view important locations—the mountain range that a Boeing 747 was passing over as its engines failed, or the path of a wildlife preserve fence as it runs past citrus orchards in South Africa. Facebook pages or YouTube videos can provide insight into someone you've never met. And publicly available documents can provide especially rich detail: I have listened to a cockpit recording and combed through a 1,300-page FAA report while writing about an airline incident.

SciLance member Bryn Nelson reconstructed a string of powerful scenes when he wrote a 12,000-word account of the miraculous survival of Bobby, a toddler whose head was crushed by an SUV in 2006. Bryn began with a police report that allowed him to build a moment-by-moment time line of the accident, the boy's emergency transport, and the open-skull surgery that averted catastrophic brain damage. That report provided a list of people to interview—Bryn ultimately talked to about thirty people—and a scaffold to hang their accounts on, which was especially important given the inevitable distortions of memory when events are recalled months after the fact.

Bryn traveled every foot of Bobby's six-hour journey, driving the ambulance routes and walking the hospital floors. He interviewed the physicians and nurses who treated Bobby in the same trauma and operating rooms where they had worked on him. Bryn also went a step beyond public records, persuading Bobby's mother to allow him to see medical records. This enabled him to ask physicians why each drug was given, and why every incision was made. The result is a narrative in which even otherwise mundane moments feel like a fast-flowing movie clip.

Into the Lair—and Out of It

It's usually worthwhile to visit key sources in person, even if you know that you won't incorporate the visit itself (or even the person you're visiting) into the story. People are often more forthcoming and generous in person—far more likely to, say, share four hours of their workday. During that time, they might pull out old photographs or maps of the glaciers where they camped, or show you the Frankenstein-ish glass-and-electrode apparatus that their PhD supervisor used to perform a series of "primordial soup" experiments. Once, a microbiologist provided me with electronic copies of several dozen e-mails he had received from members of the public after a high-profile paper was published. Those e-mails alerted me to the surprising level of public paranoia surrounding his research on the way bacteria in clouds trigger rain: fear, among a few people, that it could spawn subversive attempts to control and disrupt the weather. I would never have understood this context if I hadn't visited him.

Visiting the scientist in his or her own lair also means that you can browse the office or lab, check out the books on his or her shelves—any Chinese medicine manuals or writings of Nietzsche that deserve to be asked about?—inspect family pictures, and so on. During one visit, my question about a shark tooth in an isotope scientist's office led to a story about the unidentified human femur that was found last time the office was cleaned. During another visit, I asked about the twenty-four-inch stack of papers sitting in a physicist's otherwise spotless office. These turned out to be the writings of the colorful man who had inspired the scientific theory I was writing about—variously considered a genius, a savant, or simply nutty.

A cautionary word about offices, though. Sitting in chairs, talking across a desk or table—or worse yet, in a conference room—can sometimes inspire researchers to pull out their PowerPoint slides to show graphs of key findings. Such interactions reflect the way in which researchers are conditioned to communicate with colleagues, and they're valuable for getting background information or understanding the science. But getting great narrative material involves watching people in action.

This might involve seeing an experiment run, or visiting a field site where a scientist measures nitrous oxide bubbling out of a swamp. It might involve going shopping with a researcher for the power saws she'll use to cut blocks of ice out of a frozen lake. And you don't have to go to the ends of the earth: if you're talking to an atmospheric chemist, you might walk her outside and ask about the clouds that you see, perhaps even schedule the visit for when bad weather is expected. If your source is a physicist with a theory that's going to uproot an entire field, you might attend the lecture where he teaches his students the other theory—the one he's overturning. There are a million ways to steer a visit in interesting directions.

Getting the Story by the Roots

Science stories may be about the cutting edge, but I strongly believe in digging a story up by the roots—the historical roots. I go through the reference lists of recent research papers, find the oldest citations, and track those down. I then repeat the process until I answer my question: for instance, *Why the hell were biologists so bent on cataloging the body, brain, and organ weights of thousands of species?* Answering the question often takes me back to the early 1900s, sometimes even earlier. Taking time to do this kind of research can transform a story. This was the case when I was working on "The Limits of Intelligence," a 2011 essay in *Scientific American* that proposed that thermodynamic factors might place a universal limit on the intelligence of all living things. The historical research took a story that was largely explanatory (and, I worried, might be monotonous for readers) and allowed me to place it within a deeper narrative arc: scientists' attempts, over 125 years, to identify the physical basis of intelligence, whether in brain size, the geometry of nerve cells, or the number of cells in certain brain structures. Those yellowed, dusty journal papers also provided an entertaining window into the gruesome foundations of a seemingly spotless mathematical science: the allometric scaling that describes how body characteristics such as brain mass change across species with differing body masses. With the help of a German translator I included in the story a description of state-of-the-art techniques (circa 1880, using hammer and chisel) for extracting an intact brain from the skull of a fifty-ton whale.

Published scientific literature makes it easy to dig into history—but there are more creative ways to go about it. While working on "A Puffin Comeback," a 2010 story for *Smithsonian,* Michelle visited a small, desolate island named Eastern Egg Rock, where biologists had observed puffins for decades. There, in a tiny cabin, surrounded by the cacophonous calls of nesting birds, she spent a couple of hours browsing through a stack of notebooks where dozens of biologists had recorded their observations over the years. "Often the notes were dry and scientific," says Michelle. "But I looked up dates where I knew exciting things had happened." The journals allowed her to attach a biologist's immediate emotional reactions to what happened on July 4, 1981—the day puffins were found raising chicks on the island for the first time in one hundred years.

At its simplest, digging for the roots can mean taking time to have a researcher talk about the origins of his or her interests, or the failures experienced along the way. In one story I reported, a geologist and his son spent fifteen years trying to photograph thousands of precariously balanced rocks across the Southwest, first with remote-controlled planes, then with real ones. An interesting personal history can provide a through-line for the entire story.

Time: An Essential Ingredient

Great stories don't just require great research, they can also demand a lot of time.

There are powerful moments that might happen only once during, say, the eight weeks you spend with a team of researchers. During the Antarctic cruise I covered in 2010, a remote-operated vehicle (ROV) was launched to the sea floor a dozen times. I was tempted to skip the last ROV dive—I was exhausted by the ship's 24/7 research schedule. But I dragged myself to it, and the ROV's camera soon flashed up images of invasive crabs, swept in by abnormally warm currents, that were decimating a deep-ocean ecosystem. I got to see this discovery unfold in real time; I got to scribble and record as the biologists chattered about it. I am humbled by how easily I could have missed it.

The need for time has to be balanced against the realities of story fees and income. I'm very aware of this, especially since I use software to clock in and out of stories, tracking the hours I spend on them as though I were a lawyer or an accountant.

If over-researching means that I sometimes earn less money per hour on a particular story, then I see that as an investment in my career—and happiness. Good clips beget good assignments, and I, for one, am happier to continue pushing myself, learning to be a better writer and observer along the way. I pick one to three stories per year that I see as having real potential, and I invest heavily in those efforts.

An extreme example of this kind of investment happened in 2007, when I spent seven weeks with a team of glaciologists studying lakes hidden beneath the West Antarctic Ice Sheet. That expedition consumed way more than seven weeks of my time. Planning began two years earlier. As the trip neared, I weighed on a kitchen scale the batteries, notebooks, and every other item I needed to have dropped at the field site, so the materials could be shipped months in advance. I calculated how many hours of propane generator time I'd need for my laptop. I purchased $5,000 of camera equipment and received training on how to handle it in cold, polar environments. Every piece of electronics that I bought, I tested in the kitchen freezer.

But even these best-laid plans didn't prevent complications. I had planned to write a centerpiece feature for *Discover,* but that arrangement fell through four months before the trip, forcing me to spend weeks pitching and repitching the story, through a frustrating series of rejections, to find a new home for it (for more, see "Pitching Endurance" on p. 33). I ultimately managed to re-land the story at *Discover* in mid-2008 after returning from the expedition. This was the best possible outcome, but the months leading up to that happy ending were the most stressful of my career, both emotionally and financially.

By spending so much time repitching the story, I lost thousands of dollars of income that I could have earned by working on other stories. I earned $21,800 on stories from the trip—but incurred over $25,000 in expenses, including my time. I survived financially because I had planned ahead in the year leading up to the trip, taking on some higher-paying projects to build up a savings cushion. But even so, I carried a credit card balance for a few months after returning. My bank account bottomed out at a precarious $1,152.28 three months after the trip—not even enough to cover rent—before income from my stories began to push it back up again.

The big question for me is whether the lost money and the emotional stress were worth the outcome. In retrospect, I believe they were. With several years of perspective, I now see the very real payoffs that grew out of this difficult experience.

Those seven weeks in the field gave me an unparalleled opportunity to develop field-reporting skills. Whether I was trying to capture dialogue or shoot photos, each night I could reflect on what I did and didn't do well—and try something new the next day.

For the first time ever I also had the chance to write narrative from essentially unlimited material (a stack of notebooks, 4,500 photos, and many hours of recordings). It was a great chance to learn to write first-person narrative, rather than suffering the usual constraint of not having the requisite material. My stories from the trip began hitting print in 2008—and I believe that the quality of my writing went up a notch or two that year. I attribute it in part to the trip.

I also came home from the trip as a newly minted specialist with a new beat: the intersection of ice sheets, climate, and earth science. I had never written about earth science before—I'd never even taken an earth science course in college or high school—but I now love this specialty, and I continue to pursue it today.

And finally, the last payoff: After returning from that first Antarctic trip in January 2008, I earned the chance to go back—this time, working on a feature for *National Geographic*. I could never have imagined landing that assignment even a few months earlier. One of the factors that went into my getting the assignment, my editor later told me, was simply that I had field experience in Antarctica. I believe what got me the assignment over other, more accomplished writers may in part have been my camping and snowcraft skills. Embarking on that first trip to Antarctica had given me qualifications that I wasn't even aware of.

Gestating the Big One

One last thought: Great stories can take years to happen—and this is something that we should all take heart from. Every writer I know has an amazing story in mind that he or she just doesn't know how to tackle. In some cases it's not knowing how to write it; in others, it's not knowing how to secure access to a well-insulated person or sensitive information. Patience is key.

Four years passed between the day that I scribbled the idea for "The Limits of Intelligence" in the margin of a journal paper and the day the story was published. Initially, I didn't feel equipped, as a journalist, to cross into the unfamiliar territory of concocting a scientific theory of my own. I doubted that I ever would. I wrote several stories on the energetics of the brain—each one a major feature unto itself—before an editor at *Scientific American* finally convinced me to take the leap.

Joshua Davis waited even longer to write his marine-salvage story for *Wired,* "High-Tech Cowboys of the Deep Seas." He pitched it to *Outside* in 2001 but was turned down. At the time, it would have been his first feature, and while he could have written a story rich in color from various missions the team had undertaken, he lacked a singular event to focus on.

Davis kept in touch with his sources for seven years before the *Cougar Ace* foundered off the Aleutian Islands. That accident provided him with an intersection between a fascinating topic, a motley cast of characters with diverse technical skills, and a narrative to tie them all together. "I didn't necessarily want to wait," says Davis, but the story that eventually ran in *Wired* in 2008 was far more impressive than it would have been had he not. At the end of the day, great writing requires great excavation of characters, atmosphere, and events, and as you strive to do this, patience will sometimes be your most important tool.

Who Pays for Travel?

How to pay for that reporting trip to Utah or Australia? Ideally, the outlet that assigns you a story pays for travel. Travel plans are negotiated in advance, and normally you incur the expenses up front and the publication reimburses you. Travel budgets run the gamut, from several hundred dollars for some newspapers to $5,000 or more for some glossy magazines.

(Continues)

Who Pays for Travel? *(Continued)*

But travel budgets at many publications are shrinking, and in many cases journalists need to find creative ways to fund field reporting. When I did a four-month reporting trip to Australia in 2001, I made a verbal agreement with my editors at *New Scientist* that I would come up with a half dozen stories for them. When I handed in my sixth feature from the trip, they reimbursed me for my round-trip airfare between California and Melbourne. I then used travel money from another feature assignment, this one from *Discover*, to cover some of my flights and lodging within Australia. (To avoid any misunderstanding, I made sure that both *New Scientist* and *Discover* knew I was working for multiple publications during the trip. See Chapter 23 for more on avoiding conflicts of interest when working for multiple clients.)

In general, try to get the most out of every reporting trip that you take. If a publication sends you to a faraway location, allow a few extra days to look for other stories in the area, either for the publication that sent you or for others. Of course, be careful not to include the costs of this side reporting in your expense reports to the publication funding the trip, and mention your additional time on location to your editor.

Travel funding is sometimes offered by organizations (universities, companies, or foreign governments) interested in generating coverage on a certain topic. These travel "junkets," often organized group trips, may not come with formal strings attached, but they can still create bias or the appearance of bias in a resulting story. It's important to let editors know if travel was funded by such sources; some editors will choose to turn down these stories, and others will not (again, see Chapter 23 for more). A number of nonprofit organizations also provide fellowships and grants for individual reporting trips proposed by journalists; these funds are generally considered free of the potential conflicts of interest associated with travel junkets. Organizations offering this kind of funding include the Pulitzer Center on Crisis Reporting, the European Geosciences Union, the Society of Environmental Journalists, and others (for more specifics, see Chapter 21).

- **Make notes about mannerisms, clothing, road signs, smells, noises, emotions**—not just quotes.

- **Begin sketching your story early**. This provides a checklist of which scenes, characters, and conversations you'll need to capture.

- Equip yourself to be an information sponge. **Bring a digital recorder, a camera that shoots still and video, and of course a notebook**.

- **Think big when it comes to negotiating access**. Try to spend the night in the house with six hundred cats. Often you won't succeed, but when you do, you'll have a great story.

- If you're going to do hard field time with your sources, **set boundaries and expectations in advance**.

- **Interview multiple people about their memories of the same events**, corroborate details, home in on disagreements between accounts, and leverage them to learn more.

- **Utilize every information source**: ship blueprints, Google Earth, satellite images, cockpit recordings, FAA reports, police reports, court records.

- **Visit your sources in person—in their lair**. Not at Starbucks.

- **Ask about the chain saw on the source's bookshelf** or the scar on her hand.

- **Get sources out of PowerPoint mode**, and out of their comfort zone.

- **Get the story by its deepest, profoundest, quirkiest historical roots**: go back to papers from the 1920s, or old diaries or ship logs. Employ a translator if necessary.

(Continues)

- **Find an interesting personal history**, an unanswered question or personal tragedy that has driven your protagonist for twenty years.

- Money is of course a factor, but **more field time usually equals a better story**.

- **Some stories are worth over-investing in, even taking some financial risks for**. Pick your "big one" carefully, and it can propel your career forward in ways you might never imagine.

- Be patient. **A great story can take years to gestate**.

Chapter 7

Sculpting the Story

By Michelle Nijhuis

Whether you're researching a news brief, producing a radio short, or turning six weeks of Antarctic science into a feature story, you'll gather loads more material than will fit within your assigned word limit. Writing or producing nonfiction of any kind requires you to whittle that stack of research material down to its essential elements, organize those elements within a story structure, and communicate them in a way that makes sense to your audience. And you have to do it on time, correctly, with a minimum of crying.

But don't fear. As difficult as the process can be at times, I also find it fun and uniquely satisfying. There's nothing quite like seeing a strong story emerge from a chaotic pile of information. And the act of writing is fascinatingly complex, intensely individual, and not entirely rational— the process itself varies wildly from writer to writer, and every writer I know has a beat-up chair, or time of day, or obscure type of pencil that they think helps them do their best writing. (For the record, I have a favorite teacup. Don't even *think* about touching it.) So while this chapter can't hope to be comprehensive, I'll cover some general strategies that help me and others through the process of science story sculpture. I'll focus on writing, the medium I'm most familiar with, but most of these methods can be applied to audio and visual work as well.

Write Before You Write

Ideally, you'll start thinking about writing during the pitching stage. The best pitches, as SciLance member Thomas Hayden mentioned in Chapter 3, not only describe a great story but also propose a preliminary structure for it. A strong feature-story pitch will, for instance, identify a potential main character or characters and outline the journey those characters have taken—or might take during your reporting.

Even if your story is a three hundred–word news brief with a boiler-plate structure, it's worth taking a minute, during the pitch stage, to consider and articulate what your story is really about. Not the noun, the verb. It's not enough to say your story is about, say, salmon. Is it a story about bears that eat salmon? Salmon that eat bears? The scientist who discovered the rare bear-eating salmon, and her struggle to be believed?

Seriously: For any story I work on, no matter the length, I try to come up with a full sentence (okay, maybe two) during the pitch stage that captures my best guess at the core action. I might eventually use that sentence in a headline, or it might become part of my lede paragraph (see "Story Anatomy" on p. 84 for more on story structure terminology). Then again, I might never use it in print. And I almost always tweak it during my reporting; after all, if we knew exactly what our stories were about from the outset, we wouldn't have to do any reporting. But I do use that sentence as a lodestone as I do my research. Reporting takes all of us on fascinating detours and into dead ends, but a clear focus will lead you back out, helping to remind you what's relevant and what's not.

When SciLancer Kendall Powell profiled a father-son pair of climate-change researchers for *Nature,* she found that while the duo were viewed by many as pesky agitators, they were, in person, the "nicest guys you'd ever want to meet." She struggled to portray that contrast until she and her editor drafted what journalists call the "dek" or (if you're a Brit) "standfirst" of the story, the subtitle that runs under the main headline. "The two Roger Pielkes can be obstructionist pains in the neck, say their colleagues," the dek read. "So why is this likeable father-son pair such a welcome addition to the debate on global climate change?" That pithy summary not only guided Kendall as she wrote the story, but also ran as the dek on the published piece.

Another step I take, very early in the process, is to figure out what type of story I'm going to tell. We all recognize archetypal narratives; they're the story types that occur over and over again in books and movies and campfire tales around the world. An old dictum, often credited to Leo Tolstoy, is that all great literature is one of two stories: either a man goes on a journey or a stranger comes to town. (And those two stories are, of course, just different views of the same story.) Christopher Booker's *The Seven Basic Plots* examines the classic plots of Comedy, Tragedy, Rags to Riches, Voyage and Return, Overcoming the Monster, Rebirth, and Quest.

Sticking too closely to an archetype creates a cliché, of course, and can distort the facts. But straying too far from one of these familiar story types risks alienating your audience. These archetypes are the patterns we all unconsciously use to identify a story as a story—without a supporting narrative, a story is likely to collapse into nonsense. Even the most experimental fiction or drama usually draws on story archetypes, if only to rebel against them. I've found that putting some thought into possible archetypes at the beginning of my reporting helps me recognize useful scenes during my research, structure my first draft, and eventually find that sweet, surprising spot between cliché and confusion.

Science stories are often told as Quests of some sort, but many can also be told as Overcoming the Monster stories, Rags to Riches, or even Comedies. Remember that the "hero" doesn't have to be a person: some very powerful science stories have used animals, diseases, and even cell lines as main characters. Consider a few possible approaches, and of course always be open to changing your strategy as you research.

As SciLancer Douglas Fox described in the previous chapter, it's always useful to take advantage of downtime, in the field or at home, to organize your notes and begin to sketch out your story. During that time, I also scrutinize articles from the publication I'm working for. Even if I'm already familiar with the publication, I take another look at its overall tone and at the story structures, ledes, and kickers it favors. I also look at how its writers build scenes and bring in other sources, and whether they use the first-person voice. That way, I have the publication's particular approach fresh in my mind as I report.

Draw the Blueprint

When I return from my field research, or, with a phone story, when I sense that I'm about two-thirds or three-quarters done with my research, I will—assuming I have enough time—type up my handwritten notes, fully or partially transcribe my recorded notes, and read everything I've collected so far. Many of us find software programs such as Scrivener, DEVONthink, and OneNote useful for storing and sorting notes and background information at this stage. SciLancer Helen Fields uses OneNote, but when it's time to organize her notes for writing, good old paper works best for her: "I print out all my notes in tiny print, two columns to a page, and reread them, writing short summaries in the margins and marking promising quotes," she says.

After Hillary Rosner, another SciLancer, reads her notes, she tests out the highlights on willing friends. "I like to talk about the story informally with a friend or two, because I think that the details you select when telling someone a story over dinner should be a good guide to what's going to end up in your article," she says. "Sometimes I have no idea what these details are until they're out of my mouth."

At this stage, I start outlining my story. Ideally, the steps I talked about in the previous section have already helped me start thinking in scenes: I'll have had an eye out for a natural climax to the story, and for scenes that might start and end the piece. In my outline—usually scrawled on an envelope, definitely not as formal as the Roman-numeral version from middle school—I'll make a list of those potential scenes, either scenes I witnessed or scenes from the past that I know will be important to reconstruct. I'll also list bits of ideas, context, history, and anything else that I think needs to be included in the piece.

Most writers have developed their own approach to outlining: "I don't usually do an official outline, but I often break a story into various sections and come up with little captions for each section," says SciLancer Cameron Walker. (Magazines generally manage their readers' attention spans with subheadings, so it can be useful to divide your story into these sections early on.) Douglas, for his part, uses large pieces of blank sketch paper to map out his stories with boxes and arrows, including interesting scenes, natural breaks in the narrative that might require a subhead, and key facts, insights, ideas, and characters.

Many writers use their original proposal as a starting point for their outline. You may find, after delving deep into research, that your proposal needs to be substantially revised, or you may see that your earlier view of the story holds up surprisingly well. Either way, returning to the proposal can remind you of what your editor is expecting, and clarify your view of the story's theme. (See "A Tale of Two Query Letters" on p. 36.)

Build the Skeleton

There are several classic story structures in journalism (see "Story Anatomy" on p. 84) but all of them are chronological in some way. If you already have a story archetype in mind, and you're using a chronological structure, the order of events in your outline should be fairly obvious. (Some stories have two or more intertwined narratives, in which case the structure may be more complex, but each narrative is still usually chronological.) In general, the biggest decisions you'll have to make are where to begin and end your story.

Writers like to fret over what we call the lede sentence, paragraph, or section of a story, and with good reason. We all know that readers aren't required to read our stories, and often the first few lines will determine if readers go further. It's tempting to choose the grabbiest, sexiest scene you have as a lede, but be cautious; ledes have to not only get readers' attention but also prepare them for the rest of the story, so the most exciting scene you have might not necessarily have the right content or tone. It's also wise to save some of your most dramatic material for later on in the story, using it to draw readers through your piece.

As you outline, don't let the specific language of the lede hold you up. If you start fiddling, try SciLancer Stephen Ornes's technique: "I write a dummy lede—basically, the most banal and uninteresting introduction to the piece—just to get it over with temporarily. Then, after I've written about half the first draft, I can go back and improve the lede."

Most feature stories also have what journalists call a "billboard" or a "nut graf"—a sentence or paragraph, usually at the end of the opening section—that hints at what the story is about. Resist the urge to summarize your entire story in the nut graf. As veteran journalist and teacher Jacqui Banaszynski has said, the nut graf shouldn't give away the ending of your story, but simply tell the reader what kind of boots to put on for the journey.

While we obsess about beginnings, we often don't spend enough time sculpting our endings, or kickers, and that's too bad. Endings are our last word to the reader, and often what readers will remember most. I like to end with a small scene that serves as a coda to the rest of the story, but there are infinite possibilities: consider powerful quotes, pithy observations, or just a strong statement in your own voice. "I think the kicker is just as structurally important as the lede," says SciLancer Jessica

Marshall. "When you know the kicker from the beginning, you know where you have to end up, and that is just really, really helpful." (Writers are especially prone to clichés in both ledes and kickers, so be wary. If a line comes to mind suspiciously quickly and easily, it might well be a tired phrase.)

The work of outlining doesn't end with the lede and the kicker. Internal ledes and endings are important, too. When outlining my stories, I often break them up into five or six sections, as Cameron does, and choose a possible lede and ending for each section. That practice reminds me that just like the story as a whole, every section needs to draw readers in and usher them out. It keeps me from letting things bog down in the middle of a draft.

Once I've sketched an outline, I'll try to ease the important ideas and bits of background into the scenes. Not all will fit, but the more information that can be communicated within a scene, the more smoothly a story will flow. I cut and paste quotes into each scene, add in pieces of description and phrases from my notes, and make note of questions and uncertainties. Stephen takes a chemist's approach: "I drop in the best quotes from my interviews and the best lines from my notes so I know where they'll go. Once the outline is supersaturated, I wait for something to crystallize."

At this point, I often stop and do some more reporting, as I invariably find some factual and conceptual holes. It's a great time to ask more focused, detailed questions of your sources. "I love the feeling of the second round of interviews," says SciLancer Emily Sohn. "I know exactly what I need to learn, and I can avoid asking all those general, vague questions I asked at the outset."

Now Go!

It's certainly possible to just start writing without the sort of planning and outlining I've described. But when I write without a plan, I find that it's terribly tempting to jump straight into micro-level work, to start playing around with vocabulary and punctuation before I've figured out the main point of my story.

When I have enough of a structure in place, and enough information on hand, I find I feel much more comfortable just *telling* the story—that is, letting my personal writerly voice, or the combination of my voice and the publication's voice, take the floor and go. Especially with a long, complicated story, I want to feel in command of the information, not the other way around. It's that feeling of authority that makes my voice trustworthy. I sometimes have a moment, usually toward the end of the first draft, when I feel like I've almost physically flipped my research on its back and wrestled it to the floor. That's a good feeling.

But even as I take charge of the facts, I keep in mind that the reader and I are on a joint expedition into new terrain, one that evokes excitement and uncertainty, humility and awe. I try to use my voice to express those emotions, too. "The goal is to show how some new discovery looks to an interested outsider, writing for other interested outsiders, using metaphor instead of mathematics," writes longtime *New York Times* contributor George Johnson, author of *The Cancer Chronicles* and other books. "I want the reader to feel that we are both on the same side—outsiders seeking a foothold on the slippery granite face of a new idea."

With that delicately balanced stance in mind, I start with the outline I've developed—that saves me from facing the dreaded blank screen—and work through it, using it as raw material to build full sentences and paragraphs. This is when I let myself start having fun with description, analogy, metaphor, and rhythm (created by varying word, sentence, and paragraph lengths). These tools are especially important when you have to step back from your narrative and do some explaining. Interesting language, good quotes, and humor can help these necessary but often-dull sections—the vegetables, or what a radio-producer friend of mine calls the "sawdust sandwich"—go down smoothly.

As with outlining, I try to move quickly through my first draft, saving the finer details for revision. But I do pay attention to the word order within sentences—the most emphatic words go at the end—and to the transitions between sentences and between paragraphs. Ann Finkbeiner, who runs the graduate program in science writing at Johns Hopkins University, suggests smoothing transitions with what she calls her "AB/BC" rule: the end of each sentence should echo the beginning of the next, as in the example below.

Astronomers' biggest problem has been that they have to see stars through the earth's distorting atmosphere. The atmosphere is effectively a moving stream made of patches of varying temperatures.

Each temperature patch sends incoming starlight off in a different direction.

"This rule shouldn't be overdone and works best for descriptions of some little machine," Finkbeiner says. "But every time I get stuck in a paragraph and muddled about where I'm going, the AB/BC rule saves me." With time, AB/BC becomes second nature.

Many writers work without notes at this stage, filling in the details later. "I'm a big proponent of 'TK'—journalese for 'to come,'" says Hillary. "I use it for everything from explanations I can't be bothered to write yet, to details I can't remember and need to double-check, to quotes I need to find in my notes, to bits I see are missing and need to be further reported." And remember that you don't have to write your first draft from beginning to end. Maybe you've already talked about a side-bar with your editor: you can start with that, using a smaller, less intimidating task to get you going. Or work on a basic explanatory section that you know you'll need, using it to move past the horror of the blank screen before you tackle the challenging work of crafting the perfect lede.

Whatever you do, don't let the voice of your internal critic—and yes, we all have one—kill your momentum. At this point, you've earned your authority on your subject. Use it. "How do I stay sane while I'm writing? Coldplay and jellybeans," says Helen. "Seriously, I usually just try to keep plowing through and hope that eventually I'll end up with something. Even if it sucks, it's so much easier to revise than write."

Get Some Distance

While you need to turn off your internal critic while you write your first draft, you need to turn it on again before you hand in a draft to your editor. Once I finish a draft, I try to get some distance from it so that I can see it more clearly. If I have time before my deadline, I'll take a week away; if not, I'll take a shower before I reread it. That way, I can better spot awkward or confusing language, clichés, and slow sections that need to be cut, shortened, or spiced up.

Even changing locations or printing out the story can refresh your eye. "If I have a couple of hours to work on a story, I always end that time by printing out whatever I've written," says SciLancer Alison Fromme.

"Then, when I return to it, I read that printed copy and mark it up like crazy before I turn my computer back on."

Showing drafts to spouses and friends can be tricky, and writers have a wide variety of approaches. Some use their spouses as their very first readers; others wait until their second draft, or even later, to show the story to anyone but their editor. (See Chapter 17 for the pitfalls and benefits of sharing writing with spouses and partners.) My husband—who's not a journalist, but is a close reader and good critic—is usually the first person to read my drafts, and I almost always show early drafts to one or two SciLancers or other writer friends. These editing friendships can take time to develop—the exchange of tough, honest criticism requires a lot of trust on both sides—but when they mature, they're invaluable.

Especially when time is short, it's tempting to skip this stage and just get the story off your desk and into your editor's hands. But sending your internal critic on vacation is risky business. Consider this clearly unsupervised lede from an *Esquire* science story, aptly described by the science writer Carl Zimmer as a "noxious martini of mixed metaphors topped with an olive of ridiculous hype":

> First thing that happens when you have a heart attack, an unlucky part of your heart turns white. The blood's stopped pumping to that spot, so it becomes pink-speckled bloodlessness, coarse and cool like grapefruit gelatin.
>
> Next comes the back-alley bruise of organ death. The cells turn from white to black, all shitted up like a body pit in a war, two weeks after. Suddenly, soldier, this part of your heart is dead. . . . But the dead part can't fix itself. And the healthy part can't throw it a bloody rope. So the whole heart begins to die. . . .
>
> But now look here, a woman. She is a pretty lady of Pakistani heritage who highlights her soccer-mom layers, which you don't expect from a lab-worn doctor-lady. Hina Chaudhry believes she can do what the body can't: fix the dead parts.

Yikes. So before you submit that draft, enlist your internal editor—and, for good measure, some trusted friends and family. They won't save you from the formal editing process, but you can count on them to throw you a bloody rope.

Story Anatomy

Classic newspaper style, often called *Associated Press* or inverted-pyramid style:

Headline (or "hed"): Short and direct, with active verbs. Gives a clear sense of the story.

The news lede: What's new? Who's involved? Where, when, and how did it happen?

Most important point: Fleshes out the lede and its implications.

Substantiating points, in decreasing order of importance (so that space-squeezed editors can shorten the story quickly and easily).

Background/context/reactions, in decreasing order of importance (ditto).

Classic magazine-feature style, sometimes called *Wall Street Journal* style:

Headline: Can be more whimsical or evocative, but should be catchy, and for online stories, should include searchable terms.

Dek/Standfirst: The "subtitle" to the headline. Gives a clear sense of the story in a line or two.

Lede: Opening line, paragraph, or section that lures the reader into the story. Often includes characters or quotes. Can be somewhat tangential to main story, but should match the tone and style of both the publication and the rest of the story. Can be a long anecdote that introduces a character or characters, or can be extremely simple. SciLancer Emily Sohn once led a *Los Angeles Times* health story with two words: "Ah, salt."

Billboard/nut graf: Line or paragraph, usually at the end of the first section, which partially summarizes the story. Identifies the main news and its significance, suggests or states where the story is going, introduces conflict if any. In science news features, billboards are often variations on

"In a new study published this week," or "Scientists have long thought X. Now, they report Y."

Body 1: Context, history, or explanation. Can loop back to the lede to tie up loose ends, or loop forward to start telling the story. May include quotes, often introduces or fleshes out characters.

Body 2: Carries the story forward. Provides "what happened" information, substantiates claims, fleshes out characters and conflicts. Usually contains a quote.

Etc. . . . : This form is expandable, at least up to a few thousand words.

Kicker: A firm, crisp ending that ties the story together and leaves a sense of completion. Often refers back to the lede, or spins forward to implications or next steps in an unresolved story.

Variations on classic magazine-feature style:

Pure narrative: A story told entirely within a series of linked events, without the writer's stepping in to add context or explanation. (In personal narratives, the writer becomes a character in the story.) Often requires deep research to accurately reconstruct characters' thoughts and actions. A classic science-story example of pure narrative is the Pulitzer Prize–winning "Mrs. Kelly's Monster," by Jon Franklin, a moment-by-moment reconstruction of a brain surgery told from the perspectives of surgeon and patient.

Layer cake: A feature story that alternates between sections of narrative and explanatory sections of context or history. Pure narratives are very difficult and time-consuming to produce, and not every story lends itself to the form or to the extensive reporting access required. So when editors say they're looking for "narrative" stories, they often mean that they're looking for layer cakes—stories knit together by narrative, but not entirely dependent on it.

SciLance says . . .

- The writing process starts well before you sit down at your computer. Ideally, you'll start thinking about the structure of your story **during the pitching stage**.

- Early in the process, **come up with a full sentence** that captures your best guess at the core action.

- Also early in the process, **figure out what type of story you're going to tell**. Does it echo an archetypal narrative?

- When you return from your reporting trip, or near the end of your first round of phone calls, **organize your notes**—with digital tools, analog tools, or a combination of both.

- Try out what you consider **the best details and anecdotes** on willing friends.

- Before you start writing, **outline your story as thoroughly as possible**. Assuming your story will be told chronologically, decide where it will begin and end.

- Use your outline as **the raw material of the sentences and paragraphs** of your first draft. Turn off your internal critic, and write quickly. Allow yourself to play with description, analogy, metaphor, and rhythm.

- If possible, **get some distance** from your first draft before revising.

- When you return to your draft, look for awkward or confusing language and clichés. Look for points where your story slows down, and consider shortening, cutting, or spicing up those sections.

- When you do begin revisions, consider **asking a family member or trusted writer friend to read it**. Are their takeaways the ones you hope your eventual readers will have? If not, why not?

Chapter 8

Working with Editors—and Their Edits

By Monya Baker and Jessica Marshall

For science writers, there aren't many relationships more important —or more complex—than those they have with their editors. When you work on staff, whether at a newspaper or magazine, or at a university or other institution, your editor is a colleague, and quite often your manager or boss as well. As a freelancer, your editor is not only a collaborator, but also one of your only lines of communication with a publication, and the main advocate for your story as it moves toward print. Either way, career successes—clips and paychecks—ultimately depend on your relationship with editors.

How do you make these relationships lasting ones? Give editors what they want.

And what do they want? The essentials are surprisingly simple:

Editors want to know that they are going to get copy on time in something approaching house style and that is properly reported and accurate. Those things sound so basic that you'd think every reporter would do them. I wish they did.

—Peter Aldhous, *New Scientist*

Understanding Your Editor

An editor's mission is to produce great content for his or her publication under tight time pressure. "Our job is to get things in a magazine," says Adam Rogers, senior editor at *Wired*. "We acquire stories and we make them suitable for our bosses and what our magazine does. We tend to think as writers that all editors want to do is rewrite, to step on our art. Nothing could be further from the case."

The lesson? Good writers, whether on staff or working freelance, strive to make an editor's job easy. They turn in copy on time and at the agreed-upon length, clearly describe complicated science, alert editors to potential problems right away, answer e-mails promptly, and stay pleasant throughout edits, says SciLance member Kendall Powell, who freelances as both an editor and a writer. "I largely view my relationships with editors as 'customer service,'" she says. "Whatever I can do to make their life and job easier will hopefully end in my being rewarded the next time an editor needs a writer."

But there is another important element in an editor-writer relationship, especially for longer projects. "I start with the assumption that we're teammates, on the same side, and both trying to serve the story," says SciLancer Jill Adams. After all, the point is not to prove how much you can do in isolation. The point is to get a good story.

When the relationship is at its best, appreciation flows both ways and the story gets better with each iteration. But lofty ideals of customer service and teamwork can be hard to maintain when an editor sits on your story for weeks and then wants additional reporting plus a revised draft right away—and you've got other obligations on your calendar. It's even harder when errors creep in and your favorite quotes disappear as multiple editors work over your copy. Unfortunately, these experiences are just part of the process. Making a sustainable, rewarding career out of science writing depends on how well you can anticipate, avoid, and respond to these scenarios.

One final point before we move on to the nitty-gritty: Being accurate, meeting deadlines, and writing well are universal editorial desires. But beyond that, editors and their publications have their own distinctive preferences. So when in doubt, don't take our word for it. Ask your editor.

From Assignment to Deadline

Editors differ as to how much interaction they like before a story is turned in. Editors of daily or weekly news venues, who typically assign stories on short deadlines, told us that their writers rarely check in before filing. Feature editors, meanwhile, generally assign much longer projects and prefer to be kept in the loop during the reporting and writing process. An editor's interactions with you during the pitching stage (see Chapter 3) may help you gauge how and how much he or she wants to hear from you—whether by regular phone calls or an occasional brief e-mail.

There is one overarching principle, however, unanimously espoused by the editors and writers we spoke with:

> Editors hate surprises. If anything comes up, whether it's an unexpected twist in the story, difficulty in reaching a critical source, or a personal crisis that threatens your ability to make the deadline, your editor needs to know ASAP.
>
> —Bryn Nelson

If you're having serious problems or the story is shaping up to be substantially different from the one you were assigned, get in touch. Of course, use the editor's time well: don't bug your editor with minor questions about whether to use a particular quote, or with style questions that you can answer by reading the publication.

One way to avoid surprising your editor is to pay careful attention to your correspondence about the assignment. Whether your marching orders come in a formal assignment letter or a chain of e-mails, reread them regularly as you report and write to keep the editor's expectations in mind. (A tip: When you're writing, that assignment letter can be a useful source for a nut graf or an outline.) If you realize something is missing, go back and report some more. If you can't deliver on each specification, your editor should know before the deadline.

Some editors, like Rogers, write detailed assignment letters, ending with a list of what the writer will need to do for the story to succeed in their eyes. "I expect the writer to have that as a guidestone," Rogers says. "When the story comes in, if it doesn't have those things, it gives me the power to say, 'You didn't do this and I said you had to.'"

Sometimes editors give broad assignments: they might ask you to refresh a topic the magazine hasn't covered in a while, or to highlight a specific researcher. "They are expecting you to find the angle," explains Bryn. "They'll say, 'Here's an interesting scientist. Go find a story.'" He recalls being burned by just such a scenario. After researching the scientist and discussing interview questions with his editor, he wrote up an article and turned it in. "It wasn't what the editor had in mind. They killed it," he says. "If I did it again, I'd send the first three or four paragraphs a week in advance to make sure we were still on the same page." The point: Just because you have a vague assignment doesn't mean the editor will be happy with whatever you turn in.

Even when expectations are crystal clear at the outset, editors recognize that the story will change during reporting, and they usually want to be kept abreast of those changes.

"Sometimes writers express that they are worried about bothering me, so they don't get in touch, but I think I speak for most editors when I say that that's what we're here for," says Laura Helmuth, science and health editor at *Slate*. "I would encourage people to think of an editor as a sounding board." Conversations with editors can offer solutions you may not have considered. Rogers notes that he can sometimes help with stumbling blocks by, say, making a phone call to a reluctant source or offering research support from an intern, but only if he knows what the writer needs.

"I tend to dread those phone calls or e-mails to my editor beforehand," says SciLance member Amanda Mascarelli, "but I'm always really grateful for them afterwards, and find myself wondering why I don't pick up the phone and call my editors more often." That said, it's important to tailor your interactions to editors' individual work styles, she says.

Plan on touching base with an editor after a reporting trip, or before settling in to write thousands of words. "It is nice to have a discussion with a writer once the reporting is under the belt," says Helen Pearson, features editor at *Nature*. "It's much better to be asked questions along the way than to have a disastrous story in my inbox." In fact, unexpected twists can be a fresh source of assignments. "Contact your editor with an update when you hit a snag or roadblock in reporting and you wonder if your story should take a slightly different turn from what you'd originally proposed," says SciLancer Susan Moran. "I did this recently, and it led to a separate news story and a postponement of the original feature story until more evidence came in."

Occasionally a story falls apart when the reporter digs deeper. "A writer will sometimes send me a note and say, 'I'm starting to get a bad feeling about a story,'" says David Grimm, *Science*'s online news editor. This shows your news judgment and is better than filing a story that doesn't hold water. For a freelancer it is "doubly impressive," Grimm notes, since the writer is giving up full payment. "It really speaks to the integrity of the writer."

Still, you don't want to make your first impression with this kind of bailout. "If you're trying to make a new contact with an editor, I would say you want to make absolutely sure you've got a cracking original story for them and that it isn't going to crumble to dust in their hands," Aldhous says.

More often than not, the story does print and bears a strong resemblance to the story assigned. By giving you a byline, editors are acknowledging your responsibility for the story, and how much interaction you have with your editor will usually be your decision. "I think writers are grown-ups and I try not to be a micromanager," says Pearson. "Once they've got the commission, they can go find the story and then come back when they want to." If you really think it's important to talk something through with your editor, trust your instinct and be persistent, even if he or she is tough to reach.

Filing the Story

As you approach filing, remember some cardinal rules:

Meet your deadline and word count. That's point number one for a reason, and it's especially true for a daily site or a weekly magazine with an inflexible press schedule. Missing a deadline in this situation can be an unforgivable offense.

When reporters do fall behind, they make things worse for themselves if they disappear, says Rosie Mestel, former health and science editor of the *Los Angeles Times* and now the chief news editor of *Nature*. "I don't like it when someone goes dark just because they are running late. The editor needs to know the person is still out there and the copy is coming."

Especially for monthlies and features, editors can often give you more time if you ask for it early enough. Editors would far rather have notice and plan accordingly than to clear their desk for a story that doesn't arrive.

The lesson? Don't be late, and as soon as you seriously fear you might be, give fair warning.

As for word count, missing the mark is to some editors a sin as foul as a missed deadline. "If I assign you 4,000 words and you give me 8,000, the first thing I want to do is kill it. The second thing I want to do is send it back to you and say, 'Your assignment was to write 4,000 words. Go do your assignment,'" says Rogers.

A good rule of thumb is to file within 10 percent of the assigned word count.

Be accurate. "If I find something wrong, how can I trust that reporter again?" asks Betsy Mason, science editor for Wired.com. "I don't have time to fact-check." *Science*'s Grimm agrees. "Accuracy is the biggest thing," he says. "Bad writing can be fixed."

A related point is to be sure that you have reported deeply enough to give your editors confidence. They expect that you have hunted out critical voices from appropriate sources, asked the tough questions, and rigorously checked any claims of being first, fastest, or best. "It always worries me when I just have a sense from talking to the writer that they don't understand the material," says Pearson. Long quotes from sources explaining the science tend to be warning signs, Aldhous notes. They suggest that the writer didn't understand the subject well enough to write his or her own description. For Mestel, one symptom of under-reported stories is the use of vague terms such as "positive health outcomes" rather than specific measures such as blood pressure, glucose levels, or longer life span.

And being accurate includes crediting sources fairly. Mestel recalls encountering a jargony sentence and discovering it was lifted verbatim from a scientific abstract. "We just can't work with people who will do something like that," she says. "The people we trust are the people we turn to again and again."

Provide useful supplementary info. Editors may ask you to supply web links and other material to fact-checkers as well as ideas for photographs, illustrations, or multimedia. "Any sizeable piece in the *Times* is going to have some sort of illustration, and the more value that adds, the better," says David Corcoran, editor of the *New York Times* science section. "I always say to the writer, 'How would we illustrate this piece?' I expect the writer to work closely with the picture editor and the graphics editor to make sure that we get the best possible illustration for the space we have."

Write well, and in the publication's style. Editors told us again and again that many writers don't pay enough attention to what their publication "is."

To get the right voice, read stories from the publication you are writing for. "I notice right away if writers don't read *Wired*—they turn in something unlike anything we've ever run," says Mason. "If you haven't taken the time to read the site, that will be an obvious, huge strike against you."

Stand out. Here's what editors told us separates the best writers from adequate ones:

> *Structure:* "Features are tough to write because you're drowning in material. The outstanding writers can pull back and craft a story out of that. They can see what needs to stay and what needs to go," Pearson says. Writers should analyze story structures from the relevant section of the magazine before, during, and after reporting. They should also discuss ideas for structure when checking in with their editors.

> *Style:* Writers should follow the particular style of the publication they're writing for. For instance, British publications punctuate quotes and spell words differently than their American counterparts. "The people who straightaway blow me away are the ones who adapt to it," says Aldhous. "If I get an American freelancer who sends me an article that's been spellchecked in British English, it shows attention to detail."

> *The whole package:* While reporting, chase down images, audio, or video. If you're writing a story about bird songs, for example, ask for recordings.

Getting the Draft Back: How to Take Editing Well

From the moment a writer sends in a story, he or she is dying to know what the editor thinks. It's like the anticipation before getting back a graded test or a report card. Waiting can be excruciating. But don't interpret silence as an indication that your editors hate your story. They're probably preoccupied with the fine details of another story that's ahead of yours in the queue—or stuck in an interminable meeting and afraid to check e-mail.

Being edited is hard. Emotionally it's kind of battering. No matter how gentle the edit is, the draft is something you've kind of poured your soul into. There's a range of how personally or deeply people feel that, but what's independent is how professional and gracious they are.

—LAURA HELMUTH, SLATE

Even if you get your story back with praise, seeing the edits can hurt. Why has your favorite section been shrunk to a single sentence? What if the editor wants some more reporting to flesh out an angle? Or if the science is mangled because the editor didn't understand what you wrote? And are you really expected to send it back by the day after tomorrow?

We've all been there. This is what you need to do: Give your dog an earful, call a friend, take a walk, or down a pint (ice cream or otherwise). Then write the following back to your editor: "Thanks for the edits. I'll get on it."

This is where responsiveness and professionalism make all the difference. Your interactions with your editor as you get a story ready for publication can be the deciding factor in getting repeat assignments. "The impression you don't want to give is that revisions are a pain. They're part of the process," says Aldhous. "The speed, the willingness to make another call, to find another source, to go and do a bit more research when necessary—when that is dealt with promptly, enthusiastically, that's great."

Cursory, superficial responses to requests annoy editors and create more work. "Take edits seriously," says Mason. "I don't edit for the sake of editing, ever." Above all, be polite and cooperative.

For short news stories, or stories on tight deadline, the edit you get back may be close to the final form, and you may be asked to check only for factual errors and misleading changes. Longer stories may involve more extensive rewriting and several versions back and forth.

At some point, your assigning editor may send your story up a chain of editorial command. This may include a top editor who will edit the story with fresh eyes, a copy editor or subeditor who will finesse sentences and check for house style, and sometimes a magazine editor who makes sure content across the publication isn't repetitive or contradictory. Your assigning editor is typically the interface between you and the rest of the editorial staff. Although it can be hard to revisit the story time and again, treat these new requests seriously. If you strongly disagree with a request, concisely and politely articulate your argument to your editor to help him or her make a case on your behalf. The best writers see every stage as an opportunity to make the story better, Helmuth says.

So stay the course, remembering the ideals of customer service and teamwork, even when your story goes back and forth several times or encounters editors who contradict previous editors' comments.

A few guidelines for navigating the edit:

Pick your battles. Editors don't want to work with writers who fight over commas. In general, if the edited piece is factually accurate and you feel readers will understand it, don't object to the edits.

Remember that editorial decisions are, by definition, for the editor to make. The goal is not to show off your facility with words or include every interview you conducted; the goal is to produce a story that will carry readers of that particular publication from beginning to end.

Challenge an editor respectfully. "Good editors don't want writers simply to take their edits," Aldhous says. "It's easy for people starting out to be so glad that they're getting a commission that they aren't as assertive as they should be." Alert your editor to errors and changes in meaning that get introduced during the editing process. If you think edits have removed an important aspect of the story, explain why.

Also, if you don't understand what the editor is after, ask, don't guess. "If you're confused, and if you send back a draft that doesn't resolve the confusion, you're just wasting your time and your editor's time," says Bryn.

Be clear about what you can accomplish. Editors may have no idea how much work their requests will require. They may assume, for example, that you have answers to all their queries in your notes. If a question or proposed change requires chasing down a source, you may need more time. If so, clarify with your editor whether that time is available.

SciLance members emphasize that a cheerful, cooperative attitude makes a big difference. "I'm willing to go the extra mile when it's possible, and particularly when editors have been especially good to me at other points," says Sarah Webb. If a request seems unreasonable or will require significant time, explain why without getting huffy. Kendall Powell says, "Helen Pearson once told me, 'Kendall, I know sometimes I ask for the moon. And it's not that I always expect you to be able to deliver it, but I still have to ask just in case you actually can!'"

Finally, if the editor is really asking for considerably more reporting or side pieces outside the original scope of the assignment, you may want to renegotiate so that you get paid for the extra work. (This is where having assignment letters and expectations in writing can be really helpful.)

Suggest an alternative. Never just change an edit back to the original. If you don't like something an editor wrote, suggest an alternative. "If it was changed there was probably a reason for it," Aldhous says. "Let's forget about going back to the original wording and move on to a form of words that both are happy with and is correct."

If anything is incorrect, fix it. If your editor introduces errors, suggest accurate options. If something is wrong, be firm in the need for a change that makes it correct. You may need to explain briefly and politely that a technique has several inventors, that a study was performed with biopsies, not in patients, or that being HIV-positive is not the same as having AIDS. Be careful at this point not to add too many words to the total story length.

When in doubt, use the phone. A phone call can defuse an escalating back-and-forth e-mail exchange, and get both of you back on the same page. Writers and editors agree that sometimes that's the best way to get the process back on track. "If I think it's a situation that will turn into hours of e-mail versus five minutes on the phone, I'll try the phone first," says Sarah.

Assume your editor has good intentions. Accept that your editor understands the readers of the publication you are writing for. Remember that he or she is representing them. Also, know that the e-mails and changes from your editor may reflect things going on behind the scenes at the publication that you'll never have to know. "What's happening that the freelancer doesn't see within the magazine is that the editor is fighting for more pages, for a better art budget, for better placement, trying to keep the writer's language protected from top editors, and speaking on the writer's behalf to the fact-checker," says Helmuth. "The editor is your biggest advocate."

After the Story, the Relationship Continues

Completing an assignment is not just an end in itself. It's a bridge to the next assignment, and the next. But remember, if you're a freelancer, you don't have to keep working for any particular editor or publication. If writing for them is not worth the money—or the byline—stop pitching and politely decline additional assignments.

Conversely, when you find a good editor, latch on tight. Stay in touch and show that you're proud of your work. Scott Dodd, the editor of OnEarth.org, says that writers who use blogs and social media tools to expand a story's audience are "an editor's dream." If, as you promote your story, it gets picked up by a popular aggregator, send a brief e-mail to your editor (but not a series of them!). And remember to give thanks where due—if someone at the magazine helped with a great image or lede, acknowledge that in an e-mail or even in your online posts about the story.

Particularly after you've written for an editor a couple of times, you might ask for feedback in a way that doesn't put the editor on the spot. Saying something like, "Have you seen anything in my stories that you'd like me to work on?" or "Is there anything I could be doing differently that would make your life easier?" leaves the door open for the editor to respond or not. It shows a positive attitude and, if the editor responds, makes you better able to target the editor's needs.

Another way to stay in touch is to establish yourself as a resource, and as someone who follows a particular topic closely.

When you're working with a good editor, every story becomes a lesson in better reporting and writing. Producing a great story is hard work, and few people can do it alone, says SciLancer Michelle Nijhuis. "Good editors, and there are quite a few of them, can both make your stories better and make you feel proud of the process. The longer I'm in this profession, the more I appreciate them."

One final tip: When your fantastic story wins an award, make sure you thank your editor, says Helmuth. "This is a little secret among editors: we really listen for that. It's really gracious and it helps your reputation and it makes people want to work with you."

When I'm working regularly for an editor, I anticipate his or her weekly/ monthly needs and send ideas and forward relevant e-mails about events/findings—even if I don't have time to do the resulting story. I think that taking this approach both keeps you in the editor's good graces and makes you a go-to person.
—VIRGINIA GEWIN

✒ SciLance says . . .

- Deliver **accurate, thoroughly reported, clearly written copy** to your editor **on time** and within 10 percent of the assigned length.

- Work to **keep your editor's job easy**. Editors are busy and have to produce work to satisfy their bosses and the style of their publications. Think of your job **as customer service**.

(Continues)

Working with Editors—and Their Edits

- **Editors hate surprises.** Pay close attention to correspondence that spells out your editor's expectations for the story and **make sure you deliver** on them. Let your editors know as soon as possible if the story is turning out differently, if you hit serious stumbling blocks, or if you are going to be late.

- Remember that **your editor is your ally**. You are working together to produce a great story. Don't be afraid to connect with your editor to discuss the project.

- **Find video, images, and other extras** that can be packaged together with your story.

- **Take your edits graciously, but not uncritically.** Don't quibble over commas, but if any edits make your story wrong or misleading, speak up and suggest alternatives.

- **Never just change an edit back to the original.** Assume your editor had a valid reason for tweaking your text, and look for another option that you are both comfortable with.

- When your story gets picked up by other outlets or wins an award—or even when it just comes out a lot better than your original draft—**thank your editor**.

Chapter 9

Going Long

How to Sell a Book

By Emma Marris

I have written and published a book and lived to tell the tale. It took a long time and was hard work. But I am very glad I did it. Now that the thing has been out for a while, and whole days pass where I don't check my Amazon.com sales ranking, I feel ready to share my number-one, most important piece of advice for those considering nonfiction book writing: don't do it for the money.

That's not to say you won't make any money. Some people do. Rebecca Skloot, author of *The Immortal Life of Henrietta Lacks,* spent years on the best-seller list, and Oprah is making a movie of the book. Oprah. That could happen to you, too, if you have an amazing story, spend ten years researching, write as well as Skloot, and the stars align in your favor. But don't hold your breath.

Instead, you should write a book for one or, ideally, both of the following reasons: you are so gripped by a story, person, or topic that you just have to write a book about it; or you have a good idea for a book, would like to try your hand at long-form writing, and would like to take advantage of the platform it will give you as a book author to further your career.

That is, write a book because it is a personal imperative, or write a book to shake up and reshape your career. Or do both. Doing the first may mean some personal financial sacrifice, especially if you write the book without a contract, or sell it for a tiny advance. Doing the second may mean that you must budget a decent amount of time after the book comes out for promotion, so as to properly position yourself and the book and efficiently parlay its publication into a career boost. Doing both, naturally, means spending a lot of time on both ends—taking your time and sparing no expense to craft the book and running around shamelessly pushing your book for months afterward. It is a big investment.

But it can pay off, even if your book doesn't sell particularly well. A book has a unique power to turn a person who has written about a topic extensively in shorter formats into an expert on that topic. Once you write the book, you own it, and to some extent you own the topic, too. Sure, there are now all these other media channels, from blogs to documentary films, but a book—especially one from a traditional publishing house, as opposed to one self-published—still has an inherent cultural gravitas that sets it apart. Russell Galen, my agent at Scovil, Galen, and Ghosh, says that "having a book is like having a degree from Harvard or Oxford. It conveys credibility in a way that few other human endeavors do. You are going to be heard more clearly, more loudly." And he argues that the Internet actually increases the value of writing a book. "A book can be a foundation for a larger multimedia impact: getting on the radio, getting on TV, contributing to blogs," he says.

The combined impact can open up career possibilities. Charles Seife, who has written several books on math, physics, and cosmology and teaches in the science, health, and environmental reporting program at New York University, reckons that it can pave the way for your next move. "It helps you switch jobs if you want to, or land a full-time staff position. It does make you more serious in the eyes of many people." It is for those kinds of intangible benefits, and for the pure joy of telling a great story at the length it deserves, that one should write a book. If you can afford to. With advances for many books clocking in at low five figures or less these days, and the research, writing, and promotion taking untold months, one shudders to imagine the hourly rate. "You can probably do better at McDonald's," says Seife.

So, presuming that you have not cast this book aside in favor of the "careers" page at mcdonalds.com, let us take a look at the process of selling and writing a book.

The Process

The little tour below is meant to be a very basic introduction to the process of getting a book published—with no pretensions of comprehensiveness. There are lots of good books out there that will do a more thorough job, and if you decide to proceed with a book project, I recommend you read one or three of them, ideally guides written by agents or editors with lots of experience, such as *Thinking Like Your Editor* by Susan Rabiner and Alfred Fortunato (see more suggestions in the Resources section).

Researching Your Idea

So you've got an idea for a book. Great. So does my mailman. It'll be easier to sell if you've done lots of research and can already present the major thrust of your story along with compelling details. But how do you find the time and money for all that research? When you are a staff writer working on a feature, your salary pays for your research. Even for freelancers, magazines often pay for travel expenses when you go somewhere to research a story. It makes sense; magazine editors know that stories told from the place where they happen have a vibrant, eyewitness quality that's very difficult to achieve over the phone. But there's no such thing as "travel expenses" in book publishing. If you feel like you need to fly to Australia to make the book sing, you just have to hope you've racked up some decent frequent-flier miles. And whether your research takes you ten years or two weeks, you are likely to get the same advance.

A common way to deal with this problem is to pitch stories for magazines on the same topic as your book idea for a year or two before you write the proposal. This needn't be premeditated. If you are able to follow your interests in shorter projects, they will often naturally lead you to your book idea. "For me the process was that daily news led to features and then features led to books," says Seife. "When you realize that you have a collection of features that are thematically linked, the book sort of falls out of it."

This was more or less my process, too, and it allowed me to get paid for my advance research. Then, once I had the contract, I explicitly cost-shared a few additional stories. I told the magazine I worked for most often about the book and offered to split expenses with them if they wanted a feature about one part of it, long before the book would come out. I even ended up using some of the magazine material, with permission, in the book itself.

I recommend this approach, with the following reservation: don't count on being able to just sew together a bunch of features and call it a book. Even if you end up using a great deal of your own magazine work, you will find that smoothing out and adjusting the style, reworking beginnings and endings to hide the seams, and adding updates for those you wrote some time ago will mean considerable, even total, rewriting.

Writing a Proposal

A book proposal is a long, detailed query letter, usually with at least one complete sample chapter and a full rundown of all the planned chapters. My proposal was a kind of prose outline; my basic approach was to write a sexy and intriguing magazine-style pitch for each chapter. At the end of each of these chapter pitches, I put in a list of planned interviews and a list of related articles I had written so that it was clear I had already done a fair amount of research.

Make sure your proposal shows off any research you have done. "It should show editors that yours isn't just a vague idea, but that you've done your work and will hit the ground running," says Carl Zimmer, author of many books on biology, including a lavishly illustrated tome on science-related tattoos. Make sure the proposal is well written. Most important, make sure the narrative line is clear. Genes, stars, cells, other dimensions, argon, or jellyfish: No matter the topic, all nonfiction books—science or otherwise—must tell a story. (Remember the distinction between topic and story from Chapter 2?) Whether it is the story of how the recession affected the rice farmers of southern Missouri or how your mother's wisdom got you through being stranded in an elevator for three weeks with a box of venomous snakes, your proposal needs a narrative that propels readers forward through the pages—ideally, one that hurtles them forward with such inescapable narrative force that prospective editors end up finishing your proposal sitting in a bath that has gone to room temperature or hunched under the bedside lamp at 2 a.m. even though the baby is due to wake up at 5.

Getting an Agent

The literary agent is a misunderstood figure. Writers think of agents as some sort of mystical gatekeepers of the publishing industry, since, as everyone says, you can't get anything published unless you have an agent (which is generalizing, of course). But agents—the good ones, at least—don't see themselves that way. They see themselves as the discoverers, shapers, nurturers, protectors, and occasional psychotherapists of writing talent. You want to sell your book; an agent wants, ideally, to work for an author who is going to turn out a series of well-written, on-time books with progressively higher sales figures. So if you want to hook an agent, think beyond selling your book and sell yourself as a promising author.

Create a short list of agents you would like to work with. I did this by making a list of books that I believed had the same feel as the book I wanted to write—they were speaking to a similar audience on similar topics and at a similar level. Then I looked in the acknowledgments, where most authors thank their agents. A few didn't do that, but some Googling around helped me figure out who represented whom. Another common route is to ask friends or acquaintances who have published books for the names of or introductions to their agents. This can be dicey, etiquette-wise. Not all writers feel secure enough with their agents to want to bug them with a lot of introductions to new writers. So tread carefully. You may find you get a name but no offer of an introduction, or even a plea not to use your friend's name. Chalk it up to her being still in awe of the agent, and don't be angry with her.

The accepted process for wooing an agent is to send a query letter, generally by e-mail. This isn't the full book proposal. It is short, and similar to a magazine pitch. (See Chapter 3.) Make sure to put your story up top; show that you've got a narrative to sell, not just a topic. And take time to sell yourself as the right person to write the book. Highlight any preexisting relationships or articles or well-trafficked blogs or well-followed tweets or PhDs—anything that positions you as the expert on your topic and shows that you have a readership. This is your "platform." Be sure to mention some of the most impressive places you've published. Agents want to be able to sell a book about the scientific quest for the lost monkeys of Mongolia by award-winning *Outside* contributor Ozzie Oozing-Cred, not by Suzie No-Clips who just loves monkeys. Spend a few sentences talking about who you think would read the book, perhaps citing books that did well that you believe have a similar audience. See p. 112 for an abbreviated version of my query letter, which led to my book deal.

Agents are notoriously busy. You may hear back right away, but it might take weeks. There's no magic formula for whether or how often to follow up, but there's also no rule against sending queries out to multiple agents simultaneously. If you get a nibble from one, you might think about taking that opportunity to ping your first choice again. If no one bites, find six more agents and send out another round of queries. Keep trying!

Getting an agent is reckoned by many to be the hardest part of selling a book, but don't get complacent once you have representation. Your agent may love your idea and still not be able to sell it. Also be prepared for your agent to ask for considerable changes to your proposal before she shows it around to editors at publishing houses. That's part of her job. She wants to sell the thing, after all. And it is good practice for you. Even though Zimmer has published more than a dozen books, he and his agent still spend lots of time on each proposal, going back and forth, honing it until it is so tight and carefully researched that when he sells the book, he pretty much has his outline already done.

Your agent might also ask for pretty big changes to make the book more marketable, and there's nothing wrong with that. There's a kind of vague perception out there that you don't have to compromise, artistically, as much in a book as you do in magazines or newspapers. While it is true that the leanness of today's publishing industry and the heft of a book manuscript means that there is often less line editing, I would argue that that's probably a bad thing for readers.

And editors will also want changes to a book, from large-scale reorganizations to sometimes-annoying concessions to the public's tastes and interests. Don't forget that the book is a commercial product. "You may have this idea that you are going to write this beautiful thing and everyone is going to love it," says SciLancer Hillary Rosner, who has coauthored one book and worked as a ghostwriter on three others. "Detaching emotionally is one of the hardest parts of the process." If editors don't see dollar signs when they read the proposal, they are likely to pass. Making it commercial enough to sell doesn't have to mean dumbing it down or betraying the material, though. It means finding a way to tell the story so it resonates with as many people as possible. That's, arguably, honoring the material.

One way to do this from the get-go is to talk about your story, as we've suggested in previous chapters, with people from all walks of life: your mother, your hairdresser, people on the bus. You may find the rags-to-riches saga of the first particle physicist from inner-city Baltimore compelling on its face, but what is it that makes your accountant's eyes light up when you tell him about it?

So you and your agent craft a proposal that best showcases your story and he or she goes off and . . . I don't know. Has a bunch of three-martini lunches with editors in midtown Manhattan? I actually think no one has the expense accounts for that kind of stuff anymore. My guess is that they all sit around in their offices huddled over e-mail, just like we writers do. But there are complex networks and relationships strung across Manhattan and the rest of the world, little imaginary dotted lines that you are, to some degree, paying your 15 percent agent fee to ride on. So you wait and worry and every once in a while your agent lets you know how it is going, and you probably get lots of editors passing. Then, if you are lucky, one says yes, and you get a very pleasant phone call.

If you aren't lucky, and no one says yes, turn to Chapter 13 of this book, on handling rejection. A rejected proposal can feel like a gut punch, and even the most hardened hack should be forgiven for sulking a little and maybe, you know, throwing a bottle of bourbon violently across the room while playing the Pixies at maximum volume. But after a few weeks, the seasoned writer will either sit down and retool the proposal for resubmission, or lay it lovingly on the necropsy table for dissection and repackaging as smaller magazine pitches. (You may also want to consider publishing your book in a shorter, digital-only form. See "The Goldilocks Length" below. Self-publishing is another, increasingly popular option, though it still doesn't carry the credibility that comes with an imprint from a traditional publishing house.)

No matter your next steps, your time and energy weren't wasted; your research can be recycled and what you learned is still in your head. Isn't this one of the reasons we write—to learn about new stuff ourselves? And then you can get to work on your next proposal. "One guy I know does five proposals" that go nowhere, says Kathy Belden, my editor at Bloomsbury. "It always takes about six tries to hit the right one."

Signing the Contract

To be perfectly honest with you, I barely read my first book contract. *That's what my agent is for,* I thought. *He'll make sure it is good.* And I am sure he did. Now here is where I say, "Do as I say, not as I do." You will, of course, read the fine print, jot down questions to ask your agent, and work with him or her to make sure you're getting as much as you can for the rights you give up, not just for print books but for e-books as well. Contract lingo is intimidating, but you can figure it out.

For my second book, which was a textbook instead of a trade book, the contract was different. (A trade book is a book that the regular public buys at a bookstore or online, as opposed to a textbook, which is usually assigned by a teacher in a class.) So I hired a lawyer, recommended to me by another textbook author, to look it over.

My very amiable textbook publisher made about half the changes my very amiable lawyer suggested, and everyone was very polite and relaxed about the whole thing—if you don't count me. I was very nervous about asking for changes, because I thought it looked rude or as if I didn't trust the publisher. But this is nonsense. If you are a good businessperson, you'll look out for yourself, and the people with whom you do business will respect you for it.

Writing the Damn Thing

After the Sturm und Drang of seeking a book contract, it can come as rather a shock that once one is secured you actually have to write the book. And a book is so long. Much longer than anything you've ever written. At first, you will feel like you are knitting a sweater for a giant out of a bunch of balls and tangles of odd, assorted yarn scraps. There you are, with a bunch of mismatched needles and no pattern, and you are *inside* the sweater. It seems as though you'll never finish.

But eventually you will. In my experience, most writers make their regular deadlines because of the inevitable presence of The Fear. You pitch, you get an assignment, you do some research and interviews, you dabble with some paragraphs, you clean out the junk drawer and watch some reality TV, you Facebook, and then, just exactly when you need it, you are seized by The Fear that you will not finish the article in time. And suddenly, you are the soul of productivity. Words stream fluidly from your fingertips, and you work for hours straight until the whole thing is done, fact-checked, and copy edited. If you are really good, you even leave twenty-four or forty-eight hours for it to sit before you do one last edit. You are a pro.

The same thing happens with a book, except at a much-elongated pace. SciLancer Mark Schrope wrote a book on the BP oil spill in the Gulf of Mexico in an epic bout of intense, fear-motivated flow: six days a week, more writing after dinner, all routine maintenance on the house and yard canceled. "I worked for about six months like that," he says. "Nonstop fear. I didn't mind it. I got into it." My memories of writing my book are kind of vague and mixed up, a good sign that I did much of it under the semi-supernatural influence of The Fear.

But if Mark and I are any indication, you might mess up the timing a little on your first book. Your fear-generating apparatus is not yet tuned to the scale of a book, so The Fear may arrive just a little late. Both Mark and I had to ask for extensions on our books—him on his first draft and me on my second. I hated making that phone call. I was near tears asking for another month; I felt like unprofessional scum. But my editor and agent seemed totally fine with it. The culture of book writing is not as focused on deadlines as is daily, weekly, and monthly science writing. Stories of late manuscripts—decades late, even—are legion. But that's no excuse for us, in my opinion. We still ought to try our best to turn our books in on time, if not for professional pride, then at least for business reasons. They don't pay you more if you take extra weeks or months to write, so the longer you take, the more money you lose. If you do think you are going to be late, let your agent and editor know as soon as you are sure. They'll like it better than if you just don't deliver on time. My editor suggests budgeting eighteen months to write. And that's if you make the book your top priority every day, which might be difficult if you are also trying to make a living through other means.

Another distraction from book writing is the social media and self-branding that seems to take an increasingly large share of writers' time these days. "Journalists think that if they don't tweet for a week or blog for a month that people will forget them," says Zimmer. "This is not true. People will not forget you entirely." After all, he says, if you are blogging and tweeting to prepare the ground for the book, there's no point to any of it if you don't get the book done.

As far as how to knit your way out of a giant's sweater, that is a topic for a whole 'nother book, or possibly a master's degree and/or course of therapy with a trained professional. One thing I can say is that if your material is personally important to you or emotionally wrenching, it is wise to try to build in some breaks and even some short spells of time working on unrelated short articles. When SciLancer Thomas Hayden wrote a book about a medical team's experiences during the early days of the Iraq war, *On Call in Hell,* a book filled with death, agony, and the horror of war, he lived with it intensely for six months. "I was drained by the end," he says. "I cried during the writing of that book numerous times."

So for Thomas's second book, *Sex and War,* which also had intense, violent themes, he made sure to intersperse some lighter assignments and make dates with his wife for five in the afternoon, so he'd be sure not to work through the night on such grim material. Take his example and take care of yourself.

Editing the Damn Thing

You may be surprised by how long it takes to get edits back from your book editor. Editors are all overworked, and besides, the pace of the book business is glacial compared to that of a magazine, newspaper, or website. Try to keep busy and make some money while you wait and for heaven's sake, don't reread the manuscript. You need some mental distance from it so you can do your own smoothing and fixing on the editing round. My editor asked for a major rewrite of my book. I was disappointed, but she was right; I could see it at once. You may be a master of structuring a 5,000-word feature or a 500-word online story, but an 80,000-word book is a different beast. Be prepared to struggle with organization. Every book is different and has its own process. As with anything else, clear and open communication will always help.

Eventually you'll see the copyedited manuscript (yep, it's really starting to be real), then the publisher will send you proofs, and you can go over them with a fine-tooth comb looking for any last-minute errors. After that, you can stop reading the damn thing, at least until you have to plow through it to select excerpts for magazines or to read at bookstores.

Waiting for It to Come Out

Oh my God, books take forever to come out. Months or years. But instead of getting annoyed, make the most of the break. Save your strength and work on something else. You just lived inside the thing for however long, and you will again when you promote it. So just go write a bunch of articles about space exploration or something—unless, of course, your book is about space exploration. Once the publication date begins to loom on the horizon, you can begin building your social media presence, your website, and your other digital tools for publicizing yourself and your book. Also pay all bar debts and make up with all your estranged friends. You'll want everyone helping you spread the word. Practice saying "tweet me!" Shine up your self-tooting horn. (Welcome to the uncomfortable world of self-promotion.)

Publicizing the Book

These days book tours are pretty much dead. You might get a little tiny bit of money from your publisher to drive to a nearby city to do a reading or be asked to piggyback bookstore events on your preexisting travel schedule. But unless you just wrote about something truly hot, or unless you have the time, money, and moxie to create your own book tour, you'll be doing a lot of your promotion online. You have to have a Facebook page, tweet, and join whatever new social media platform is en vogue when your book appears.

You'll also want to send copies to all your friends in the media business, even though the publisher will send copies to a list of media outlets. There are two reasons to do this. First of all, it is always nice to have a free book arrive in the mail. The second is that some of them might then decide to pitch something about you and your book, and if they sell it, then you get the publicity and they get the word rate and everybody wins.

The Goldilocks Length

A book is not the only forum for stories that need more space than a magazine feature. And some stories are better suited to a length in between the 5,000-word feature and the 75,000-word book. Alas, there has long been a lack of outlets in this range, so these 30,000-word stories sometimes get padded until they reach the 75,000-word range—which can be annoying for the reader.

Luckily, the Internet and digital readers are helping fill this vacant niche. As this book went to press, the marketplace of projects, initiatives, and startups publishing long-format journalism was both vibrant and in flux: the Atavist, Kindle Singles, and Byliner are just three of the many current attempts to marry long-neglected story lengths with new distribution and funding models.

Coauthoring

One way for a writer to get involved with books is to be asked to cowrite a book with someone else. Generally the someone else is the "expert" and the science writer is the skilled writer and communicator. These collaborations can be fantastic, but make sure you know what you are being offered. They come in different flavors.

First, what kind of authorship are you being offered? Does the "expert" want you to ghostwrite the book, which means your name will not be associated with the book and you may be prohibited from revealing your involvement? Does he or she want to write the book "with" you? This is code for "the hack writes the book, the famous guy goes on the lecture tour." Check out the covers of books written by Hotshot McFly "with" Schlumpy Scrivener and compare the font sizes of their names. Not to say that this arrangement is never a good deal; just know what you are getting into. Or does the expert want an equal coauthor with the word "and" linking the authors' names?

Second, how will you be paid? If the book has already been sold, the publisher might offer you a flat fee and a "work made for hire" contract. Such an arrangement is appealingly low-risk, but also has a finite reward. Does the author want you to work on an unsold proposal? If so, will there be any payment to you if no publisher bites? Alternatively, the author may offer you a royalty share for either a sold or unsold project. This is higher-risk, but higher excitement. Thomas arranged a royalty share for *Sex and War,* a book he coauthored with Malcolm Potts. He says it was "the right emotional decision," since he thus had more invested in the project.

It is wise to meet your proposed collaborators face-to-face to get a feel for them. One SciLancer did a quick-turnaround coauthorship job with a guy who was kind of a jerk. She invested only three or four months in the project, and it paid well, so she was happy with the outcome. But imagine being yoked to a blowhard or a flake for a year.

Hash out the expectations for all parties at the beginning of the collaboration. How will the work proceed? What is the schedule? Will you be paid more if the project takes longer than expected? What will you do and what will the other authors do? Who gets final say on the edits? Thomas also recommends, for "with" projects, a clause that provides for access to the coauthor, something like "the coauthor will be available for so many hours per day or per week for X period." Otherwise, you might spend months chasing Hotshot McFly around trying to get enough material on tape to shape his or her immortal words into a story.

Textbooks

An emerging area for nonfiction writers is writing or collaborating on textbooks. I am writing one as this book goes to press, and Zimmer has written several. If you have a trade-book agent, he or she will likely bow out of any textbook deals, so you will have to work them out on your own. And there are many other ways in which the textbook is a different beast from the trade book. "The advantage in the trade book is that you can write as eloquently as you can," says Zimmer. "The disadvantages are that trade publishers are not interested in helping you make the book look good or updating the book. Textbooks offer the opposite. Clear, concise, elegant writing is a strength in textbooks, but you aren't going to be able to go on for pages and pages telling the adventures of some Arctic explorers. But on the other hand, textbook publishers love to make their books look good." And the textbook business model is all about putting out frequent updated editions, which means that the new stuff you've learned about your favorite topic always has a home.

The editing process is different for textbooks, too. Often a slew of experts in the field will be called in to check your work, which is both terrifying as it happens and extremely comforting once they've signed off.

Edited Volumes, Best-ofs, and Other Compilations

Check the back of edited volumes and writers' organization listings for calls for submissions to these kinds of compilation books, as they are a great way to gain exposure and get a foot in the book world. They don't pay much, if anything, though. Hillary has written a few of these, for fees in the neighborhood of $200 for reprints, or $0 for writing a contribution from scratch. She was able to sell that contribution to a magazine, though, with no objections from the book's editors, so it worked out. Make sure you ask about reusing material up-front when you agree to contribute to a volume.

SciLancer Douglas Fox has made a point of submitting his work to *The Best American Science Writing, The Best American Science and Nature Writing,* and similar anthologies. Submission instructions are usually tucked somewhere in the previous year's volume. He's had a couple of his articles anthologized, for small fees in the few-hundred-dollars range.

As with all things book, though, it isn't the money that is the reward. Since appearing in anthologies, he's had half a dozen book agents contact him to talk about representing him. He has also used his inclusion in the anthologies when introducing himself to new editors, and the result, he says, has been "an uptick in being taken seriously."

Books Are Long-term Investments in Your Career

Selling and writing a nonfiction book is tough work for generally low pay—at least your first time out. As my editor says, "Don't ever plan on making a living doing it." But the nonmonetary rewards are not to be sniffed at, from increased name recognition to making your mother proud. I plan to write more books, if I can sell them. They feel weighty. Hell, they are weighty—assuming they're made of wood pulp and not pixels, which is admittedly a big assumption these days. You can hold 'em in your hand and use stacks of them to prop open the door.

There's nothing mystical about writing a book, as I mentioned; it is in many ways a lot like writing a very, very long magazine piece. If you are a good writer with an attention span on the longish side of the notoriously short journalistic average, you can probably do it. But no, you can't have an introduction to my agent.

Sample Query Letter

October 4, 2008

Dear Ms. Fancypants Agent,

Most people think of the natural world as a place where humans are not. I am writing a book that will change how readers see the "natural" and "human" worlds—a book that will transform how they think about everything from tigers on TV to what they plant in their own backyards. *Rambunctious Garden: Saving Nature in a Post-Wild World* argues that cherishing nature only when it is "untouched by man" is an outdated trap that thwarts new, bold plans to save the environment.

I've covered environmental stories for the world's leading scientific journal, *Nature,* since 2004, and in recent years I've been questioning what conservationists are trying to conserve and why. Many environmentalists and conservationists tell me that they are trying to save the "pristine" or "wild" places. But these terms are vague, outdated, and limiting. And I'm not the only one who is ready for a change.

[*Several paragraphs omitted here outline the structure and content of the book.*]

This is an optimistic book filled with quirky detail. The reader will meet scientists, environmentalists, activists, nature documentary film-makers, and others, all with their own ideas about what is important in nature and how to get it. We'll travel around the world to visit false Edens, designer ecosystems, and empty-lot jungles.

The research for this book is already partly done; I have written more than a dozen long stories on this general theme for *Nature.* I can synthesize the science confidently. I know many leading ecologists and conservation biologists well who are interested in these ideas and would want to be a part of the story. And I can write. The tone will be authoritative but light, crisp, and accessible without being overly cute.

Rambunctious Garden is a Big Idea book that will mix interesting theory with surprising and compelling anecdotes, an approach that has met with success in books such as *The Omnivore's Dilemma, 1491, Out of Eden,* and *The World Without Us.*

I hope you'll be interested in representing me. I'm enclosing some of my stories that hew most closely to what I'd like to do in the book, and I am at work on a sample chapter.

I look forward to hearing from you.

Sincerely,

Emma Marris

The Six Steps to Authorship

Here's some advice I sent to SciLance on recognizing a book idea. And yes, it is based on personal experience.

Step 1. Have a nagging feeling that the way you and most people think about something is off-base.

Step 2. Obsess about this, collecting examples.

Step 3. Get so that every time you have more than two or three drinks, all you can talk about is your obsessive idea.

Step 4. Get so that all you can talk about is your obsessive idea, even when you are sober. At this point, your significant other may start looking across the table at you with this look that says, "Really? Again?"

Step 5. Sell your obsessive idea to a publisher.

Step 6. Pray that you can maintain the obsession for at least another year.

SciLance says . . .

- Don't write a book for money. Write it for the less tangible benefits, and especially **because you're passionate** about the story.

- **Subsidize your book research** by pitching feature stories on related topics.

- Finding an agent is tough, but good agents won't just hawk one book; they'll **invest in your long-term career**.

- **Even great book proposals get rejected**. Sulk for a while, then get to work repurposing your research as something else: a series of magazine stories, say, or as a long-form piece designed for e-readers.

- Set strict writing goals for yourself, **to keep on pace without regular deadlines**.

- Consider **collaborating with an established expert**, to learn the format and share the financial risks.

- **Being an author means publicizing your work**. Get comfortable with that before your book comes out.

- And finally, really **don't do it for the money!**

Chapter 10

Multilancing

By Robert Frederick

Multilancing—reporting a story in more than one medium—can be immensely rewarding. For one, you get to think about storytelling in multiple ways, which can improve your overall storytelling ability, like learning a second language can help you better understand your first language. In addition, you get a lot of variety in your daily work. You may also have multiple opportunities to sell the same story, because editors in different media don't generally view one another as competitors. A multimedia reporter can sell a print version of his or her story to *Nature* and an audio version to the Canadian Broadcasting Corporation's *Quirks and Quarks*. And reporters who can deliver a story in multiple media to the same editor may open up yet more opportunities. For example, says SciLance member Douglas Fox, "Being able to take photographs for some of my field-reported stories has landed me print assignments that I otherwise wouldn't have gotten."

Whether or not you decide to become fluent in a second—or third—medium, trying it will help you in the same way that knowing a few words or phrases of a foreign language can help you in your travels. "Occasionally I see stories in my head as visuals," says Cameron Walker, a SciLance member and a print journalist who has experimented with video. "I've always tried to write in scenes, but videographers' distinction between the 'A roll'—the person being interviewed—and the scenery and descriptive shots of the 'B roll' has stuck in my mind, and now I try to build that combination into my stories."

In this chapter, I'll talk about the advantages as well as the challenges of reporting in multiple media. (For advice on learning the specific technology and techniques of different media, see the Resources section.)

When to Multilance

Before plunking down money for a new camera or microphone that you don't yet know how to use, take some time to reflect. What kinds of media do you personally like to consume? If you're not drawn to watching video, for example, chances are you won't like producing it, either. If you do enjoy consuming a particular medium and think you might enjoy producing it, too, learn more: talk with people who produce it, take a class on it, or rent any needed equipment and try it out.

The best time to try a second medium is after establishing yourself in your first medium. That's because you'll need to be able to afford the time and equipment to learn and practice that second medium. After all, you're competing with professionals who specialize in a single medium—though again, more opportunities can arise for multilancers. The worst time to try another medium is out of necessity: financial desperation is a powerful but ultimately unfulfilling motivator. I know from experience that it's much better to learn another medium out of love and curiosity.

My first media love was radio. I listened to it all the time, and I still do. When I tried it out, spending a summer as a science journalist at a National Public Radio (NPR) member station, I found I really liked producing it, too. That summer, I even had a piece about NASA's upcoming mission to Mars run on NPR's *Morning Edition*. But I was heartbroken when after six months of radio freelancing—podcasting hadn't been invented yet—I had to turn to another medium out of financial desperation. I chose print because there were so many more outlets. My learning curve was steep, and competing with professional writers was tough.

I sold a few print stories, and those led to well-paying gigs as an editor and technical writer. But with lots of downtime, I started learning HTML for coding and designing websites, deciding that I was going to make it as a science writer by specializing in multimedia itself. I would be the person who could do it all, on the cheap (at least to start), and of exceptional quality. Gradually I would make multimedia my career.

This was an ambitious plan, and for the next few years the reality of it hit me like a daily hangover. No one was hiring multimedia freelancers; editors were convinced that jacks-of-all-trades were masters of none, an enduring misperception. Bit by bit, however, I learned a few things about photography and about video storytelling and production, all in the same way that I'd picked up HTML: I found free lessons on the Internet and clients who were looking for a deal. In this way, I was paid to practice, and found I loved these media, too. I invested time in my clients' projects until I delivered a superior product, and eventually I was able to charge the same as my competition.

Of course, delivering a superior product for less than what others charge is a good way to break into the business, and get client referrals and more clients. Be careful, though, as doing this regularly can undermine standard freelance rates, and could upset the very group of professionals you are seeking to join. (See the Resources section for places to find current information about multimedia rates.)

Sell Your Content: Starting Out

Thanks to advances in technology and the democratization of the Internet, the barrier to producing and distributing content is much lower than in the recent past. But when you're just starting out in a medium that is new to you, you have to do more than learn how to produce and distribute it. In addition to crafting your stories with the tools and techniques appropriate to that medium, you need to learn to recognize the sights, sounds, and other distinguishing elements of a good story in each medium you practice—no easy feat, particularly given the varying demands of different media outlets.

One of my first opportunities to learn this came while freelancing a piece for NPR about a technology dispute between two companies. During my reporting, I heard about a government-funded project to adapt positron emission tomography (PET) scans to screen for breast cancer. I knew I was way ahead of any press release about it, and I confirmed that with the press agent at the national lab that was developing it. On the strength of my NPR credits, I got an interview with the relevant scientists and started reporting it as an audio piece: recording radio-quality interviews, using question-asking techniques to get short interviewee responses delivered with a lot of intonation, and recording sounds that I could use to set scenes. I soon realized that NPR was not the best place for this story; just defining PET and PET scans would take the better part of a minute, and a typical NPR piece is only three to five minutes long.

As a multilancer, though, I had another option: I pitched a print story to the *Dallas Morning News,* a large regional newspaper in a city that is home to cancer research and a major breast cancer foundation. I got the assignment, and delivered what became the cover story for that week's health section, timed to coincide with the foundation's annual charity walk in Dallas. Using the audio I'd collected during my initial reporting, I also sold a few radio stories to regional markets, which would take pieces a little longer than NPR as long as the story was tied to something local—in this case, upcoming charity walks in other cities. These stations posted links to my *Dallas Morning News* story on their websites, expanding the audience for the print story.

Then, while reporting the *Dallas Morning News* story, I learned about efforts to develop a new way of delivering cancer drugs and an upcoming paper to be published about it in *Cancer Research*. I knew this would also have to be a print story, because finding relevant sounds to help set the scene would be very difficult. But the story was too complex for a mass-market outlet. On the strength of my recent work with the *Dallas Morning News*, I pitched *ScienceNOW* and did that story, too. My audio journalism career had been under way for a couple of years, but now my print journalism career was really getting going, too.

As I learned, selling your content when you're just starting out in another medium is hard work. I understand from others who have done it that it's like starting your career again. In my case, I *was* at the beginning of my career—I wasn't a master storyteller in any medium. That's why I think it is so important to establish yourself in one medium before starting another: a jack-of-all-trades can become a master of many, but it is far easier on the wallet to master them one by one.

After my fourth year of multilancing, the opportunity I had been preparing for arrived: multimedia host, editor, and producer at *Science* magazine. I leapt at the job and got it. And among all the many positive experiences I had, it was there that I also learned—from the accomplished freelancers who approached me about audio, photos, and video content—how to add multimedia content to an existing assignment. It's the approach I use today.

Sell Your Content: Adding It to Other Work

Selling additional media components for an assignment you already have is the best way I've found to build up your skills in another medium and get paid for doing it. Always ask your assigning editors about multimedia opportunities: you may learn, for example, that a print magazine collaborates with a television, radio, or online show, or that a publication has separate editors for print and online content, each buying content separately from freelancers. Keep in mind that you probably won't get professional rates—or even standard contract terms—in your second medium, at least to start.

"I've never had an editor offer me a 'package' assignment for photography and writing," says SciLancer Amanda Mascarelli, a print journalist with some photography experience. "Typically, editors just ask me if I can take my camera along and look for good photo opportunities. Afterwards, I send along photos and have been paid separately for those in addition to the agreed-to story fee."

As you build a portfolio in your second medium, however, you should ask for more formal arrangements and proper fees. To do so, get to know your new medium's editor in the same way that you get to know an editor in your primary medium. Learn the second editor's style and requirements, and if you can without offending your assigning editor, interact with the second editor directly (see Chapter 8, "Working with Editors—and Their Edits"). Thoughtful networking may even lead to independent assignments in your second medium.

Multilancing Challenges

At the beginning of this chapter, I compared one benefit of multilancing to the benefits gained by learning a second language: you get to know your first medium better when you pick up a second medium. But sometimes you're working in a medium that isn't familiar to your source, or just doesn't make sense to him or her. It's like trying to talk to someone who doesn't speak the same language.

The medium all scientists understand is print: all scientists write, and many have students and hold lectures, and so a scientist interviewee likely will be quite comfortable with your jotting down notes as she tells you a poignant story. But suppose the scientist gets a wonderful expression on her face in the middle of that story. If you grab your camera, snap on the wide angle, and lean in close for a shot, what was a familiar experience may become one that upsets the interviewee and even ends the interview.

When SciLancer Bryn Nelson is acting as both writer and photographer, he always lets his sources know that he might be interrupting the interview to snap some pictures. "It's exceedingly difficult or impossible to try to capture that image later," he says. "As long as people know what to expect, it hasn't been a problem."

Another challenge to multilancing is the time you need to switch back and forth between media, during which you can miss a great quote, sound bite, or image because you haven't got the right equipment at the right time, or even because you're dividing your attention between the multiple media. "When I do a site visit for a story—whether it's two hours or a full week—I find that my time is pretty much filled trying to do reporting and digging for the print story, let alone tackling anything else," says Douglas. "I find that even shooting still photos, if I put a lot of effort into it, cuts into my ability to do the reporting I need for a written story."

Gisela Telis, a SciLance member who works in print and in TV production, says TV stories take a different kind of thinking: "It's like you're fitting together a puzzle instead of telling a story, and the puzzle is in multiple dimensions because it's the narration but it's also the visuals and the audio. It was overwhelming at first," she says, "but it's really, really satisfying when it comes together."

For me, that immense satisfaction makes multilancing worthwhile. After four years of multimedia work at *Science* magazine, I am back to full-time multilancing. I do things now a little differently than I did when I was starting out. Like many others, I find it difficult to work simultaneously in multiple media at a professional level. Instead, I choose carefully which media I think best matches the story. If I'm reporting without yet having an assignment, then I do my preliminary reporting in a way that enables me to sell a story to as many outlets as I can: I know that I can produce both print and audio stories from a recorded phone conversation, but I can't produce a good audio story from notes of that same conversation.

There are challenges, sure, and lots of reasons not to multilance. But if you have a great story, using more than one media can increase your work's value—and the fun you'll have doing it.

- Before you start working in another medium, first **establish yourself in your primary medium**, because you'll need to support yourself in learning that second medium.

- When choosing a second medium, **ask yourself if you like** *consuming* **that medium**. If you don't, then you'll never be as good as your competition (or as attractive to your editors).

- **Try producing in that second medium** in a low-cost, low-risk way: talk with people who do it, take a class, rent the necessary equipment, and give it a try.

- **Choose your medium carefully.** While a good story is a good story, one medium may be more suited to your story than another.

- **Let your interviewees know** if you plan on switching media mid-interview.

- **Avoid simultaneous media-capture** when possible because you really can give your full attention to only one medium at a time.

- **Ask your current editors** about multimedia opportunities that may be behind the scenes.

- **Add on to your story** with multimedia, rather than relying on multimedia to sell your story.

- **Know the standard rates** for your multimedia work. Undercutting the competition is understandable when you are learning a new medium, but not when you are a professional.

- **Try to work directly with editors in other media** by getting to know them in the same way that you know editors in your primary media.

Chapter 11

Just Write the Friggin' Thing Already!

By Anne Sasso

In a perfect world, one where climate change didn't exist and the chocolate fairy did, my writing process would flow serenely, like a gentle forest stream, from idea, pitch, and assignment to research, interviews, and deep thoughts and on to writing, publication, and wide acclaim. But my world is profoundly, disappointingly imperfect.

My stream is full of whitewater eddies that swirl me in circles, overhanging branches that snag my hair and clothes and threaten to poke out an eyeball, and broad, flat stretches where I bottom out and have to hop my butt along the gravel, trying vainly to regain momentum. I often head down side tributaries, wasting entire afternoons as I lose myself in dense undergrowth. Sometimes there's even a circus on the banks, enticing me with its sideshows: Patagonia Sale! People You May Know! Retire Rich!

Like the obstacles that muddy the smooth flow of my imaginary stream, procrastination, in its many forms, wreaks havoc on my writing projects. It drives me nuts—and overcoming it requires the same gut-wrenching struggle every time.

When my tolerance for procrastination wears out, I start talking to myself . . . and then I start to write. When it's over, I wonder what all the damned fussing and foot-dragging was about, and I vow that next time I will do it better, faster, and more enlightened-ly. But when the next writing project rolls around, it's Groundhog Day: Procrastination Edition.

This cycle has repeated itself for years, and if you've been writing for any length of time, you know I'm not alone. I've come to realize—or perhaps I've just resigned myself to the fact—that this is the way it is. So

I had better learn to understand it and turn it, as best I can, to my advantage. If you have any desire to maintain your sanity as a writer, I suggest you do the same.

Percolation, Not Procrastination

While procrastination can strike during pitching, reporting, or revision, it comes most often during the writing stage. "I go through a slovenly, self-loathing stage right about the time I need to be writing—usually when I'm stuck on my lede," says SciLancer Amanda Mascarelli. "I question my career choice and pick fights with my husband."

The irony is that we—most of us, anyway—love to write. We love being fully engaged in putting words on page or screen. The concentration is seductive, meditative. We are junkies for that feeling, but we struggle to find entry into it. We beat ourselves up. We do the laundry. We know we're not being productive and would really prefer to leave our office and go for a walk, catch a few waves, or meet a friend for coffee. But we're WORKING, dammit! And so we often punish ourselves by keeping our butts in our chairs, browsing our way into ever-greater states of guilt and self-loathing.

I've found that procrastination has several faces. So far, I've identified daily procrastination, which can range from creative procrastination to totally lame or distractive procrastination, and prioritization procrastination, which takes place over longer time scales, like that of a career. You may discover others.

For me, each project has a creative phase when I'm allowing all the research and ideas I've gathered to simmer in my subconscious. It's an immensely enjoyable phase. Possibility and brilliance lie latent within the mélange. On my more enlightened days, I give myself time in the garden, take a pottery class, or join a friend on the ski slopes while I allow ideas to settle and structure and story to emerge.

I love SciLancer Thomas Hayden's description of this stage: "It's procrastination as Zen practice: a way of using pleasant distraction to disperse mental clutter and access deeper thoughts or narrative intuition."

This creative procrastination is a very necessary phase of the writing process. It nourishes the inner *terroir* that sustains our craft and, I believe, distinguishes a competent-but-unremarkable piece from one that sets the heart soaring with pride. We skip it at our peril.

Distractive procrastination, on the other hand, is creative procrastination's evil twin. It emerges when the motivation to tackle a tedious task is lacking. In my office, bouts of distractive procrastination look like this: Check e-mail. See if anyone's posted anything new to Facebook. Watch video shared by my neighbor of animals doing crazy shit. Run downstairs to stoke the woodstove. Put the kettle on for tea. Grab a handful of chocolate-covered almonds. Check e-mail. Check Facebook. Get two paragraphs into a story and remember the kettle. And so it goes.

Creative procrastination often looks suspiciously like goofing off. Whereas distractive procrastination at its finest—paying bills, vacuuming, reading the *Wall Street Journal*—can appear surprisingly productive. Distractive procrastination isn't all bad. It's a clue, I suspect, that we haven't allowed ourselves enough creative procrastination, and aren't quite ready to enter the writing zone. But how does a writer know when she's ready?

Getting into the Zone

I often don't know whether I'm ready to write until I actually put pencil to paper. So while it might sound comically obvious, my first step toward the writing zone is to just start writing.

I call this the Natalie Goldberg Method, or NGM—because, hey, every science writer needs at least one acronym in her piece, right?—after the writer whose book *Writing Down the Bones* kept me writing early on. The idea is to put pen or pencil to paper and keep it moving for a set amount of time no matter what drivel emerges. Goldberg prescribes it as daily writing practice, but I use it as a springboard to dive into active writing. Sometimes I even hear Natalie's voice: "Ten minutes on invasive species. Go!"

If I'm still struggling with the material. If I've started to write prematurely. The flow is choppy. I only last for a quarter to a half a page before stalling out. The false starts are frustrating. And tend not to be all that good.

When my pencil starts sprinting across the page and the words are coursing faster than I can write, I know I'm there. I've crossed the threshold, that almost-magical point when procrastination—of either type—clicks over into productive scribbling. Hallelujah! When I'm in the flow, when I'm ripe, my hand keeps moving and I can fill several sheets before I lift my head and stare out the window for a few minutes. Then another idea will land and click into focus, and I'll be off again. Soon, I have a barf draft—a rough draft spewed on the page—and the end, while still far off, is most definitely in sight.

Sometimes there's an in-between phase where I struggle with one section of an article, a lede maybe. I apply the NGM but find myself rewriting the same words in different combinations. As I fiddle obsessively, it often feels like I'm not ready to write, that I'm pushing too hard. But as I immerse myself fully in the intricacies and cadence of the section, I find that the deeper parts of my writing brain are quietly performing alchemy on my piece. When I do eventually nail that section, the other pieces of the story seem to fall into place and almost write themselves.

But what if you deploy the NGM and you just can't write? If I still haven't much clue what I need or want to say, then I dive back into the research. If I know what I want to say but I haven't quite figured out how, then I need another little swim in the creative procrastination waters.

Distractive procrastination can also be a sign of a deeper, darker, more distressing problem: sometimes I just don't want to write what I have to write. That's when distraction procrastination acts like spring runoff, turning my stream into a chaos of dashed expectations. Instead of just holding my breath and praying to survive, I must resort to more drastic procrastination hacks.

Deadline as Procrastination Slayer

It would be lovely to wake up each morning, visit with Natalie (Fifteen minutes on shale gas. Go!), and know whether my muse is ready to canoe downstream today or not. Alas, that's not the writing world that I inhabit. Like most working writers, I have deadlines to meet and bills to pay, and there aren't enough hours in a week to take too many off from writing.

That's why SciLancers have devised ways to wrestle distractive procrastination into partial submission. Fear appears to be one of the best motivators: fear of letting our editors and our readers down. Fear of writing a lame-ass piece at four in the morning because we spent our working hours shopping for cute boots on the Internet.

Or fear of blowing past a deadline. Douglas Fox stares down his deadlines from early on, making sure that he plans enough time to complete a feature and then let it "rest" for a week or two before he picks it up again, revises it one last time with fresh eyes, and turns it in. Monya Baker sets fake deadlines "just to get the benefit of the 'I'm late! I'm late!' adrenaline before it would actually annoy my editor," she says. For Virginia Gewin, the adrenaline rush associated with a feature deadline usually kicks in about forty-eight hours beforehand, sending her into a mad, sleepless, singularly obsessed state until she has to just hit send.

Robert Frederick, on the other hand, powers through procrastination by planning something fun to do afterward. "There's only a carrot, no stick," he says. Thomas Hayden lights a fire under himself—literally:

> My mom used to tell me to start the day with a $20 bill, and to make a deal with myself that I would either do the thing I was avoiding or burn the money. No fooling, I've sat there with the bill and the lighter and really thought about "buying" my freedom. I haven't burned it yet, though. There's something about the absurdity of actually doing it that makes me square my shoulders, curse under my breath, and make the phone call or whatever it is.

Taming Procrastination

In most of my writing work, I can't wait for deadlines to loom before I write. I have to manage my time and my workflow to maintain my business and my sanity. That's when I, and other SciLancers, deploy an assortment of other tools to overcome procrastination.

I am a compulsive list maker, so I will often break a seemingly insurmountable writing task into more manageable chunks—write the description of the protagonist, explain why the scientific breakthrough matters, show why the purple velvet coat is so important. Hannah Hoag likes to make a "quick but detailed list that maps out what needs to be done and when." Douglas tops his list with a big to-do (write 3,500-word feature) and follows it with an assortment of easy, inane items. He then methodically crosses those smaller tasks off his list, eliminating potential distractions and preparing himself for the big one.

Often I will assign deadlines for the chunks and reward myself for completing them: finish a draft of the hurricane prediction section by three and you can stroll around the garden, eating fresh peas and sun-warmed raspberries. Cameron Walker makes a "really fancy hot chocolate" that she permits herself to drink only when she's in the writing zone.

When Jill Adams finds herself mired in a bout of distractive procrastination, she likes to call a friend and chat about whatever she's supposed to be writing about. "I 'hear' myself and realize what's interesting about the article, and *voilà!*" She's fired up and ready to write again.

If my distractive procrastination is particularly intractable, I will set time or word limits. I must produce five hundred words before I can break for lunch, or I must write for one hour before checking e-mail again. Then I just keep my butt in my chair and grind it out. It's not fun, or especially pleasurable, but it allows me to fight my way out of my pit of destructive procrastination. And I don't necessarily stop when the goal is achieved. The hardest part is often just getting started, Bryn Nelson says. "Once I'm an hour or so into the writing, I can get into a zone and start cranking on it."

Some SciLancers make use of the very tools that distract us to create pacts with other writer friends and engage in group bouts of timed writing. They agree by instant message, on Facebook, or through a Google+ hangout to buckle down and write for forty-five minutes, say, and then share what they accomplished when the time is up. Helen Fields likes knowing that she's not the only one working—"like I have supporters, people on my team, and I'm accountable to them." (See "I Started My Own Group and So Can You" on p. 28.)

Others find they must shut down the Internet to get serious writing done. Sarah Webb creates "psychological space" to work by using apps that limit her access to sites that distract her.

When all else fails, I resort to two Hail Mary techniques: sleep and inspiration. I will abandon a project and sleep on it. In the dark hours of the night, the surly critics that squat in my head transform into creative superheroes, solving structural problems and designing innovative turns of phrase. Invariably, I wake at 3 a.m., stumble to my desk, and scribble furiously until I've extracted their brilliance and they get cranky again. I'm always grateful for the breakthrough. I just wish I could schedule it for, say, Tuesday at 10 a.m.

For inspiration, I turn to two books: Roy Peter Clark's *Writing Tools: 50 Essential Strategies for Every Writer* and Natalie Goldberg's *Thunder and Lightning: Cracking Open the Writer's Craft*. They are craft books, but it's the authors' wisdom and matter-of-fact voices that soothe me. Whether it's the content that helps or simply the act of pulling a familiar book from my bookshelf, opening to a random page, and reading for ten or fifteen minutes, I don't know.

What I do know is that sleep and The Books along with a load of laundry and a handful of chocolate-covered almonds usually gets me safely past the procrastination roadblocks and back on course.

When There Are No Deadlines

The writing life is also fertile ground for another type of procrastination, one that generally appears when there are no deadlines, editors, or clients in sight.

Prioritization procrastination kicks in when there's a project that I really want to do—a book project, a pitch to a premier publication, a foray into new media—that keeps getting pushed down the to-do list by regular day-to-day projects.

Again, judiciously applying deadlines, lists, and rewards, and tackling manageable chunks can overcome this form of procrastination. Over the years, I have sought out opportunities (fellowships, writing retreats, and workshops) that have allowed me to work on pieces of larger projects. Progress is agonizingly slow but it's there—and I always feel reinvigorated by the break from my working writing life.

Learning to Love Procrastination

As I've matured as a writer, I've come to realize that some phase of creative busywork is essential to my process. While I'm avoiding writing, my mind is actively assembling the puzzle: elucidating themes, making connections, deciphering overarching patterns and forms. If I relax into it and allow it to happen organically, there's a satisfying grace and weight to my work that is often lacking when I force myself to write on a tight schedule.

Distractive procrastination still consumes far too much of my time. And I still get frustrated with the unpredictability and inefficiency of creative procrastination. But I still haven't developed the equation that calculates how much percolation time is required for a 2,500-word article (I was trained as a geologist, not a mathematician, and geological time scales are not at all helpful here).

I still struggle to discern when I need more creative procrastination. I still often feel guilty, although I am getting much better, when I engage in it. I still substitute distractive procrastination, trying to trick my subconscious into doing the winnowing and restructuring while I'm cranking out invoices—multitasking to cut corners. But I have learned that good writing takes time and patience. For it, I cannot take shortcuts.

This leads to another deep, dark secret: I cannot make a living by nurturing every piece with enough creative procrastination to reach its fullest and most glorious potential. I don't have the time and I would go broke if I did. So I compromise, and recognize that some articles are just tended more carefully than others. That's part of the decision-making that every working writer faces, often on a weekly if not a daily basis.

For now, I'm doing my best to give myself permission to enjoy the creative procrastination phase and not fret when I get tangled up in the weeds, caught in a distractive procrastination eddy. Eventually I resort to telling myself to "just write the friggin' article already!" And I always do.

Thirty Books in Thirty Days

By Emily Sohn

The first call came on a mild April day. An editor I had never worked with before offered me a medical-writing gig that would take an estimated ten to fifteen hours per week. I thought about it for a few hours. I said yes.

Less than a week later, a regular client wanted to know if I'd be willing to double my workload. Could I write twelve news articles a month instead of six? I hesitated for a day or two, thinking about the fast-approaching days of summer, the lost opportunities to enjoy outdoor time during Minnesota's short warm season.

Again, I said yes.

And then the third call came. This time a publishing company asked if I could rewrite a series of thirty children's books. The catch? The books were scheduled to go to print in just a month.

And so it came to be that I agreed not only to write thirty books in thirty days, but also to submit a dozen news articles and log dozens of hours of medical writing during the same stretch of time. Suddenly procrastination wasn't my problem. Panic was.

While that month was nutty, and I spent far more late nights at my computer than I will admit here, I learned enough from what I affectionately call my Productivity Experiment to consider it worthwhile.

By accident or intention, you too may find yourself with an intense need for more hours in the day. You will wonder how you are going to meet all those deadlines. And you will suffer from aches in your rear end from sitting too much while simultaneously upping your intake of wine or chocolate.

Freelancers are especially vulnerable to these deluges, but it can happen to any writer: cool opportunities have a way of arriving all at once. Once in a while, you may decide it's worth it to work like crazy.

Figuring out how much is too much will depend on a complicated formula that might weigh financial payoffs, high-profile bylines, a passion for certain subjects, and the need for sleep. The variables in the equation differ for everyone, as does the solution.

As for coping with a deluge, SciLancers' collective experiences illustrate some helpful strategies: during the reporting phase, consider outsourcing. Find a transcription service, for example. Unemployed journalism students may offer an affordable and helpful source of hourly research on useful web links, research papers, and potential sources.

Pouring your efforts into one project at a time from beginning to end helps some people focus. Personally, I like to conduct interviews for a bunch of projects all at once and then set aside chunks of time for writing each, one at a time.

When it comes time to churn out words, tune into your daily rhythms. Write during the times of day when you concentrate best. Save fact-checking and other less taxing work for the times when you tend to feel less creative. And shut down major distractors and time wasters, such as social media and e-mail. Politely let your close friends and family know that you'll be out of touch for a while.

(Continues)

Thirty Books in Thirty Days *(Continued)*

When you emerge from a deadline downpour, make sure to steal at least a little time for yourself—and the people you've been neglecting.

Even when the assignment load gets really crazy, things often have a way of working out. In the midst of my Productivity Experiment, when countless nights at the computer had induced a mild kind of depression, my editor sent me layouts of the kids' books. They looked fantastic, and pride in the project buoyed me. (The paychecks had started to arrive, which was also helpful.)

Soon after that, the publisher decided to put off printing half the books for several months, giving me just the break I needed. Around the same time, the medical-writing gig petered out. Suddenly I was left with what was still an objectively large amount of work—and yet I felt free and unburdened. Being busy had made me more efficient. I was amazed to find that I could now complete stories in a fraction of the time it used to take. I truly appreciated the ability to relax again during evenings and weekends. And I had developed confidence that I would survive the next busy period, whenever it came.

It was then that I realized the great value of being too busy now and then. Periods of intense productivity allow you to see what you are capable of. And once in a while, everyone deserves to feel superhuman.

SciLance SAYS . . .

- Every writer encounters procrastination. It often leads to guilt and self-loathing but it doesn't have to. The sooner you **learn to distinguish useful from damaging procrastination**, cultivate the former and find ways to tame the latter, the better off you will be.

- **Creative procrastination is an indispensable tool**, allowing your mind to assemble the pieces of a puzzle, your article, into a pleasing, coherent whole. It often improves the quality of a writer's work.

- **Distractive procrastination can be debilitating**. It's often a sign that you aren't ready to write a piece or that you just plain don't want to write it.

- A firm deadline is the only surefire cure for any sort of procrastination. **Professional writers are always motivated by deadlines**.

- When distractive procrastination strikes, try:

  Making **a list of the tasks** at hand and breaking up a large project into manageable chunks.

  Assigning deadlines to complete the chunks and propel you forward.

  Rewarding yourself for reaching goals, to motivate you to get things done.

  Setting a word-count or time goal, then just forcing yourself to write. **Getting started is often the hardest part**; once you're going, words usually continue to flow.

  Setting **a writing date with a group of friends**. Knowing that others are also working and will hold you accountable can be a fun way to beat paralysis.

  Calling a friend and **describing your project**. Hearing yourself speak about the project can be the inspiration needed to start writing.

- If all else fails, **put the project aside and sleep on it** . . . but be prepared for inspiration to strike in the middle of the night. Get up and take notes.

PART II

THE SANE SCIENCE WRITER

The Loneliness of the Science Writer

By Stephen Ornes

One day in the fall of 2007, I was interviewing a planet-hunter for a medium-length news article with a fast-approaching deadline. Quick turnaround, decent money, interesting topic. I'd been following the field for years and had interviewed this astronomer before. I was after a choice quote or two to enliven the story.

The process should have been fast.

Instead of simply asking a few questions and getting my quote, though, I kept the conversation going. The obliging, amiable astronomer was young and seemed familiar.

I asked meandering follow-up questions. I became chatty (which is fine for a profile, but not on deadline). I nearly asked him if he'd seen any good movies lately. We'd been having a pretty heady chat, and now we were buddies, so why not keep the conversation going?

To my credit, I didn't ask the astronomer about movies. But that's only because in the moment before those words became sounds, a nagging voice in my head arrested my train of thought. I was starting to confuse a *source* with a *friend*.

These days, when I'm tempted to assign strangers the roles of friends, I recognize it as a symptom of my own loneliness—and as one of many telltale signs that it's time to change my environment.

Whether you write in a busy office or at your kitchen table, the choice to become a writer is a choice to toil alone. The actions of choosing words and wrestling with your own mind prime the soil for the invasive weed of loneliness. And *science* writing, by its very nature, requires us to dig into obscure and sometimes not-so-glamorous subjects, which can make research a lonelier journey still.

Perhaps you're immune to loneliness. Perhaps you can toil indefinitely without craving human interaction, except for the soothing voices of scientists who do interesting work. That's entirely possible. But if writing about science does occasionally bring on the blues, the rest of this chapter is for you. Here, I offer a smorgasbord of suggestions for ways to combat the creeping demon of loneliness.

1. Change Your View . . .

After my revealing interview with the astronomer, I decided I needed to inhabit a new workspace for a while, one outside my home. I rented a small office in an old stone church near my home in New Haven, Connecticut. My small window looked out on a stately magnolia tree, and my world seemed a lot more expansive.

Even a short visit to a coffee shop or café can relieve loneliness. "I find that just being around other people, in the same room with them, and being able to people-watch, helps a lot with isolation," reports SciLancer Douglas Fox.

. . . But Beware of Café Culture

"Coffee shops can help by putting you near others, but it's easy for that time to become unproductive or for it to just turn into procrastination," says SciLancer Jessica Marshall. "A bad Wi-Fi connection, distracting people at the table next to you, or background noise that makes phone calls difficult—these are the pitfalls of the coffee shop."

2. Find Your Folks

While some of the subjects science writers cover can alienate or bore polite company, others draw a crowd. If you take the time to tell your friends what you're working on, you may be surprised by their interest. "Very, very often, whatever cocktail or party group I'm in, people ask questions about my work," says Douglas. "Maybe they're interested in new research on the subtleties of how sexual intercourse really leads to babies. Or artificial sweeteners. Or maybe they want to be a writer themselves. Disinterest is usually not a problem."

3. Cultivate a Hobby

Having an interest in something other than your own writing can provide a much-needed change of focus. "Taking pottery classes was part of my strategy to get out of my 'alone funk,'" says SciLancer Sarah Webb. "The studio is in my neighborhood, so I've made local friends." Like Sarah, SciLancer Anne Sasso regularly gets her hands dirty in pottery classes and in her garden. Plus, she's a passionate player in a local hockey league.

4. Toot Your Own Horn

One way to engage other people in your work is to tell them about it more often. (For nice, modest, midwestern types, this may require considerable effort.)

"When I landed my first story in the *Boston Globe* years ago, I rounded up all my friends for a night at a local bar to celebrate," says SciLancer Jennifer Cutraro. "That's probably akin to coworkers going out to celebrate landing a big client or wrapping a big project. People who don't work in our field might not understand how much work goes into any published piece."

5. Who Are the People in Your Neighborhood?

Anne says she doesn't often suffer bouts of loneliness, though she has been known to toil for days at home, eating the same thing and forgetting to turn on lights. Though she lives in rural Vermont, she knows her neighbors and can always find someone to chat with.

Like Anne, I find solace in my own backyard. I used to strap my infant son into the Baby Bjorn and go on marathon walks through town, exploring and talking. Investigating the neighborhood where you live or work may have a professional benefit, too: you never know where a new story idea may appear.

6. Organize a Night Out

A regular lunch date or beer night with friends can go a long way in keeping loneliness at bay. "It doesn't have to be with other science writers, but I think it helps a lot if you can combine some shop talk with some non–shop talk," says SciLance member Thomas Hayden.

Douglas seconds Thomas's recommendation, and says just setting up such a night out can lift morale. "When I'm down in the dumps, I find that even the act of sending out an e-mail about a beer night two weeks from now—and then watching the 'yeah, I'll be there!' replies start coming in—can give my morale an immediate boost."

7. Get a Group

Genuine community, whether online or in the real world, can help vanquish writerly loneliness. After I rented an office outside my house, my next step was to join a writing group in New Haven. It wasn't exclusively for science writers, but it was a great way to socialize with people who cared about writing.

But how to find a community? See the Afterword for advice about setting up your own online group, or try these places:

- The National Association of Science Writers (NASW.org) hosts discussion forums about all things related to science writing.
- Meetup.com provides an online gathering place for groups of all flavors—including people interested in writing.
- Freelance writer David Hochman hosts an online group called UPOD (upodacademy.com), where freelancers gather to talk shop.

8. Spend More Time with Your Kids/Spouse/Dog

"The cure for freelancer loneliness," says SciLancer Emma Marris, "is to have children. Now, when I have the house to myself, there is practically a physical sensation of pleasure."

"I live with a man, three children, and a dog," says SciLancer Jill Adams. "They drive me crazy sometimes, but I rarely feel lonely."

9. Get Involved with Social Media, Unless It Makes You Feel Worse

Science writers love to tweet, retweet, post, blog, and comment. Tools such as Facebook, LinkedIn, Twitter, Foursquare, and Tumblr can help you build a network of virtual colleagues, a running fount of story ideas, and an audience for your work. (See Chapter 24, "Social Networks and the Reputation Economy," for more.)

The rule for social media tools seems to be—as with almost anything else—moderation. "A little bit of Facebook or Twitter during work can give me a nice warm, quick fuzzy of connectedness, and it's definitely useful professionally," says SciLancer Michelle Nijhuis, "but I don't think it goes very far in the emotional satisfaction department. It's kind of like a cup of coffee when what I really need is a nap."

SciLance says . . .

- Figure out how much human interaction you need and want, and **plan your work schedule accordingly**. Put some effort into finding the right mix of a social and working life.

- Try **working in a coffee shop**. Or a park.

- **Tell your friends** what you're working on.

- **Get a hobby**, especially if writing used to be your hobby and now it's your work.

- Writers' groups are a good place to **find people in the same situation**. Consider looking for one at Meetup.com or joining the National Association of Science Writers (NASW).

- Science writers **gather every year** at the annual meetings of NASW and AAAS, among other meetings. These gatherings offer an easy way to meet other writers, hone your craft, and get a pulse-check on new developments in your subject areas.

- **Tweet**—unless it consumes all your time.

- **Change your clothes**. Shower. File on time. Repeat.

Chapter 13

Good Luck Placing This Elsewhere

How to Cope with Rejection

By Hillary Rosner

One morning in early April, as I sat at my desk reading yet another "no, thank you" reply to a story pitch I'd sent out, it occurred to me that I might never write another article. The last time an editor had assigned me a story—had said yes to a pitch and then followed up with a deadline and a contract—was December. For nearly four months, I realized, my rejection rate had been 100 percent.

In my inbox that morning were three more brush-offs. The first was a flat-out "this won't work for us" rejection of a feature I was dying to write. The second was less cut and dried but a rejection nonetheless. The third wasn't even from an editor, but I took it as a clear sign that all hope was lost: my occasional housecleaner wrote to tell me she couldn't fit me into her schedule.

Rejected by my housecleaner! During a recession!

Of course, these three rejections had nothing whatsoever to do with one another. But I lumped them together. And took them personally. Clearly the universe had a grudge against me. I might as well just give away my laptop and retreat into my ever-messier house.

Oh, and then later that week I landed some assignments and was busy making travel plans and juggling deadlines—and wouldn't you know it, I'd completely forgotten about the universe and my stalled career. (My house, unfortunately, was still dirty.)

Learning to cope with rejection is one of the hardest parts of being a writer. We all deal with it, whether it comes in person from your boss, on the phone from your agent, or via e-mail from an editor you may or may not have met. Rejection is hard on both staff writers and freelancers, but it can have the greatest impact on those who don't earn a regular paycheck, because its sting is both psychological and financial.

Even your idols, even the writers whose careers you'd give anything to emulate, the ones who seem to float from one exotic locale to another on a magic carpet of 10,000-word story contracts—even they still deal with rejection. An editor friend of mine recently had to reject an op-ed piece from Robert Redford because it just wasn't groundbreaking enough. Okay, Robert Redford probably didn't fret too much over that little rejection. But it's a nice reminder of an essential truth: just because an editor turned down your article does not mean you're a failure.

Let me repeat that, because it's really the crux of the matter. In the vast majority of cases, the editor is not rejecting *you*. She is rejecting your *story pitch*. It is crucial to remember this distinction. Rejection feels intensely personal when you're on the receiving end, even though the person on the doling-out end is simply doing her job—which is to commission stories that are the best possible fit for the publication.

Editors are inundated with submissions and pitches. As *New Yorker* editor Alan Burdick explains it, "They have a limited number of slots to fill, and are buffeted by mercurial publishing winds that may blow in or against your favor on any particular day. That's just the business. Also, editors are notoriously conservative. They prefer story ideas that will definitely work over ones that might work."

There is a nearly infinite number of reasons your story won't work, and most of them have nothing to do with your worth as a writer. Which is why there is no more important advice for coping with rejection than this: *do not take it personally.*

Consider a few—out of a gazillion—possible reasons your story might be rejected:

1. **A similar story has already been assigned.** Maybe you've written a feature pitch tied to a recent headline—and yours is number four in the editor's inbox. Or maybe at the very moment you press send, the editors are walking out of a meeting at which they've assigned something on a subject similar enough to yours that yours just won't fly.

2. **A conflicting story has already been assigned.** Your 3,000-word profile of a famous scientist who unburdened himself to you about his childhood abuse and its relationship to his work may not fit when the publication just commissioned a special package on why parents can be a scientist's best inspiration.

3. **Editorial decisions aren't entirely rational.** Maybe the editor in chief has told the staff, "I really hate frogs. Don't ever come to me with a frog story." Which is unfortunate, given the subject of your pitch.

Even the pitches you think are watertight, the stories that feel like gifts from the journalism gods, can meet rejection. I recently pitched a story I believed was a sure thing. It had all the essential elements: a compelling main character, a paradigm-shifting idea, and an exotic backdrop, plus a link to Greek mythology and a submersible underwater robot. A robot! What more could you want? I sent the pitch to an editor I've worked with before. He loved it. He took it to the editorial meeting, hopeful it would sail through—and discovered that another editor had just assigned the same story to another writer. Oops.

Learning to persevere in the face of rejection is one of the most valuable lessons of writing. But it's easy to tell someone not to take it personally—and far more difficult to put that into practice. Still, there are ways to set yourself up beforehand so that the inevitable rejection won't be such a blow:

Always have multiple eggs in your basket. No matter how terrific your story idea, there's always a chance it won't sell. Anywhere. So don't bet the house on one pitch. Successful freelancers are constantly pitching. SciLancer Monya Baker used to reward herself with an afternoon off (and a bag of potato chips) after submitting ten well-thought-out pitches.

Plan ahead. Hoping an editor will approve your pitch will not make it happen. While having confidence in your own ideas and abilities is essential, no amount of wishful thinking is going to help your pitch meet success. You have to maintain a positive outlook while also recognizing that rejection is a real possibility. The best way to do this is to be proactive. What are you going to do when the answer is no?

David Dobbs, a successful freelance journalist who writes about science for *The Atlantic* and *National Geographic,* among other publications, has a brilliant strategy. He knows his story stands a good chance of getting rejected, so he plots his next move ahead of time. Which publication would be his second choice? Before he sends out his pitch, he tweaks it as needed to send to the next publication on his list, if necessary, and even addresses the e-mail so it's ready to go. Then he stashes that e-mail in his drafts folder and hits send on his first choice.

If the first editor rejects his pitch, Dobbs might be disappointed. But he doesn't need to waste time trying to decide which other magazine might want it, or reshaping the pitch. He already decided—while he felt buoyant and hopeful about the article's chances. All he has to do now is pull out the second e-mail, consider the third publication down the line, draft the third e-mail, and send off the second one. Since he began this strategy, Dobbs says, his "lag time before repitching went from days or weeks to minutes." The result? He sold more stories. (See Chapter 3 for more on pitching.)

Have a pet project. One hazard of always trying to please editors or to fit into a publication's particular style and narrow range of subjects is that you can sometimes feel like you've lost all agency, as though every decision depends on someone else's whims. Rejection only amplifies this problem, because it makes you feel powerless to execute anything.

The antidote is a project (or several) that you own—something intellectually satisfying that you can work on without anyone else's approval. It could be as simple as researching a topic that interests you, and casting a wide net within it for a story. Sure, eventually you'll have to pitch the story. But for now it's just a fascinating mental exercise that enables you to do creative reporting (which will inevitably turn up juicy new leads). Or maybe it's a blog, about any subject you want. Perhaps it's a movie script you're writing, or a novel. The point is simply to have a longer-term project on hand that you can work on—and enjoy—without needing the green light from an editor.

Recast rejection as success. It might sound silly, but it's just a question of perspective. When my friend Hannah Nordhaus, author of *The Bee-keeper's Lament,* was starting out, her mother gave her some valuable advice: "Rack up rejections and consider them a triumph in themselves. It shows that you tried." As Nordhaus set about establishing herself as a freelancer, her mother suggested she aim for a set amount of rejections over the course of a summer, and to declare herself a success when she'd received that number of rejections. "It's a good way to see rejection as a rite of passage rather than proof of your shittiness as a writer," says Nordhaus. "And by making it commonplace, it does seem to hurt a little less."

Another writer, a longtime *Wired* magazine contributor who's now a journalism professor, managed to put a similar idea to work. The first time he pitched a story to *Wired,* the editor—a friend of a friend—took the time to explain in detail why the pitch wasn't quite right for the magazine. The personalized rejection had a big impact on him. "It made me feel like writing for major magazines, as a career option, wasn't just possible, but probable. The right rejection can mean as much as, or maybe even more than, an acceptance note."

Admittedly, sometimes rejections just suck. An editor's reply can feel as though she barely even skimmed your agonizingly crafted pitch, or somehow missed your point entirely. In those cases, it's best to simply buck up and move on.

But there are other clever ways to turn rejection into a positive engine for change—to actually come away a better and more successful freelancer and journalist.

Don't make the same mistake twice. Rejection is an opportunity for reflection. Seize the moment to reevaluate what you submitted, and try to discover things you might have done better. Was your story really a good fit for the magazine? Was the pitch as strong as it could have been? Did you read it aloud and send it to a friend before shipping it off to the editor? Reflecting on what might have gone wrong can be a powerful lesson in the art of pitching.

Build a relationship. Relationships with editors are among your most important assets. While rejection is rarely personal, success very often is. If you have an established relationship with an editor, she's far more likely to provide feedback on why a pitch won't fly—or better yet, encourage you to rework your idea if she sees a seed of something promising in it.

When an editor rejects your first story pitch with a few words of encouragement, send her another. And another after that. Act while you're on her radar screen, and use the rejection as a way to establish rapport and show that you're full of great ideas. Once you have her attention, ask her what holes she has in the lineup for upcoming issues. Enthusiasm will get you everywhere: you never know when she'll need a writer for an assignment and think of you first. (Just don't confuse enthusiasm with stalking.)

Recast your story. Is there a better way to frame your story? Sometimes we become so enthusiastic about an idea that we miss the real story, the far better story, hidden within it. Look below the surface. Is there a better way in? Are there questions you haven't answered—questions whose answers might yield a masterpiece?

I once labored over a pitch for a story about the Svalbard seed bank, the "doomsday" vault that holds copies of seeds from around the world. My story was about the vault's founder and champion. But to my immense frustration, I couldn't sell it. Then an editor asked me where the seeds come from: Who are the people who go to the far reaches of the planet collecting native crop seeds from village women, or finding new genetic material deep in the rain forest? I had no idea—and realized it was a brilliant approach to the story. I did some research, and finally sold the article.

If your pitch is rejected, take another look at it. There might just be a more interesting angle, a more marketable concept, or perhaps a whole new story buried within your pitch.

Channel your frustration. A young freelance journalist I know, let's call him Smith, attended a liberal-arts college that didn't use letter grades. In a written evaluation one semester, one of Smith's professors had this to say of his work: "Smith is a writer who lacks clarity, focus, and structure."

While that comment on its own didn't propel Smith into a journalism career, it was, he says, "a motivating force that made me want to prove myself."

Smith still channels that sentiment, using rejection as a catalyst for ambition. In this way, rejection actually motivates him to "send the awesome idea to someone else." So take a lesson from Smith, and view the pitching endeavor as a grand challenge, a test of your true grit, or a provocation from a naysayer. (Make a bet with yourself: "A hundred bucks says you'll never sell that story!")

Find your inner mobster. It's okay to get mad. Just don't do it publicly. We all become emotionally attached to our stories, and when an editor shoots them down, we get pissed. But this is business, and it's crucial to maintain that perspective. So "channel those TV and movie mobsters and learn not to be upset about it," advises SciLancer Robert Frederick. In other words, it's just business. Do not reply to an editor when you're angry or feeling defensive. Go to the gym, drink a cocktail, take your dog for a walk: do whatever you need to calm down. And then get back to work.

♦ SciLance says . . .

- Rejection is an **inescapable component of writing**. To succeed, you must learn to cope with it.

- Do not take rejection personally. **The editor is rejecting your article idea**, not you.

- Don't bet the house on one pitch. Be sure to always have **multiple story ideas in progress**.

- Plan ahead before you pitch. Decide beforehand **where you'll send the story next** if the first editor rejects it.

- Always have a **personal project to work on**, one that doesn't depend on the whims of an editor.

- Try to **learn from rejection**. Reflect on why the story didn't work, and how you might make your pitch—and your story—better.

- **Build relationships** with editors.

- Don't reply to a rejection when you're feeling angry or defensive. **Always be professional**.

- Remember: **It's not personal!**

Chapter 14

Beyond Compare

By Michelle Nijhuis

This is a story about two writers. A story, in other words, of envy.
—Kathryn Chetkovich

When I became a journalist, I was an amateur at envy. As an only child, I'd escaped sibling rivalry. In school, I'd avoided most competitive sports. I'd gone to a college where grades were firmly deemphasized, to the point where students considered it uncouth to discuss them. Sure, as a middle-schooler I'd longed for other girls' designer jeans and clear skin and armfuls of Swatch watches—but who hadn't?

In journalism, though, I discovered something I wanted a lot more than a pair of jeans. I wanted to tell stories about science, I wanted them to be read, and yes, I wanted to see my name in print (preferably in a large, attractive font). At the beginning of my career, almost every story by another writer felt like a tiny threat, evidence of something I should have pursued but hadn't. At the small, brainy publication where I started out, I found myself envying other reporters' bylines and word counts, and jealously guarding mine. At the same time, though, I loved and respected my colleagues, and—at least most of the time—truly wished them well. How was this possible? It was confusing and painful for me and, I'm sure, no picnic for those nearby.

I've come a long way with envy in the decade-plus since then, but even so, the preceding paragraph wasn't easy for me to write. Envy is embarrassing. Envy is a by-product of our quest for love from the world, which means it's about insecurity and loneliness and all kinds of incredibly common things we'd rather not feel, much less own up to. "To experience envy is to feel small and inferior, a loser shrink-wrapped in spite," writes *New York Times* science journalist Natalie Angier.

But a writer who's never once felt the cold burn of envy is, well, lying. Though envy is a common human failing, writers and other creative professionals are especially prone to it—and probably have been ever since prehistoric cave painters started sizing up their neighbors' work. Envy is a hazard of the natural ambition to do something we love, something we think matters.

When writerly envy is unacknowledged or untamed, it's toxic. Members of SciLance say that envying and being envied has at times reduced them to tears, kept them up at night, and broken up friendships. But we've all learned that if we wrestle with envy a bit, it loses its power quickly. Sometimes it can even be a writer's best ally.

· · ·

Let's say you're in the airport, and you spot a flashy cover story in Dream Publication X. Not only is it about a subject that you've been researching and planning to pitch for a while, but it's also written by a younger acquaintance. Which of the following describes your first reaction?

a. *"Oh, wonderful! Can't wait to read it!"*
b. *"Hmmm . . . well, maybe this story will get my editor interested in the subject, and I can find a different angle to pitch."*
c. *"Argh, I'm such a lazy idiot! I should have gotten that pitch together months ago!"*
d. *"*%&^!! What right does that pipsqueak have to write that story?!"*

"I have never felt (a), or almost never," says SciLancer Cameron Walker. "Sometimes (b). But usually (c). And probably most often (d). I certainly don't want to read some huge cover story on underwater basket weaving, because now I think underwater basket weaving is stupid. And I probably don't want to pitch it either, because I will look like a copycat. If I do read it, I will hit myself in the head with the rolled-up magazine several times, either because I think I could have done a better job or because I couldn't have."

Let me pause to say that Cameron is one of the nicest people I know. She's a lovely writer, with a varied, thriving career and a beautiful family. She doesn't seem like the kind of person who swats herself with magazines. But like most of us writers, she sometimes does. Fortunately, she has the guts to admit it. Often, simply acknowledging a flash of envy—even quietly, just to yourself—is enough to extinguish it.

Another strategy is to separate writer from writing, as Hillary Rosner suggested in Chapter 13. When you get the urge to bonk yourself over the head with other people's magazine stories, realize that it's their *work* getting the plum newsstand space in the airport. It's not them, or their face, or their children. And while we all like to have our work recognized, someone else's recognition doesn't mean you won't get yours in time. Really, it doesn't. There's plenty to go around. Envy doesn't know that, though. Envy, in its grunting, lizard-brain way, sees everyone else's victories as threats. It's up to you to tell it otherwise.

If scolding your envy doesn't work, consider reaching out to its object. Seriously: Part of the reason you feel envious is that someone else did something cool, right? (If you envy praise or attention that seems undeserved, see below for directions to the airport bar.) If you genuinely admire the object of your envy, though, why not give him or her a compliment? Chances are, he or she will be sincerely flattered—because the real person behind that showy cover story or ecstatic Facebook update almost certainly suffers from the very same insecurities you do.

Talk to another writer long enough, and you'll probably realize that what looks like breezy success took a lot of hard work to achieve. I found that my own envy diminished dramatically when I left my staff job, struck out as a freelancer, and started commiserating with my fellow freelancers about rejection and isolation. As writers, we're all struggling with the same things, and remembering that is a great cure for envy.

But sometimes none of this works. Sometimes, maybe when your own work or personal life is none too rosy, that cover story you spot in the airport really gets under your skin. That's when it's time to call someone who knows you and your faults and likes you anyway. Whether your confessor is your mom or a trusted writer friend, confide your envy. Indulge in a little schadenfreude about how unhappy or underpaid or prematurely wrinkled that seemingly successful writer must be. Take a cue from Anne Lamott, author of the writer's bible *Bird by Bird,* and quote the poet Clive James: "The book of my enemy has been remaindered / And I am pleased." Laugh at your tiny-mindedness. Then head to the nearest airport bar, buy yourself a drink, and leave your envy sitting quietly on a stool.

. . .

At a meeting of your local writers' group, a friend and longtime colleague announces that she's landed a feature assignment with Bigshot

Magazine X. You've been pitching Bigshot for years, and had a pitch rejected by a Bigshot editor just last week. Which of the following describes your first reaction?

    a. *"Oh, wonderful! She deserves it!"*
    b. *"Hmmm . . . well, at least we all know it's possible to land an assignment there."*
    c. *"Argh, I should have worked harder on my Bigshot pitches, and sent more of them!"*
    d. *"*%&^!! How unfair! I should have that contract! I've been pitching them for years, and this is her first try!"*

"I'll feel some combination of all of the above, usually expressed as 'OMG, that's so awesome!'" says SciLancer Amanda Mascarelli with a laugh.

Why does a friend's success so often inspire envy? "There are few successes more unendurable than those of our ostensible equals," writes the modern philosopher Alain de Botton. We can't envy everyone, de Botton explains. We just don't have time. So we save most of our envy for those of similar status, the people we instinctively see as our closest competition. As Gore Vidal so pithily put it, "Every time a friend succeeds, a little part of me dies."

Envying a friend can feel especially shameful and confusing. This is your friend, after all, a person you like and support and who likes you back. How can you, a supposedly nice person, resent her good fortune? The answer is that you can, and you will—but you can and will love her at the very same time. Maybe some people learn this from their siblings or their high-school teammates, but I learned it from my fellow science writers. Most of us find that with a little experience and honesty, the envy fades and the love endures.

"When I lived in New York in my twenties, I had a tight-knit group of writer friends," says Hillary. "Most of them have written books by now—some, multiple books. They've all had lucrative writing contracts and other successes. So I constantly measure myself against them, and often feel like a failure by comparison. I've certainly felt envious at various times. But it's not that I wish them less success. It's just that I wish I felt as successful as they seem to me." (For the record, Hillary has done plenty of enviable things, including winning prestigious fellowships, cowriting nationally best-selling books, and living in beautiful Boulder, Colorado. Her New York friends probably envy her sometimes, too.)

With my closest writer friends, I share these conflicting emotions. Not too long ago, a friend of mine was nominated for a National Book Award. I read the news early one morning, while sitting at my kitchen table. I was in my bathrobe, my face was unwashed, and my hair was sticking up. I was pointedly ignoring my screaming toddler. My first thought, I'll admit, was "Hmph. *Someone's* having a good day!"

But then I called my friend and said, "Oh, I'm sitting here in my bathrobe having *such* embarrassing feelings about you. And I am so happy for you. And proud!" By the time I got to the third sentence, I really meant it. I knew how hard my friend had worked, and I knew what a great book he'd written. I knew he'd felt his share of envy over the years, too, some of it even toward me. So I knew I could trust him with my envy, and that owning up to it would make it disappear—allowing me to enjoy his success along with him.

With experience, it gets easier and easier to nod to envy, familiarly and oh-so-briefly, then to skip ahead to the fun of cheering for a deserving friend. (And hey, there's a bonus when you arrive at the party: you get a vicarious ego boost just from keeping such exalted company!)

Don't chase away your envy too quickly, though. Envy is dumb, but because it speaks from your unconscious, it knows a few things you don't. If you envy a friend's big cover story, maybe you should pitch such stories more frequently. If you envy a colleague's best seller, maybe you should finish that book proposal. If you can alchemize envy into a sense of friendly competition, it can be a powerful guide and motivator.

"Of course I have those zero-sum feelings of envy when someone else does something great," says SciLance member Douglas Fox. "But after the perfunctory wound-licking, it pretty quickly gives way to genuine gladness for the other person, and then to the competitive thing: 'Okay, so this person got that story into Magazine X. Give me a month, or a year, or three, and I think I can, too.'"

There's an even more practical response to envy: now you know someone who's done something you want to do. She's proved it's possible, and she might even bring you along. "I'll often think, 'Great, if an editor at a magazine I want to work for likes my friend, that's good for me,'" says SciLancer Robin Mejia. "Maybe my friend will be able to help me with some inside information on different editors, or on the assignment process. Kinda selfish, but there it is."

Beyond Compare

I might have been an amateur at envy when I started out in journalism, but now I'm a certified professional. In my expert opinion, no writer should let envy shame him or her into isolation. I know that you can feel envy and still be a generous, loyal friend and colleague. In fact, you can use envy to remind yourself of the importance of generosity and loyalty. (Jedi mind trick.) You can scold your envy into submission, or laugh at it, or use it to break through procrastination, or all of the above. Just remember that if you feel it, your friends probably feel it as well. Have the confidence to believe that you, too, can inspire envy at times, and be sensitive to that possibility. Toot your horn gently.

Most of all, though, love your work for its own sake—not for the recognition it brings you. When SciLance member Monya Baker was in high school, she liked ballet. "I was no good at it," she remembers. "My body is all wrong, my sense of rhythm nonexistent, but I went to class maybe six days a week. I still didn't get parts that less dedicated but more talented dancers did, and I had to work at not letting that bother me so I could enjoy the dance." Today she says ballet taught her most of what she needed to know about science writing: work hard, enjoy the process, and learn to appreciate your own peculiar talents.

Measuring Success in a World Without Performance Reviews

By Alison Fromme

Comparing yourself to other writers isn't always productive. But what about comparing yourself to . . . yourself?

As a graduate student in biology, I counted a lot. I sat for hours at a dissecting microscope, cracked open snails, and tallied how many were infected with parasites. When I started out as a freelance science writer, I needed numbers to tell me I was headed toward something resembling success. I listed, counted, graphed, and analyzed everything I could think of related to my work. I even started to write myself annual reports.

Why bother? I've found that writing an annual report lets me systematically review what I've done, and plan where I want to go. For instance, one year I congratulated myself for increasing my earnings. But thanks to my pie charts, I realized that my journalism work had dwindled in favor of lucrative corporate projects, and I was forced to confront my definition of success. Did I want to continue to take the easy money and forgo more interesting projects? Or could I strike a better balance?

As my work changes, day by day and year by year, I'm still asking these questions. But counting as I go helps keep me headed in the right direction—without having to kill any snails along the way.

Think an annual report might be for you? For a freelancer, a table of contents could look something like this:

Summary and major milestones

Review of last year's goals

Gross income by quarter, by client, and by type of assignment

Expenses, both covered by clients and out-of-pocket

Net income, including an hourly rate breakdown for each client or project (yes, this means you have to keep track, on paper or with one of several available apps)

Clients retained, lost, and gained

Pitches sent, assigned, or in progress

Contacts, including editors and useful new sources

Professional development activities and costs, ranked by usefulness

Goals for next year

SciLance says . . .

- For writers, **envy is a universal job hazard**. Don't suffer it alone.

- Sometimes **simply acknowledging envious feelings**—even to yourself—can make them go away.

- Remember that **envy is dumb**: it sees other writers as threats, not allies. It's up to you to tell it otherwise.

- To treat a persistent case of envy, **call a friend (or your mom) and confess**. Laugh at yourself. Have a drink.

- If you envy a friend—and all writers do sometimes—realize that **you can feel envy and still be a generous, loyal friend**. With trusted friends, consider confessing your feelings. They're likely to be flattered, and may even reveal that they envy you sometimes, too.

- Get **familiar with envy**. With time, you'll learn to recognize it, dismiss it with a shrug, and move on.

- Use envy to **show you what you want**. If you envy a friend's book, for example, get to work on your stalled book proposal.

- Adopt a practical attitude: the friend you envy may be willing to **share her experiences and knowledge**. (If she is, just remember to return the favor.)

- Have the confidence to believe that **you, too, can inspire envy at times**. Toot your horn gently.

- Most important, learn to **love your work for its own sake**—not for the recognition it brings you. Recognition is unreliable, but your own satisfaction in your work is yours to keep.

Chapter 15

An Experimental Guide to Achieving Balance

By Virginia Gewin

I remember those early elementary-school experiences on the balance beam—balancing was active, not passive. It meant wobbling all the time, and sometimes I fell off.

—SciLancer Robert Frederick

Like many science writers, I trained—for five long years—to be a scientist. I can wield a pipette, design a study, and suck microbial enzymes out of soil with the best of them.

Then my PhD imploded. The government research facility that housed my three-years-in-the-making experiments abruptly shut down the study. And I realized I didn't want to fight for a research career, even after having pursued one for so long. It was a blessing in disguise: I discovered that my true passion was writing about the important topics I'd studied, such as agricultural sustainability, ecological degradation, and climate change.

What I didn't know at the time is that when I chose to pursue science journalism as a freelancer, I wasn't just making a career move. I was choosing a new lifestyle. It's filled with undeniable perks: working from home, being my own boss, and setting my own schedule are just a few. But at times it mirrors the drudgery of research: I'm tied to a laptop instead of a lab bench, always working to beat deadlines, and setting schedules only to have them crushed by distractions and procrastination.

Whether you work freelance or on staff, full- or part-time, science writing has a way of intruding on all aspects of life. The creative process and the "smart" devices that allow anyone to work anywhere let jobs creep into home life, and staff writers and freelancers alike often find themselves staying at the keyboard till long, long after night has fallen. Especially when you work from home, the science-writing lifestyle requires some well-tended fences to prevent excessive trespassing.

The members of SciLance have run several experiments—most of them inadvertent—as we've tried to achieve balance between writing and the rest of our lives. As a good former scientist, I've gathered and analyzed these results. I hope that reading about SciLancers' experiments with balance here will save you the pain of becoming your own experimental unit, and help you shave years of frustration off your own quest for balance.

Experiment 1: Trying the *Ex Situ* Office

Surely the easiest solution to separating life and work is simply getting an office outside the home, right? The *ex situ* office has some advantages, as Chapter 12 makes clear. But my data suggest that offices close to home—within slipper-footed walking distance—work best.

A few years ago, I was thrilled to try sharing an office on an up-and-coming street in Portland, Oregon, with two other local freelance writers. I was venturing out of my home-office cave and into the "real" world— coffee shops, fresh air, conversation with flesh-and-blood humans. It was intoxicating.

Unfortunately, the arrangement also increased my stress. I work about thirty hours per week, often at odd times of the day. I'll do interviews at 6 a.m. Pacific time to catch sources in Europe. I'm just as likely to find myself up and working into the wee hours when on deadline. In between, I might well have a busy day of domestic chores with little or no "work" at all. To avoid commuting more than once a day, I had to maintain some form of a home office, too, which made it harder to keep track of my notes and materials. In addition to its actual rent, it turned out that my hipster office had a hidden cost—it made me inefficient.

Michelle Nijhuis and Stephen Ornes both have freestanding offices in their backyards, an enviable setup that combines physical separation with convenience. Other SciLancers, especially those of us with families, say

I liked having a rented office away from home in a lot of ways, but I wasn't getting to enjoy the advantages of free-lancing. I had to look at least reasonably present-able at the office, and while it was nice to see people, one of the downsides is that you have to make chitchat with all the random people who stop by your desk. I decided that it was really much better to work at work, and see friends at other times.

—MICHELLE NIJHUIS

their secret to success is a home office door that shuts—and preferably locks. "Having a physical delineation between the office and the rest of the house has helped mark off office time for both me and my partner, especially during those days when we're both at home," says Bryn Nelson. For Emily Sohn, a home office with a closeable door was a must-have when her family was house shopping. "My door has a little metal sign on it that says EMILY SOHN: FREELANCE JOURNALIST," she says. " I like it. It makes me feel official."

But in some places, having a door or even four walls to call your own can be an unachievable luxury. Big-city rents, for example, can make an extra room prohibitively expensive. As a result, several of us have offices in the corner of a living room or bedroom (more about office options in Chapter 16). While an office in shared space can be poached by, say, piano practice or breakfast, Sarah Webb says it can also foster balance by forcing her to put work aside when her husband gets home. "Having my office in the living room actually helps with work-life boundary issues," Sarah says. "Unless I'm really pushed, I'll shut things down by dinner time." (See Chapter 17 for more about the emotional issues that arise around domestic office space.)

Experiment 2: Imposing Time Boundaries

If physical boundaries don't work for you, the next best thing might be setting hard-and-fast boundaries in time, clearly defining hours for "work" and "life"—basically, mimicking a nine-to-five work schedule.

"Clocking out" is a foreign concept for most journalists, particularly in the early days of their careers. Most of us spent years taking on every assignment that came our way, and when you're a new freelancer or a new intern at a staff job, there are days when the work starts early and goes very late indeed. "I used to hardly set any hard-and-fast boundaries about work hours," Douglas Fox recalls. "I was a single guy living alone and loved the freewheeling flexibility of freelancing. I'm a night person who could sometimes work a really productive noon to 2 a.m. workday during crunches."

But once writers are established and, ahem, older, some of us start to draw lines in the sand. Most SciLancers try to not work on the weekends—at least one day. Many of us limit the amount of time spent working at night. And we try to get the most out of our time at work, for instance, by making valiant attempts not to get distracted by e-mail.

When I'm away from my office, I'm unreachable. If I'm out of my office, I'm out. I'll deal with whatever needs dealing with when I return. In that sense, I am fully committed and present to whatever it is that I am doing.

—ANNE SASSO

Robert Frederick doesn't allow himself to work early in the morning or at any time in the evening. He even takes an hour for lunch—a rarity for any reporter. And he makes sure there's no mistaking when his workday is over. "I'm typically wrapping things up between 5 and 6 p.m.," he says. "And even though it sounds corny, at the end of my day, I actually make a sound like that of a factory horn—*baaaaaannnnnt!* And once I've made that sound, I don't do anything work-related until the next day."

Interestingly, however, several of us have found that rigid boundaries suck the fun and flexibility out of science writing. This is a creative endeavor, after all. When we report is often decided by the schedules of our sources—and the inspiration to write sometimes strikes outside predetermined working hours. As our science-writing careers have developed, we've learned when and how we write best.

"My 'aha!' moments and bursts of productivity—often inspired by mild panic over an impending deadline—don't always fit neatly into a defined schedule," Bryn says. He likes to keep his boundaries fluid enough to accommodate bursts of productivity. Others find that breaking up the traditional workday with other tasks can help. "What works for me is to incorporate some household tasks into my day, but to be disciplined about it," says Gisela Telis. She'll even set a timer and do thirty minutes of chores before going back to work. "If the activity is physical yet meditative, like a lot of household chores can be," she says, "I'll come back to my work refreshed and more productive."

For Kendall Powell, flexibility also means being able to take a moment during her nonworking hours to complete a quick work task. "I like being able to pick up my work whenever I have a moment long enough to concentrate," she says. "I find that makes me more efficient, and helps free up other times when I don't want to be working." Kendall usually spends some small part of her weekends, holidays, and even vacations working, but sees it as a way to keep her workload manageable and her year free of income gaps.

My big struggle now is the smart phone. It's always there, begging to be checked. My husband and I have made a pact to keep the phones off on vacations, even just long weekends. I sometimes succeed at that.

—EMILY SOHN

Experiment 3: Taming the Smart Phone

The smart phone has made science writing better in just about every way imaginable. The ease of responding to a quick yet urgent e-mail query from an editor while enjoying a day at the zoo with my kids is bliss. Not having to search for a Wi-Fi signal at a conference to meet up with an impossibly busy source is downright delicious. Recording a call with only one additional swipe of the same device is a little piece of heaven.

The only downside is the Svengali-like hold the smart phone has on me. I check e-mail—all the time. Many of us do. I justify the quick checks for the comfort of knowing that all is right in my world. And my habit is often validated when a "quick check" gets me a time-sensitive assignment. For example, one of the outlets I write for often assigns online news stories. Even if I happen to be out, I can respond quickly with a yea or nay—ensuring that I either get the job or that my responsiveness encourages the editor to keep the offers coming. But inevitably, I get sucked into "just one more e-mail"—which erodes my downtime.

Still, the intrusive little smart phone can set us free to rejuvenate. "I'm trying really, really hard to give myself license to step away from the computer when I'm spinning my wheels," says Hannah Hoag. When the writing just isn't working, she'll walk away from her desk to read, or go for a walk or a run—and with smart phone in hand, she can take a break guilt-free.

Experiment 4: Turning Down Work (Gasp)

In the world of science writing, turning down work is a kind of blasphemy. As a freelancer, you never really get over the fear that if you turn down one assignment, you may never get another one. And as a staffer these days, telling your boss you can't take on yet another story can feel like begging for a layoff notice. But sometimes you have to be sacrilegious to stay sane—especially if the quality of your work will suffer due to competing deadlines.

We tend to forget that turning down work can also send a positive message: "I'm in demand." And because assignments tend to come in downpours and droughts, if you're ever going to master the delicate art of moderating your workflow, you're going to have to learn how to say no. I've had several periods in my career when offers poured in on top of regular gigs. Since I didn't have to spend time on pitches, all my working hours magically became paychecks. But there was always a point at which my work started to suffer. It was usually when I agreed to write easy stories on topics I didn't care about rather than pursuing the ideas that consumed me.

We were leaving for a trip the next morning, and a magazine I wanted to break into e-mailed and asked for a quick-turnaround news story. I spent that whole day reporting and writing the story, and filed after midnight, exhausted. Ultimately I didn't feel like it was my best work. It didn't lead to a hoped-for feature assignment, either, and I stressed my husband. That was a big eye-opener for me.

—AMANDA MASCARELLI

Saying no is particularly hard for freelancers. For all the supposed control of being your own boss, much of the freelance lifestyle is beyond the writer's control. Thomas Hayden likens the lack of control to being back in high school—when you were at the mercy of six different teachers' schedules of assignments, exams, and projects. There's simply no way to moderate unexpected editor requests, shifting deadlines, or conflicting magazine schedules.

It can be especially difficult for freelancers to clear the calendar for vacations (see "How the &%@ Do I Take a Real Vacation?" on p. 163). As a consequence, we often take what I call mini-vacations—long weekends with laptop in hand, during which we can get away with editors none the wiser. But I've learned that mini-vacations cheat me out of real quality downtime. Some of us unplug on a routine basis: Jill Adams makes sure to spend at least one week unplugged in the mountains every summer. "It reminds me that I can ask editors for time off, I can disconnect from social media, I can read long books and contemplate the clouds, and I can come back rejuvenated," she says.

Experiment 5: Giving Your Brain a Break

One of the biggest, and most common, balance blunders is to deprive your brain of the breathing room it needs to function best. Sure, you can bang your head against a keyboard for hours on end, but sometimes it's better to let your subconscious be your guide. Given some time and space, the deep recesses of my gray matter can generate a lede or simplify a story structure.

For me, a hike is a guaranteed way to let my mind meander right past writer's block. For Emily, the type of exercise doesn't matter as much as making time for some kind of physical activity. "I regularly take an hour in the middle of the day—just before or after lunch—to swim, bike, or otherwise move my body," she says. "It powers me through the afternoon slump, soothes the stress, and keeps me so much happier."

Exercise is, not surprisingly, a favorite activity of many writers. But many of us find redirecting our mental energies into other creative pursuits to be equally invigorating. For Robert, one rejuvenation strategy is drawing. On paper. For Sarah and Anne, it's working with clay. And sometimes keeping the creative spark alive means simply being mindful of your daily windows of inspiration.

The single best thing I've done to create balance in my work and life as a full-time freelancer is to dedicate eight hours of my work time each week to creative projects that are for my enjoyment and may or may not lead to work.
—ROBERT FREDERICK

Experiment 6: Having Kids

Having kids is a surefire way to impose boundaries between work and life: see Chapter 18 for more on this most drastic of experiments. Most of us SciLancers who have children have dialed back the overall number of hours we work, the amount of travel we take on, and the level of perfectionism we seek.

But babies are just one of the clearer reminders that life is all about change. It should come as no surprise that in an ever-changing world, and in a dynamic business like science writing, finding balance is a never-ending quest.

I don't really want to travel for work anymore. That used to be one of my favorite things, but since having kids, I just don't want to be away. I've only traveled for a night or two here and there, and don't take the kind of joy in it that I used to. Funny.

—THOMAS HAYDEN

How the &%@ Do I Take a Real Vacation?

One of the tenets of the freelance lifestyle is that you work only when you want. It's true, but it's a half truth. Just like the one about being your own boss. As Douglas Fox points out, you have multiple editors at different media outlets, all with their own demands, deadlines, and druthers. Fitting those obligations into your vacation plans can, to say the least, complicate things, especially when you are traveling with family or friends.

As a result, I went five years without a proper I'm-out-of-cell-phone-and-Wi-Fi-range-for-at-least-a-week vacation. Making one happen was both financially challenging and invigorating: I found that to ensure my sanity and leave no strings left unattended once I unplugged, I had to plan for three phases.

The Ramp-Down: Once your vacation dates are set, make sure you can meet all of your deadlines before you leave. This is trickier than you might think. If you set your deadlines too early, you'll have dead time before vacation when you can't feasibly start something new without getting sucked back into someone's

(Continues)

How the &%@ Do I Take a Real Vacation?
(Continued)

publication cycle. If you set deadlines too close to your departure, stress is all but certain. Once the deadlines are done and stories put to bed, it's time to enjoy. One good rule of thumb: Try to coordinate the last read of a story for at least two days before departure so you are in the clear. Use any leftover time to start the pitch you will send out upon return.

The Full Relax: If you take only one or two real vacations a decade, you need to disconnect from work completely. It may seem difficult or impossible to do, but your professional life won't dry up because you were offline for ten days. Alert key colleagues that you'll be out of touch, then enjoy the hedonistic bliss of not answering the phone or checking e-mails. You might even set up a separate "friends and family" e-mail address, so you can stay in touch with the people in your life who aren't sending you new work.

The Ramp-Up: Jumping out of the media cycle isn't as hard as jumping back in. Editors assign work at their leisure—not yours. It can take awhile after returning to get pitches in play, assignments on the books, and checks coming in the mail. The point is that while you deserve a bona fide vacation, it's wise to plan for an extended disruption in your flow of work and money. But chances are you can also bank on a boost of productivity that only a recharged mind can deliver.

Balance, Schmalance

By Liza Gross

Enjoying lunch with my two sisters one afternoon, I mentioned that I was writing a short piece about finding the right work-life balance. They looked blankly at each other, then at me, before collapsing into gut-busting hysterics. My older sister, tears streaming down her face, barely managed to get out the words: "You're kidding, right?"

I wish I could say that my sisters overreacted, but the truth is I don't have an off switch. I didn't think it would be so hard to freelance on top of my full-time job as front section editor of the journal *PLOS Biology*. You might say I was delusional. But I think I'm probably like most science writers.

As a longtime staffer at publications including *Wine Spectator*, *Parenting*, and *Sierra*, I'd always considered freelancers a somewhat mysterious lot. So many decisions and changes were made in-house, how could anyone not on staff possibly keep up—or break in? But as I got to know more freelancers, the mysteries of the enterprise began to fade as the realities, daunting as they were, became apparent. And my desire to do more on-the-ground reporting in far-flung locales—something that wasn't practical given my other duties for the journal—proved a powerful motivator.

I wasn't ready to conquer the business end of freelancing, but I thought I could figure out what (at least a few) editors wanted. So I started freelancing while working a full-time job that often requires overtime. What's funny is that I thought I could do all this while maintaining some semblance of a normal life.

Since then, most of my vacations have been busman's holidays. Every freelancer I know has a website, so I spent one Christmas vacation building one from a WordPress template. At every opportunity, I've squeezed in regional reporting on weekends or days off, taken advantage of local story opportunities, and tacked on side jaunts after conferences or other work-related trips farther afield.

For me, the notion of finding balance between work and life is a false dichotomy. When you're insatiably curious and see stories in even the

(Continues)

Balance, Schmalance *(Continued)*

most offhand remark, it's time to admit that writing *is* your life. It probably helps that my husband is also a writer, so you might say that storytelling is a conjugal bond. But if you have an unremitting urge to tell stories, to unearth information that the public has a right to know, or simply to explore and write, you'll find the time. It's true, I'm sometimes tired. But I've never felt more fulfilled. And that's nothing to laugh at.

SciLance SAYS . . .

- **Pay heed to your work habits** when deciding between an office inside or outside the home. Will the presence of other people make you procrastinate? Will household chores distract or invigorate you?

- If you choose a home office, **play around with your schedule until you make it work for you.** Better yet, geek out: keep a diary to identify when bursts of creativity are strongest and adjust your schedule accordingly.

- Find a way to **tame the smart phone.** Are you more comfortable setting specific times to check messages or turning it off completely on weekends or on vacation?

- Realize that **you have no control over your clients' publishing schedules**—be they weekly, monthly, and/or quarterly. Plan accordingly.

- Don't be afraid to **turn down assignments if you are overbooked.** You will preserve the quality of your work and send the signal that you are in demand.

- **Give your brain a break.** Exercise or take on new endeavors to keep creative juices flowing.

Chapter 16

Creating Creative Spaces

By Hannah Hoag

Most freelancers work from home, and an increasing number of staff science writers do, too, at least part of the time. Setting up an office that works for you is an essential and sometimes undervalued part of your productivity—and happiness—as a science writer. Before you declare your home office open for business, consider what you need to do your job.

The Essentials

Many writers are true minimalists when it comes to equipping their offices. They're right to be so: to report and write a news story or a feature from home, you don't need much more than a computer, Internet access, and a telephone (landline, Internet, or mobile).

When you equip your office, start by choosing a computer that is going to work for you. If you do even a modest amount of field reporting, you'll want the portability of a laptop. If you can't stand staring at a computer screen the size of an envelope or mashing away at a diminutive keyboard on a daily basis, invest in an external monitor and keyboard for your laptop. Working from two screens or one large screen allows you to have two or three documents open side-by-side, instead of clicking or tabbing between your interview notes and your story document.

Coupling a small laptop with an external monitor also means that you have one hard drive (on your laptop) that contains all your documents, meaning you never have to shuffle files between laptop and desktop computers. You'll probably save yourself some money, too. But if you go this route, make sure you back up your laptop to an external drive (or two) daily, so that if you drop your laptop or it's stolen, you still have all your research materials.

For me, owning a light laptop computer is a must. I find myself on the move a fair amount over the course of a year, either working in cafés during the regular workweek or on the road, reporting stories in the field, or attending conferences. I know others who feel the same way about their netbooks—personal computers with a small but full keyboard, and some Internet capabilities—or tablet computers, which can also be outfitted with external keyboards.

For my primary computer, however, I use a desktop with a wider screen. Its hard drive holds everything I need, from applications to research materials going back for years. And it is hooked up to an external hard drive, where my data is backed up daily. Some time ago, I tried the laptop-monitor setup, but I couldn't find a screen I liked within my budget. So when I want to work on my laptop, I move the files I need to my password-protected web-based file hosting service that gives me storage space on the cloud, where I can access them from any computer I choose. There are many different such services and most offer a decent amount of space for free, with the option to purchase more. Moving files is a bit of extra work, but it also means my laptop doesn't contain much sensitive information, a potentially significant benefit if it is ever lost or stolen.

There was a time when every office had a scanner, printer, and fax machine. These days you can usually get by with one—or none—of them. Forget the fax: press releases arrive by e-mail and there's almost no reason to send a fax these days. If you're working with a client—or a government agency, especially—that relies on one, there are fax-to-e-mail services that will let you send and receive documents. A scanner isn't essential, but it can put you on the path toward a paperless office; I use mine to organize clips and return signed contracts by e-mail. You can also reduce paper use by creating a digital signature to affix to contracts, using online note-taking and archiving software to store web clippings and PDFs, and reading long articles on your computer screen or tablet. For most freelance science writers, however, printers have been harder to cast aside. Though I'm trying to change my ways, I still prefer to scribble notes in the margins of printed journal articles instead of doing it electronically on a PDF file.

Consider the features of the chair and desk you add to your workspace carefully—you're going to spend a lot of time with them. Read up on the best ergonomic settings that will keep you comfortable and allow you to move about easily. You may also want to consider a standing desk. Desk-tethered office workers burn more calories when standing, and some research suggests there may be other health benefits. Many stand-up devotees report they are alert, attentive, and energetic throughout the day, and avoid the all too common midafternoon crash. Test it before you commit, though—high-end standing desks can cost thousands of dollars.

Talking to the World

If you're going to be a reporter, or a science writer of any kind, you're going to need to make lots of phone calls. Improvements to the sound quality of mobile phones have prompted many science writers to do away with their landlines for interviews. Another option is to sign up for a voice- and video-calling program that runs over the Internet, such as Skype, Google Voice, or another voice over internet protocol (VoIP) service. I use Skype almost exclusively now.

These VoIP applications offer other advantages, including portability and the potential to record the phone call directly to your computer's hard drive with a third-party application such as Audio Hijack Pro. It's an easy and important archiving solution for a minor investment. (See Chapter 4 for more about recording phone calls.)

VoIP can turn your laptop—or your smart phone—into your primary communication tool. With a smart phone, I can Skype from a hotel in Guyana for only a few cents and avoid exorbitant long-distance and roaming charges. Not everyone considers a smart phone as a necessary tool in the freelancer's toolbox, but it has changed the way I work for the better.

Whether you opt for a traditional phone line or an Internet service, seek out a good headset with an adjustable microphone and a mute button. By keeping your hands free to type or take notes, you'll save yourself neck pain—and physical therapy bills. Consider whether you want one that connects to your phone, or to the 3.5-millimeter jack or USB port of your computer. Wireless headphones will allow you to stroll while you interview.

Deadlines Don't Belong on Gum Wrappers

A good calendar, paper or digital, is crucial for monitoring deadlines, interviews, and incoming checks. I schedule all my reporting and writing activities in iCal, the calendar application that comes with a Mac. There are many calendar options for other operating systems. Google Calendar is an especially popular option because it is free and web-based. Web-accessible calendars are also handy if your computer goes on the fritz or your dog decides your leather agenda looks tasty.

I use a large whiteboard for my major deadlines and a handful of significant to-dos. In the bottom corner, I also keep notes on the types of stories specific editors or magazines want, story ideas that I want to pitch, and the deadlines for awards or fellowships that interest me. The notes keep me moving after I've filed a story or when I need a change of pace; I just look up and know what I need to do next.

Spreadsheets are another popular way to organize your writing business or your daily tasks. (See Chapter 19 for more on recordkeeping.) Microsoft Excel, Google Docs, and Open Office are some of the most widely used spreadsheet programs. With a little effort you can create color-coded worksheets that track the status of an assignment, the number of hours you've spent on a project, your business expenses, and income. You can also keep track of all the phone calls you make to sources for your stories, annotating the entry each time you interview another one. The bonus is that they're easily searchable, which means you can track down the cell number of the immunologist in Florida whose name you don't remember.

If you're in this business for the long haul, you're going to accumulate thousands of journal articles and other documents. Many of them you'll read once (or twice) and never need again. But if you develop a beat or an expertise, you'll refer back to some key papers over and over again. A simple file cabinet or hanging-file box is handy for keeping piles of paper from overshadowing your office, and you can organize electronic documents in a reference manager like Mendeley, EndNote, Papers, or DEVONthink.

Hang Out Your Shingle

Where will you put your chosen technology to work? Even if you're employed by an organization that provides you with a desk to write from, there are benefits to setting up an office of your own: taking an afternoon away from your noisy newsroom to work on a particularly difficult scene, or a morning to read academic journal articles and government reports, can be a sanity saver.

When you launch your career as a science writer, there's a good chance you'll make your home office in your bedroom, in a nook near the kitchen, or even inside a closet. My first at-home office was little more than a corner of my bedroom outfitted with a desk lamp, a laptop computer, a cell phone—and a long-distance calling card. I was an intern in Washington, D.C., unable to afford luxuries, and this arrangement worked. But long term, the bedroom office can be an obstacle in the never-ending quests to achieve work-life balance (see Chapter 15) and avoid domestic disasters (see Chapter 17).

After I left my bedroom office in Washington, D.C., I made sure that every apartment I moved into had a spare room or a substantial nook where I could set up an office and spread out my work. One of my favorite offices was a tiny six-foot-by-six-foot room off the kitchen of a ground-floor apartment in Montreal. It was compact, but I could reach anything I needed—the printer, a recently signed contract, or the file folder of writing guidelines I had collected over the years—by spinning my desk chair one way or the other.

When a separate room isn't available, creating a private, pleasant spot for work can be challenging. Most writers crave natural light, and often carve out an office space near windows or balcony doors. While you might upset living-room furniture arrangements—and uptight roommates—working near a window protects your eyes and brain from fatigue. (And when your bed is only a few steps away, fatigue busting is of utmost importance.) You can create the illusion of a separate space using bookcases, arranging them like walls around your desk to delineate your workspace from the rest of your house or apartment. Alternatively, if your work is infringing on the rest of your life, you can use a screen to shield your desk—and your teetering pile of books and papers—from your dinner parties.

In an office of any kind, posting photographs, paintings, or other visual paraphernalia around your workspace can create a calming or inspiring environment. "I like to put up a few pictures that encapsulate the mood of a big project or my current interests," says Emma Marris. Other SciLancers hang souvenirs of previous reporting trips on their walls to remind them of the real people and places they are writing about.

When you work from a home office, how do you get editors you never see to notice you? See Chapter 20 for more about networking, but one essential tool is an online business card—a website or some other digital presence. A website or professional profile allows strangers and acquaintances to find you, and it lets you point editors toward your résumé or work. Your site doesn't have to be elaborate, but it does have to be professional and showcase your skills, experience, and talents. You can pay hundreds or even thousands of dollars to have one designed, uploaded with your material, and kept current. Or you can set a simple one up for free in under an hour.

Your website should include at least three things: a summary of your experience and expertise, links to or copies of your best work, and most important, contact information. Make it easy for an editor to get in touch with you by including a contact form or your e-mail. (You may want to remove the symbols when you write out your e-mail—i.e., name [at] host [dot] com—to avoid spam.) Look to free website-building platforms, such as Google Sites and About.me, or blogging software, such as WordPress, Blogger, and Tumblr to help you build a personal page and hang out your digital shingle.

Another networking essential is an old-fashioned analog business card; many online services allow users to design and print their own high-quality cards for a reasonable price. Your card should point editors, colleagues, and sources to your website and to any social-media IDs you want to publicize. (For cautionary notes on the professional use of social media, see Chapter 24.) Carrying cards at conferences or other gatherings can help turn fleeting connections into long-term contacts.

My Own Private Office

Renting a space outside of your home is worth exploring—depending on your location, it might be a reasonable option or it may be prohibitively expensive. In some areas you'll find you have to pay for your own Internet access, buy insurance, and sign a long lease to get a space you can call your own. (See Chapter 15 for more about the advantages and disadvantages of *ex situ* offices.)

If you find a solo office lonely, you may want to seek out coworking spaces in your area, which allow independent workers to share large workspaces with other entrepreneurs. Often the spaces operate on a membership basis, with monthly fees tied to the level of access, space, and privacy you get. You won't pay extra for utilities or Internet service—and some coworking spaces even offer free coffee to their tenants—but you may have to pay extra to use the board room (good for interviews), the fax machine, or the photocopier.

Since I began working as a freelance science writer in 2003, I've set up and worked out of seven different offices. I've had the bedroom office, the nook office, the office-office, and even the office-down-the street. Though each had their advantages, I'm now happily back in a home office, checking the mail when it arrives and making a cup of coffee when the mood strikes. I've found that any office arrangement can work—as long as it fits your personal working style.

SciLance says . . .

- Writers have to **think about how—and where—they do most of their reporting and writing** before buying a computer. Find one that suits your style.

- Take the time to set up your workspace. Consider ergonomics **to keep workplace injuries and medical bills to a minimum**.

- Cut back on your phone bills—**use a VoIP service**.

- Establish an online identity. Even **a simple website can boost your visibility—and income**.

- Don't let your success spin your schedule out of control. **Keep track of those nasty deadlines and interviews with a solid scheduling system**. We won't judge you if it's analog—just don't use the backs of envelopes.

(Continues)

- Before renting your own office space, **be honest with yourself and do the math**. Can you afford the rent? Are you better off claiming part of your home as an office space for your taxes?

- Consider **coworking**. Meet people, work hard, and save a little money.

Chapter 17

Avoiding Domestic Disasters
By Bryn Nelson

Experience is the name everyone gives to their mistakes.
—Oscar Wilde

The passenger seat of a '99 Chevy Lumina is a poor excuse for an office.

This is particularly true when the air conditioner has failed and you've slammed the power inverter for your laptop in the car door. This is exceptionally true when you and your increasingly grumpy partner are racing across southern Montana with camping gear and fine china stowed in the trunk, a small greenhouse of wilted houseplants languishing in the backseat, and a critical deadline looming like a runaway semi.

Let's get the obvious out of the way: a working vacation that doubles as a cross-country move with your partner is just plain dumb. And never is that clearer than when you're desperately scanning the horizon for any roadside inn with Wi-Fi so that you can send off a draft before that final red sliver of remaining battery power winks out.

As we saw in Chapter 15, balance can be an elusive goal for the science writer. But finding the right equilibrium between a demanding, sometimes unpredictable career and life with a spouse or committed partner presents a special set of challenges all its own. The blessing of having a portable occupation—with an office that can be virtually anywhere—can also be a curse when your workspace overflows into your partner's territory or is regularly invaded by him on a particularly busy day. As one SciLancer has framed it, "How do you politely tell your spouse to 'Get the *&%$ out of my office already'?"

Collisions between work and domesticity may make entertaining stories at cocktail parties, but unchecked, they can threaten your most important relationships. The good news is that many of us have been there and can offer some advice on what you should absolutely never do (e.g., check your work e-mail during a romantic dinner)—and how you can head off potential conflicts before they materialize.

Setting Expectations

One of the first keys to avoiding domestic dysfunction as a science writer, especially one who works from home, is to properly define yourself as a professional to your significant other. To establish and reinforce your professional identity, try:

- Referring to your clients by name. And in this case, obscurity can be a good thing. Your partner may not know what the European Congress of Clinical Microbiology and Infectious Diseases or the Institute of Electrical and Electronics Engineers actually does, but the names certainly sound important.
- Selectively inviting your significant other to science-writing outings or events that illustrate the importance or coolness factor of your job.
- Reminding your spouse how busy you are by sharing your work calendar, whether through a shared smart-phone app or a printed copy. Providing an account of upcoming deadlines, meetings, and major interviews can do wonders for instilling a new awareness of the demands on your time.

Even when your partner understands your obligations, tension can arise over responsibilities for chores and other domestic issues. Unfortunately for the freelancer, physical proximity often trumps workload as the main deciding factor. "Even with the most considerate partners, it can be far too easy for the home-based partner to end up dealing with a repair, moving the car for street cleaning, or fill in your favorite chore here," says Sarah Webb.

Other SciLancers recommend setting aside time to do chores together, at either the beginning or the end of the day, so there are no hard feelings about who has to do what. A polite but direct approach also works:

"These days," says Sarah, "I try to be clear that I'm dealing with work pressures, too, and that we need to negotiate."

Establishing Your Own Space

We explored the particulars of a productive workspace in Chapter 16. But you also need a strategy for defending your home office. While the "Do Not Enter" sign decorated with a skull and crossbones worked when you were nine, you may now need a more delicate and creative touch.

Some of us SciLancers have figured out how to keep our partners at bay through the clever use of clutter. "My office is so messy that Dan rarely enters it willingly," says Monya Baker. Susan Moran agrees: "My husband is repelled by my piles of paper and magazine clippings."

Marking your territory with piles of journal articles may not work for everyone, though, and tottering towers of magazines and papers can create their own interpersonal hazards, especially when they migrate into common spaces. (An outing to your favorite home organization store to buy storage bins, or an agreement to regular purges, can help forestall the creep of those *National Geographic, Wired,* and *New Yorker* back issues.) Keeping your paperwork within your own workspace also gives you more leverage when negotiating the ground rules over other space issues.

Start negotiations about space with your partner by talking about your working style. Are you easily distracted? A morning person? A perfectionist? Some writers, for instance, need a closed door to concentrate, while others like overhearing activities in the rest of the house. Some like to limit interruptions to certain hours of the day. During a recent talk with my partner, I realized I had never explicitly told him how annoying it is when he comes into my office without knocking. A simple conversation cleared up months of misunderstanding.

Many science writers are also chronic procrastinators—see Chapter 11—and rely on the adrenaline rush of a deadline to complete a project. If you're in this category, it's particularly important to make sure your partner understands that being "on deadline" is something sacred for writers.

Technology also raises boundary issues: Will your computer be used only for work, or will it sometimes be enlisted for household use? If the latter, you can save yourself much gnashing of teeth with an up-front discussion about what's acceptable—checking e-mail or playing music at specific times, for example—and what isn't. In addition, you'll want to regularly back up your files onto an external hard drive or use online storage. An accidentally deleted file, a downloaded virus, or a spilled mug of coffee could lead to a full-scale domestic fiasco.

Figuring out workspace issues when you merge households can be daunting, particularly when both of you require a desk and home happens to be a small urban apartment. When Sarah moved into her future husband's New Jersey apartment—and office space—she nearly lost her mind. "In those early months," she says, "we spent a lot of time less than two feet from each other, sharing a crappy DSL connection. There were moments when I had to explicitly say, 'Stop streaming those $&*! videos on YouTube.'" For Sarah, sanity was restored by an apartment with a high-speed Internet connection and desks at opposite ends of the central living space. Importantly, the desks were positioned along different sight lines, so that she and her husband could easily talk but couldn't see each other while they worked.

If your office doesn't have the luxury of a door that closes, you can construct physical buffers with screens and furniture (read more about setting up your own office in Chapter 16). You can create a partial sound barrier with headphones for you and your partner, a white-noise maker, or noise-canceling speakers—or even just a fan. If all else fails, an afternoon at a coffee shop, a university library, or other accessible worksite, such as a coworking office space, can help preserve the peace at home.

Constructively Engaging Your Spouse

Just when you've figured out how to keep your significant other out of your space without hurting his feelings, you may suddenly realize that you need him back in the office—for just a few minutes, of course.

My partner is my human thesaurus, forever fielding such questions as, "What's another word for metaphor?" Sarah calls her husband the voice of reason during moments of stress, and her "biggest morale booster." She can't imagine being married to someone "who thought I should get 'a real job.'" Many of us are blessed with just such a kick-ass one-person support staff. The challenge, of course, is working out an arrangement that is healthy for both of you.

Some SciLancers use their partners as general sounding boards. "I often bounce story ideas off Phil, or rely on him for basic career advice— how to reply to a particular e-mail, what to tell an editor, where to pitch a story, and so on. He thinks I never take his advice. But I do!" says Hillary Rosner.

On morning walks with his wife, Robert Frederick talks through his plans for the day, identifying work priorities and asking for input. "Because we're in different fields, we're very good at boiling down what the other wants to say because we have to identify the main point in order to make sense of the whole topic," he says. "That's been especially helpful to me in thinking through pitches, presentations, and story ideas."

Recruiting your spouse or partner as an editor can be wonderfully useful, but it's also a risky proposition. Hillary rarely sends off a story without using her husband as a front-line editor. "I constantly rely on him," she says, "even though it drives me completely nuts, and often ends with an argument of some sort." One problem, Hillary discovered, came from a basic miscommunication. "He assumed I knew he was starting from a baseline of liking most things I write, so he only gave negative feedback. Which I took to mean that he thought nearly everything I wrote was terrible."

Michelle Nijhuis discovered that editorial misunderstandings can spring from a single word, as in this recent dialogue with her husband:

JACK (FINISHING DRAFT): It's nice. I really like it.
MICHELLE: Huh. What's wrong with it?
JACK: But I said I really liked it!
MICHELLE: You said it was nice. Nice is bad.
JACK: What are you talking about? Nice is good.
MICHELLE: "Nice!" is good. "Nice" is bad.
JACK (ROLLING EYES): Did you want me to read it or not?

We deal in words every day, so it stands to reason that we would be most sensitive about having our partner point out an awkward phrase or be less than effusive in praising our prose. The solution, again, lies in communication. Ask your partner to start off with some compliments, then get into the criticism. And make sure you tell him or her what you're looking for: Do you want an in-depth review of structure, narrative, and grammar? Or do you just want him to make sure everything makes sense?

Another key role for a writer's partner? Therapist. "These days, Jack's biggest contribution to my professional mental health is to make me laugh about the crazier parts of my job," says Michelle. "He makes up nicknames for problematic projects, and imagines little melodramas that remind me how silly the business can be." Anne Sasso says her husband is her biggest defender. "He gets very incensed on my behalf when clients are taking advantage of me or being abusive," she says.

Whether you're asking for advice, editing, or therapy, make sure to be considerate of your partner's time, too. And if you can, return the favor. Monya Baker says her husband, Dan, is her best editor and particularly good at coming up with titles. In exchange, he sometimes asks her to review his lengthy research-grant applications when he's on deadline.

Knowing When to Say When

You've filed that big story, stepped away from the computer, and headed to the kitchen to help make dinner. If work is just down the hall, though, it can be difficult to leave it behind. To avoid off-hours angst with your partner:

- Let your partner know ahead of time when you're likely to have to work late (remember that it has essentially the same effect on your household as staying late at the office).
- If you absolutely must check your smart phone during dinner, never do it at the table. Instead, excuse yourself and briefly do it in the bathroom.
- Turn your phone off well before bedtime to alleviate insomnia and preserve the peace.
- Dinnertime can be a great opportunity to discuss upcoming projects or deadlines that might affect personal time. Just make sure your partner is ready to hear about work, and don't let your shop talk dominate the conversation.

"Going" Pains

You already know from Chapter 15 why science writers find it hard to take true vacations. It's even harder when you and your partner have different expectations about working on said vacation. If e-mailing during dinner is a no-no, imagine the dirty looks you'll get if you try it on the beach in Maui. When essential work is likely to encroach on vacation time, telling a partner well in advance what to expect can often head off unnecessary tension. Working during an unavoidable, don't-you-dare-back-out-on-me family vacation can land both you and your partner in your own special circle of hell. Amanda Mascarelli recalls the family friction she encountered when she had to deal with edits on the biggest story of her career while in India for her brother-in-law's wedding. "Now I try very hard to see potential conflicts coming and avoid them whenever possible," she says. "But my family has also learned that the unexpected is just one of the joys of my lifestyle."

Likewise, if you choose to bring a partner along on a work trip, be honest and up-front about your commitments, and be reasonable about what you can fit in. If the trip promises to be extraordinarily hectic, consider adding a day on the front or back end to allow for quality time with your partner. Settle as many unknowns as possible before the trip to minimize unpleasant surprises: for instance, will your partner be on his own during the day only, or will you have responsibilities at night, too? Also keep in mind that moving from business mode to personal mode can be difficult on work trips, especially when you have to toggle between solo work decisions and shared decision-making.

When well thought out, though, working vacations can be both professionally rewarding and personally satisfying. "Working vacations are fantastic," says Emma Marris. Her husband comes along, carries the luggage, takes pictures, and explores cities and countries while she works. "They take us to off-the-beaten-path places and put us in touch with locals, in the shape of my scientist sources, who can recommend the right places to eat and things to do."

In some instances, work life and home life intertwine in a way that reminds us why we love both our jobs and our partners. Emily Sohn and her husband took a monthlong honeymoon in Madagascar, including a week in a remote forest with a lemur researcher and her students. "The college kids at the research station thought we were totally crazy for spending part of our honeymoon that way," Emily says, "but my husband was in heaven, getting to see wild animals up close and learn about them from the world's top expert on them. That's when I knew for sure that I had picked the right guy. I got a couple good stories out of it, too."

As for my less-blissful encounter with a steamed partner in a stifling Montana parking lot, the vacation ended happily enough. I successfully sent in my draft, the china survived, the houseplants recovered, and we had a marvelous time in Yellowstone—interrupted only by a call to another editor. From that day, however, I learned the four basic rules of avoiding unnecessary domestic strife: be prepared, be honest, be reasonable, and above all, be willing to laugh at yourself.

SciLance says . . .

- Establish and **reinforce your identity** as a professional writer by emphasizing your specialty and setting clear expectations about what your work entails.

- Share your work calendar to **make sure your partner is aware** of major deadlines, meetings, and interviews.

- Define your physical workspace to minimize distractions, then try to stay within those boundaries to **avoid unnecessary conflicts** about encroaching on mutual living space.

- Talk about how your working style might **affect your workspace needs** and dedicated working hours.

- **Don't share your office** with the person who shares your bed (or at least use physical buffers in the office to maintain your sanity).

- If you use your partner as an editor, **provide plenty of upfront instruction** about what you're looking for to prevent hurt feelings.

- Value and acknowledge your partner's time and expertise as **vital contributions** to your business.

- Try to organize your working hours so that you **quit well before bedtime** to alleviate insomnia and preserve the peace.

- When essential work encroaches on vacation time, **tell your partner what to expect** in advance to help defuse the tension.

- **Laugh** often.

Chapter 18

Children and Deadlines

A Messy Rodeo

By Amanda Mascarelli

Looking back, it seems fitting that my introduction to blending free-lance science writing with raising children—a tricky art we SciLancers call "babylancing"—began with a bang of sorts. It was February 5, 2008, and my first child's due date was still one week away. That morning, I fired off one last e-mail and triumphantly announced to my husband: "I'm officially on maternity leave!" I treated myself to a lunch out, oblivious to how scarce such spontaneity would be after the baby arrived.

My cell phone rang. I eyed the phone suspiciously, then answered. The caller was an editor from a well-respected website. A writer friend had passed my name along to him; would I be available to cover the Colorado Democratic caucus in my Denver neighborhood that night? I hesitated—briefly—explaining to the editor that, really, I was supposed to be on maternity leave. Then, of course, I accepted the assignment.

That evening, I made my rounds of the caucus meetings, collecting quotes and scribbling frantically. But I was on another imminent deadline—and this one was nonnegotiable. I filed the story at 11:40 p.m. Less than five minutes later, my water broke. The ensuing phone call to my editor produced by far the speediest editing turnaround I've ever experienced.

And so the juggle was on—the rodeo, really, that I would experience over the next few years as I stumbled and flailed along, trying to make sense of the messy business of balancing children and deadlines.

When my husband and I contemplated starting a family, freelancing sounded like a dream arrangement for a new parent. I could work from home, spend plenty of quality time with our kids, and continue doing the writing that I thoroughly enjoyed and on which we were financially dependent. But that's about as far as we got in our "planning" process.

Every family is different, and each has to find its own way through the potentially treacherous waters of work, child care, family time, and shared responsibilities. Collectively, the babylancers of SciLance have produced some thirty offspring—and the number is growing. Not one of us will tell you that being a science writer, staff or freelance, while raising young kids is easy. But the career does lend itself to flexible work hours, and that can be a great perk if you use it wisely. Especially for freelancers, if one arrangement isn't leading to harmony, we can make adjustments to our workloads, our hours, or our child-care arrangements to find a more tractable approach.

For some SciLancers, the flexibility of freelancing helps smooth the transition back to work after having a baby. "It was nice just to do something with my non-parenting brain, but be able to ramp up slowly," says Cameron Walker. "I think if I had suddenly gone back to an office after being at home with a baby for several months, I would have freaked out and quit."

Kendall Powell says that freelancing lets her enjoy kids and career in equal parts. "As I look at my other 'mom friends' who have to make an excruciating choice between staying home full-time with their children or returning to a forty- or fifty-hour per week job, the flexibility of my freelance schedule seems like it offers the best of both worlds," she says. Kendall didn't want to rush back to full-time work, but didn't want to be a full-time stay-at-home mom either. Freelancing three days each week allows her to maintain that career, while still spending two weekdays with her children.

Mark Schrope, a father of three teenagers who has freelanced since 1999, says that working from home allowed him to focus on his career while still being present for his children. "Even though I was working crazy hours like lots of people (my father included) have done to start a business, I was actually in the house," Mark says. "I was seeing the kids multiple times a day—every time I went to the bathroom or stopped for lunch. So I didn't feel like an absentee father."

Baby Steps

Some countries, including Canada and the UK, offer government-funded maternity leave benefits to self-employed workers. In the US, when you don't have a traditional job with benefits, you also do not receive any government or insurance-based financial support to help subsidize an actual "leave" from work. Being your own boss also means you're on your own financially and must plan ahead accordingly.

In my early babylancing days, I hired a sitter (a local university student) to come to my home three half-days per week. Over the months, as assignments flowed in and my output increased, I needed more child care and began working four or five half-days per week—along with a whole lot of late nights. The sitter showed up at 8 a.m. and stayed until 1 p.m., at which time my son, Miles, would take a semi-reliable long afternoon nap. I scheduled all my interviews for when the sitter was on duty, and reserved his naptime—which could last anywhere from one to three hours—for e-mails, transcribing, research, and, if I was in a pinch, writing. Once in a while, I took a nap myself. And a few times, in the very early days when I desperately needed to do an interview and had no child care, I called up my eighty-year-old neighbor, Phyllis, to keep my son occupied for a few minutes.

When Miles turned eighteen months old and was beginning to climb the walls at home, he began attending a toddler program two half days each week. Then, just when I'd restored some semblance of sanity and balance to my work life, my daughter Isabella was born. That's when things got really interesting: after another ruefully short maternity leave, I again worked almost full-time, taking advantage of part-time sitters and my husband's flex schedule, during which he worked four days and watched the kids for three days. When Isabella turned fifteen months old and Miles was almost three, they both began attending full-time day care and preschool about thirty to forty hours a week, and those became my primary working hours. I worked this mostly full-time schedule (plus the occasional unavoidable late night and weekend) until my two children were three and almost five. Then my third child, Mia, arrived, throwing another buck and twist into my babylance rodeo. As to how that plays out, I'll have to report back.

When Three (or More) Is a Crowd

Despite the inherent challenges of sharing a workspace with a sitter and my children—the distraction, the noise, the inability to extricate yourself from them once they spot you tippy-toeing to the bathroom—I'm grateful that I got to enjoy my two older kids in the house while working for as long as I did. Being able to work while still hearing their laughter from across the house or just taking a break to drop in for a quick snuggle brought me deep satisfaction. Virginia Gewin feels the same way. "I loved having a nanny in the home because I could hear how things were going and therefore not worry," she says. "It also eliminated transport-related work delays, and meant I was paying for actual child-care time rather than travel time."

I love working from home with the kids banging around up-stairs. Popping up for a hug and a wrestle is a way better work break than scrolling through Twitter!

—THOMAS HAYDEN

But that's not to say that having the children at home while you work is all coos and giggles. Hearing your baby cry from across the house and not knowing why—or worse yet, hearing him cry for you—can be excruciating. And it's not very conducive to the free flow of thought, let alone composing complete sentences. It can also be hard to resist stepping in to trump the nanny. "The hardest thing for me in the early days of working at home with nanny and baby there was not interfering," says Emily Sohn. "It's so hard to hear everything and not want to go in and micromanage: 'Don't give him that much milk—he'll spit up! I think he's tired! Don't you think it's time to give him some fresh air? Have you done tummy time yet?'"

As my babies grew into toddlers, having them at home was no longer a tenable arrangement. Hidden away in my office or not, my kids knew I was there. Suddenly there was no such thing as just dropping in for a quick cuddle and then dropping back out of sight—no matter how much they enjoyed playing with the sitter. Just the sight of me slipping furtively past for a bathroom break or to grab a snack in the kitchen would set off tirades that no amount of soothing or distraction from the sitter could appease. Seemingly overnight, I became a fugitive in my own home office. It's a feeling every parent with a home office knows well: "I have often waited in my office until I heard the sound of footsteps heading upstairs for naptime—regardless of my own extreme dehydration or near-crisis bladder situation," says Adam Hinterthuer.

One fateful day, I was on an important phone call with an editor. Just a few minutes into the call, I could hear the wails of my then nearly three-year-old son drawing ever closer to my door. He'd managed to escape the sitter, and proceeded to beat on my door, crying out for Mommy. It must have been less than thirty seconds before he was whisked away, but the time felt geologic to me. I sat there stunned, floundering, apologetic . . . explaining to the editor that, really, I have a sitter, my son is just having a bad day. That's when I knew that the days of sharing my workspace with my kids had ended.

The Infinite Varieties of Child Care

There is a nearly limitless array of options for child care, and their costs vary widely. Depending on your location and the age of your child, you may be able to swap shifts with spouse or partner; use nanny/sitter shares and co-ops; hire mother's helpers or sitters in your home; pay for day care, drop-in care, or limited hours at a local preschool, YMCA, or Parents' Day Out setting; or employ any combination of the above. Some of us find that working several short days is best for our reporting and writing, while others prefer to work fewer, longer days.

If you're like me, you might find that no matter how you slice it, paying for child care is like taking on a second mortgage. But if you want to work, even a little, it's essential. Every working parent has sometimes had to attempt to work with kids at home and no child care due to a sickness, a snow day, an untimely holiday, or any number of other reasons. But expecting yourself to be a parent and a productive writer at once is a recipe for a particularly deep, sometimes disorienting sort of stress.

"I've essentially given up on trying to work when my daughter is at home," says Jennifer Cutraro. "Inevitably, on days when I'd hoped to count on her to take a nice long nap so I could finish a phone call, she'd wake up early and need my attention. I'd say the remedy is to not expect to get any work done while you have a young child at home. When I can remind myself of this, and keep boundaries in place, I'm much happier."

Even with the best-laid child-care plans, you may need to swap your reporter and parent hats with ninja-like speed. I once pulled off an interview in the car (as a passenger) on the way to a (real) rodeo with my whole family in tow—because it was the only time the source was available. While my son pointed out passing trains, I had my headset and voice recorder on and managed a very successful interview.

Baby Brain

Before I had kids, I was an incurable night owl. I've always been notorious for delivering my copy rather close (read: dangerously close) to deadline, and when need be, I worked caffeine- and adrenaline-fueled through the evening and into the wee hours. But no one warned me that in my new life with kids, I would lose what were once the most productive hours of my workday. The hours between 6 and 9 p.m. are now consumed with the dinner-bath-book-bedtime routine. After that, rather than being focused, I'm usually utterly exhausted. And if I do push through and stay up—as I admittedly still often do—there's no such thing as sleeping in. The hours between 10 p.m. and midnight are still some of my most productive, but now I pay for it the next day.

Given the way writing refuses to fit into a nine-to-five schedule, it's not surprising that I've got lots of company. "It's just really hard to finish an assignment during the regular workday," says Jessica Marshall. "Like others, I was used to calming down and writing in the early evening and needing to pore over the story many, many times before I finally sent it in, assuring myself that each sentence was right." Now that she has children, though, she says, "that time of day is now dead to me, and I have not yet recovered. I have yet to fully swallow that 6 p.m. to 1 a.m. is no longer available to me. Really, Jessica, it. is. not."

Many new parents find that their brain cells also just don't work as efficiently as they did pre-kid. "I always feel overwhelmed," says Adam. "The problem with the parental juggling act is that while one ball may be safely in hand, the others are on their unattended trajectories through the air."

It's important to recognize your newfound limitations and adjust your commitments and workload accordingly. "When you come back to work, remember that you're sleep-deprived," recommends Hannah Hoag. "Don't assume that you can go back to your regular work pace." Some of us have found that focusing on short, quick-turnaround assignments can be a good antidote to the impaired mommy or daddy brain. "The longer features still make me feel like I've been beaten up at the end," says Virginia. "Nice short pieces make me feel like I am able to accomplish something."

Michelle Nijhuis found the entrepreneurial side of her science-writing business especially tough during the first year or two of parenthood: "If someone had just handed me projects, I could have done them no problem," she says. "But all my creative energy and gumption were focused elsewhere, so it was hard to come up with new ideas and pitch them."

Travel Essentials: To Pump or Not to Pump, and Other Quandaries

Before my kids came along, I traveled regularly for assignments, and the only thing I had to worry about was who was going to walk my dog during the day. But traveling gets more complicated with kids in the picture. "Travel just weighs on my heart in a way that it never did before," says Douglas Fox, who sometimes spent weeks and even months on field assignments before becoming a dad. "Travel is an inextricable part of what I do. But it's hard to leave my family behind. I'm still taking on traveling assignments, but thinking through more carefully when the travel will occur, and trying not to stack trips too close together."

For me, some reporting opportunities are simply no longer an option. For example, I recently turned down a spot on a ten-day research cruise with guaranteed dives on the *Alvin,* a research submarine that makes trips to the seafloor. It was an opportunity I'd wanted for well over a decade, ever since my research days in a marine biology lab. There was simply no way for me to be away from the kids for nearly two weeks—and I really didn't want to be away from my family for that long, either. A few months later, I heard a story from that research cruise on NPR and gave a long, resigned sigh. These are, of course, the inherent trade-offs of parenthood. But the loss of income, or important opportunities, can sting.

As long as you're not going to the bottom of the ocean, though, there's no shortage of creative ways to manage work travel with young kids. You might bring the whole family along, pairing a reporting trip with a mini–family vacation. Or you might consider bringing along a parent, in-law, or friend to watch the baby while you work.

But don't be surprised if traveling while your children are young—particularly if you are nursing—puts you in some compromising positions. I once had to use a breast pump in a boat on rough seas, standing up, in a bathroom smaller than a phone booth. It wasn't a pleasant experience, but it *was* strangely gratifying in that "I can have my career and feed the baby, too" kind of way.

Whether you wait to travel until your baby is fourteen months old, as I did with my first child, or five months old, like I did with my second—

When I travel, my well of patience for my kids is refilled. I also feel like it helps reestablish me as a contributing professional member of the household.

—JESSICA MARSHALL

or whether you travel after weeks or even years—we can't say enough about how refreshing it is to enjoy some uninterrupted reading time on the airplane, to be reminded of what it is that you enjoy about your career, and to be rejuvenated by colleagues.

No one said this would be easy—and it's not. But like us, you can find your own way of making this work. You can have your children and your career, too.

I went on my first business trip—to a National Association of Science Writers meeting—when my son was seven months old. I was glad I went. It gave me confidence that everything was going to be okay at home without me. And it reconnected me with the work I had come to feel distanced from. I was surprised that instead of wanting to sleep a lot, I ended up staying up late having real conversations with real adults. It was wonderful.

—EMILY SOHN

SciLance says . . .

- The flexibility of freelancing can allow you to **design your work schedule** to suit the needs of you and your family.

- When it comes to babylancing, "balance" isn't a realistic goal. But if one scenario isn't working, **experiment with other options**, such as swapping five half workdays for three or four full days.

- Try to **reserve naptime for activities that can be turned on and off quickly**, such as proofreading or sending invoices, rather than tasks that involve deep concentration, such as writing.

- **At-home child care can be a dream arrangement or a total distraction** (and sometimes both in the same day). Only you can decide if it works for you.

- **When you find yourself feeling like a fugitive hiding out in your office**, it might be time to consider other child-care options.

- Trying to juggle child care and work at the same time is a recipe for stress and unhappiness. **Make child-care arrangements, and treat them as a cost of doing business.**

- **Don't expect the same level of productivity** that you had pre-kids. Adjust your workload accordingly, and don't over-commit.

- Allow yourself to **ramp back up to work slowly** after the arrival of a newborn, and acknowledge the limitations of your tired "baby brain."

- Travel will almost certainly be curtailed by the arrival of a new baby or by the needs of growing children. But you can **be creative with balancing family and work travel**.

PART III

THE SOLVENT
SCIENCE WRITER

Chapter 19

Minding the Business

By Anne Sasso and Emily Gertz

● "Let's say that you invest $1,000 this year and the bank pays you 10 percent," Anne's dad said as he sat across the kitchen table from his pre-teen daughter, scribbling on a piece of paper. "At the end of the year you'll have $1,100. Now if you leave that money in the account, the next year you'll earn $110 in interest. Leave that in the following year, you'll get $121. The number grows each year. That's how compound interest works. It's the secret to saving for retirement."

These kitchen-table financial lessons were a part of Anne's childhood. By the time she was grown up and running her own business, she already understood many of the basics of how to make it as a freelance science writer. Emily has also benefitted from her dad's experience as a small-business owner as she's developed her business and retirement strategies.

Not all science writers have entrepreneurial parents, of course. But that doesn't mean we can't learn to navigate the business side of the profession. If you're a freelancer, you're a small-business owner, whether you think about it that way or not. And if you've got a staff job, business know-how may help you choose an employer with good prospects for long-term success, and plan defensively for expected and unexpected turns in the economy.

Here, we'll cover the pros and cons of incorporating, the basics of good record keeping, and how to deal proactively with insurance and savings.

Business Structures: One Size Doesn't Fit All

As Anne's dad often counseled her, business owners need to prepare for their tax bill—by selecting a business structure, keeping records and receipts, and attending to some accounting basics. We'll focus on the US for specific terms and regulations, but the principles apply no matter where you're based.

Since most freelancers are one-person shops, there are only three types of business structures to consider: sole proprietor, limited liability company (LLC), and corporation. The three structures differ in the protection they offer your personal assets from potential lawsuits and in their effects on your tax bill.

Let's deal with protection first.

If you're already freelancing—signing contracts, paying business expenses, cashing checks for the articles you write—the Internal Revenue Service (IRS) considers you a sole proprietor. This is the default setting. You must fill out and file a Schedule C form with your income taxes every year, to report your income and expenses—"profit and loss" in tax lingo. You also need to estimate your annual taxes a year in advance, and submit quarterly payments to both federal and state tax collectors throughout the year. (If you don't submit quarterly, expect to pay an additional percentage of your total tax amount as a penalty.) Other than meeting these requirements, there's nothing special that a sole proprietor must do.

Operating as a sole proprietor is probably the best way to start a freelancing business, because you're operating legally and the paperwork is minimal. If after a few years you decide that freelancing isn't for you, dissolving your business is as simple as going back to work for someone else.

But there's a catch: as a sole proprietor, there is no difference between you and your business. This means that if someone wants to sue your business—for libel, say, or breach of contract—your personal assets are fair game, too.

The happy reality is that most freelancers will never be sued. But a few are, and fighting even a groundless lawsuit can be time-consuming and expensive. Once you begin to accumulate wealth in the form of a house or retirement savings, you may start to worry that your work puts those assets at risk. Moving beyond sole proprietorship to form a business entity—a company or corporation that is separate from you the person—can offer protection as well as peace of mind. Anne's lawyer, Jim Foley Jr. of Deppman & Foley in Middlebury, Vermont, calls this sort of protection a "magic shield."

There are two shielding options available to freelancers: the LLC, short for "limited liability company," or the S Corporation (or S Corp;

the S refers to the part of the Internal Revenue Code under which the corporation is taxed). Both options offer comparable legal protection.

A corporation is easier to set up, says Foley, but its management requirements are rigid. Setting up an LLC is more involved but it's much easier to manage. Setting up either an S Corp or an LLC requires that you, your lawyer, or another designated agent (such as a "formation service") file paperwork with the appropriate department or office of your state government.

Forming an S Corp: An S Corp requires the creation of bylaws as well as a shareholder agreement. These are standard forms that set out in detail how to run the corporation, and can be obtained from a lawyer, formation agent, or a legal publisher such as Nolo. Since the forms are standardized, setting up the S Corp is fairly straightforward, which can help to minimize legal fees. The downside is there's no room for exceptions to the rules in how you structure the corporation.

Do you need a lawyer or registration agent to incorporate? You can certainly do it on your own, and save a little money in the process, with help from local small-business resource centers and online resources. Filing the paperwork with your state is easy enough. Drafting the bylaws, shareholders agreement, or operating agreement is more involved. Publishing the required public notifications and obtaining proof of publication from the newspaper isn't hard to do, but it can be easy to forget about. It may be helpful to have a lawyer on the sidelines to review the paperwork and ensure the process doesn't get derailed by mistakes.

For tax purposes, both income and profits are treated differently under LLCs and S Corps. Let's take a closer look.

If you earn a salary, a portion of each paycheck goes to income tax, Social Security, and Medicare. Your employer also pays for its portion of your Social Security and Medicare contributions, as required by law.

As a freelancer, you're on the hook for both the employer and employee portions of Social Security and Medicare taxes, which the government refers to collectively as a self-employment tax. This self-employment tax is rolled into the quarterly income taxes that the federal government expects you to pay.

An S Corp provides the opportunity to treat income and profits separately. With this structure, the IRS expects you to pay yourself a "reasonable" wage, which is subject to self-employment taxes. Self-employment taxes cover your income tax obligation as well as your Social Security and Medicare contributions. Any profits generated by the company also pass through to you at the end of the year. These are considered "distributions" by the IRS; you must pay income tax on them, but they are not subject to the Social Security and Medicare contribution portion of self-employment taxes, so you'll pay a lower rate overall.

The ability to pay yourself a low but reasonable salary and then take the extra profit as a distribution at the end of the year can significantly lower your effective tax rate, and reduce the size of the quarterly checks you write to the IRS. The trade-off is that taking a lower salary also reduces the amount you pay into Social Security each year, which means you'll get smaller checks from the government when you retire. Forming an S Corp helps you lower your tax and other obligations now, in other words, but in doing so, you're implicitly agreeing to shoulder more of the responsibility of saving for retirement yourself.

Forming an LLC: States often require an LLC to create an operating agreement, a document analogous to corporate bylaws. The operating agreement states the name of the company, where it is based, and who is involved (usually just you, as multiple officers are not required). It also defines the purpose of the business and how it will handle funds, establishes a schedule for meetings, and outlines how the company will be dissolved. If you work alone, the agreement is a legal record of how you plan to conduct business. If your LLC has multiple members, the rules can get much more complicated, because the rights, powers, ownership stake, tax responsibilities, and other details for each officer must be defined. Although there are no standardized LLC operating agreement forms, many lawyers have developed basic templates, Foley says, which help to reduce complexity and cost. These should be sufficient for most freelancers' purposes. That said, you could create from scratch the rules that govern how your company will operate. This offers greater flexibility, but means that the operating agreement will take more time to draft.

Like a sole proprietor, an LLC files an IRS Schedule C form at tax time, detailing profits and losses from the business. If you are the only officer of your LLC, all profits from the LLC flow through to you, its owner. They're considered income and are subject to self-employment taxes. In this scenario, the IRS does ease things a bit by offering the option to treat the LLC as a "disregarded entity" in terms of tax forms, essentially allowing you to file your taxes as a sole proprietor while also operating as an LLC. You'll want professional advice if you decide to explore that option.

The LLC structure also offers some tax advantages, according to Foley, especially for higher earners. Say, for example, that an exceptional income year threatens to bump you into a higher tax bracket. Because the LLC structure isn't as rigid as the corporate one, there are ways to legally move income around that reduce the company profits and thus avoid that higher tax rate. You should consult a lawyer or accountant to learn more about this.

The LLC structure also offers greater flexibility in estate planning, for instance, allowing you to pass on your estate to your heirs before you die (and thus minimizing their estate-tax bill). Again, consult the professionals to learn more and get help. It's worth knowing what the options are, even if, like most science writers, your payment comes in the form of professional satisfaction as much as tangible assets.

Finally, if you've already formed an LLC but wish you could take advantage of a corporation's ability to avoid some of the self-employment taxes, you're in luck. The IRS will allow you to treat your LLC like an S Corporation for tax purposes. It sounds like the best of both worlds, but there are complexities. Ask an accountant if this option is right for you, especially if you're earning more than $50,000 per year.

Bottom line: If you're a freelancer, have been in business for at least a few years, and have assets such as a home, it's worth taking the time and investing the money to set up a "magic shield." You'll want to talk to an accountant to decide which structure is right for you.

Bookkeeping Basics

To take advantage of the income-sheltering options available from your business structure and the tax code, you have to get serious about keeping track of your income and expenses. Simple, regular bookkeeping is also the secret to tracking the success, or failure, of your science writing venture.

Some SciLancers take to accounting naturally, while others have struggled to keep reliable books. But we all agree it's a crucial part of being a science writer. "Filling out and filing spreadsheets is no fun at all, and administrative tasks are certainly not creative," says Emily Sohn. But forcing herself to act and think like a professional has helped Emily figure out what she's worth and demand that value. "Sometimes I just imagine that

I'm a plumber," she says. "I fixed your toilet. Now you pay me. If you change your mind about what kind of toilet you want, I'm happy to redo it—as long as you pay me extra for my time."

Stephen Ornes loves measurements and takes his business tracking to a joyful extreme. He keeps spreadsheets on current income, past income patterns, projections into the future, and best- and worst-case income scenarios. He also tracks average time interval from assignment to average payment per assignment. "These models help me set benchmarks for myself that give me peace of mind, even though they may or may not be useful in other ways," he says. "I know it's time to pitch, for example, if I see that I have less than $10,000 owed to me. Seriously, the mental peace I feel from all these numbers is worth it. It makes me feel legitimate."

You can do substantially less and still achieve significant financial peace of mind. Spend a little time each week or month recording your income and expenses and you'll find that setting rates, chasing down overdue checks, covering the bills, and paying taxes accurately and on time will be much easier.

Fortunately, for a one-person business the bookkeeping tasks are pretty simple. What follows is a quick look at the essential aspects of one-person business accounting—enough to get you going, help you formulate questions for an accountant or fellow freelancer, or pick out a more specialized how-to guide.

Single Versus Double, Cash Versus Accrual

There are two basic ways to keep books: *single entry* and *double entry.* For most freelance writers, who have no investors to please or inventory to track, single entry is more than sufficient. As the name implies, it involves making one entry per transaction—purchase of printer paper, say, or receipt of a fee for an article—in your bookkeeping system.

The next choice is between two accounting methods: *cash* or *accrual.* In the cash method of bookkeeping, you make an entry in your records only when money actually comes in or goes out—once you've handed your cash or debit card over for the printer paper, or deposited the magazine's check in the bank. With the accrual method, you enter income and expenses as they occur, not when payments are made or received. So, for instance, when you buy a computer on credit, you account for it right away, not when you pay the bill. And you add an article fee as income when you send in the final draft, not when you receive your fee.

Cash accounting is the simplest method. But for some freelancers the accrual method has some added utility. Freelance journalism work is often paid *upon publication* rather than *upon acceptance,* with articles appearing in print or pixels months (even years, in some dreadful cases) after you've submitted your final draft. Accrual accounting won't help make the money come any faster, but it can give you a better picture of your overall financial state than your bank balance alone will do. The most important thing isn't what style of accounting you choose, however, but that you use it to do regular accounting.

Once you have selected cash versus accrual, it is hard to switch, since these methods of record keeping have fundamental differences. So consider carefully which will best meet your needs, and which you'll be most likely to maintain well over time.

Tracking Income and Expenses

For both income and expenses, there are several basic items of information you'll need to record: the date, a description of the transaction, the amount, and the category of income or expense. One way to set up categories for expenses is to label them according to how they may be deducted from annual taxes.

Similarly, if you have multiple streams of income that may require different treatment at tax time, you may find it helpful to include that information in the category column.

Written Versus Computerized Bookkeeping

When considering whether to keep manual books or an online accounting ledger, ask yourself: Which are you more likely to maintain from day to day? For some, it is easier and quicker to write down income and expenses in a preprinted ledger kept on the bookshelf. At tax time, it takes only a few hours to convert that information into tax-readiness.

Compared to manual bookkeeping, computerized methods can take a lot of time to learn and set up. Their virtue is in their flexibility: many systems allow you to view your financial books and create reports from different perspectives at the touch of a button; search for entries; and easily categorize entries for tax purposes.

Because computer tools and programs appear and disappear quickly, we won't make specific recommendations here. (Microsoft Excel spreadsheets are standing the test of time, though, and can be great tools for bookkeeping.) Talk with fellow science writers about the programs that work for them.

Do You Need an Accountant?

The ups and downs of freelance income make it tempting, even necessary in some years, to tackle income-tax filing on our own. But tax laws have become so complex and changeable that unless it's your full-time job, it's hard to keep up, and easy to make costly mistakes. That's where an accountant comes in: a professional whose job it is to keep up with the tax rules, breaks, and changes that can help you pay what you owe and no more.

An accountant who specializes in working with freelancers will know more about tax rules affecting and benefiting the self-employed than your average storefront accounting firm. He or she can help you optimize your income (see retirement planning, below), itemize your expenses to greatest benefit, and deal with extra complexities, such as homeowner or medical expenses.

Again, asking your colleagues for recommendations is a good way to start. Professional associations for journalists, writers, or freelancers may also be useful: Emily Gertz, who is a member of Freelancers Union, often uses the group's online listings to search for services.

Paying the Tax Man

Paying taxes is part of the freelance gig—whether you write part-time, as a sideline to a staff job, or even just once or twice a year as a hobby. Despite the complexity of the tax code, the basic equation is pretty simple: all income should be recorded and most of the expenses related to earning that income can be deducted. What remains is taxable income.

I knew I was legitimate when I saw my tax bill from the first year. Ouch! But a good ouch. The ouch of legitimacy.
—STEPHEN ORNES

Since freelancers don't get regular paychecks, taxes aren't collected when you're paid. Instead, the IRS expects freelancers to make quarterly payments of estimated taxes for the current year in April, June, September, and January. The onus is on freelancers to do so, and the penalty for failing to comply can be severe.

Without planning, it is easy to be caught without enough cash when those payments come due. Anne puts 15 percent of every check into a separate bank account for quarterly taxes. She has arrived at the 15 percent figure through trial and error over a number of years, and it seems to be about right. This way the money is available at tax time and she's not panicking because a client is late with the check that she was counting on to pay her taxes. Anne manages such a low effective tax rate by putting as much as the law allows into her retirement fund (see below), carefully tracking deductions, and, unfortunately, having a somewhat elevated business overhead that comes from paying a crew of designers, transcribers, proofreaders, and assorted other professionals for their help with projects.

Emily also puts aside money. Thanks to the home mortgage deduction, as well as deductions for business use of her home, she's able to reduce her effective tax rate each year. The detailed pros and cons of taking a deduction for business use of your home are beyond the scope of this chapter, but if you're a homeowner, you'll want to raise the issue with an accountant.

Your quarterly tax payments are based on the amount of income tax you paid in the previous year. As long as you follow that rule, you'll stay on the right side of the IRS. That said, it's worth monitoring your income and modifying payments as needed. Having a much better year than last? Increase your quarterly payments. Taking a hit? Reduce them.

By carefully monitoring how your current income compares to the previous year's, you can probably avoid the need to come up with a big chunk of cash to make up a shortfall at tax time, or giving the government too much of your money throughout the year. Sure, you'll get any overpayment back as a refund. But wouldn't you rather keep your money in your pocket, working for you, than tie it up in an interest-free loan to Uncle Sam?

Write 'til You Die

The writing world is full of talented professionals who continue to produce well past the typical age of retirement. Still, many of us SciLancers envision a day when we're in a position, once again, to write for the simple joy of putting words on paper.

"I don't see retirement as leaving my job and ceasing to work," says Robert Frederick. "Instead, I see retirement as a time when I have the financial freedom so that I never have to take a project I don't want to do, and can drop a project if I find I don't like it."

If that's your vision, a little retirement planning will go a long way toward achieving it. But in the daily sprint of science writing, there's little time to think like a marathoner. Mark Schrope, for example, says he thinks about retirement a lot: "And the thoughts are generally things like, 'Wow, I really ought to do a better job with retirement.' I try to make IRA contributions, but have failed miserably."

As Anne's dad knew during their kitchen-table talks about compound interest, the earlier you start to save, the more time your savings have to grow, and the more you'll have to tap when you eventually retire. It might seem impossible to save now, but doing so is all the more important if, like most science writers, your income is modest.

Fortunately, squirreling money away for retirement fits well with our other major business mission: reducing taxes. That's because the government allows us to defer the taxes paid on money we set aside for retirement until we start to use it. With less or no income then, we'll theoretically be in a lower tax bracket, and thus save money when it's finally time to pay.

If you have a staff job and your employer offers a 401(k) or other optional retirement savings plan, contribute as much as you are allowed by the plan, or at least what is needed to maximize the match from your company. Employers often offer a match only up to a set limit, but whatever they do match is essentially free money. For freelancers, the Individual Retirement Account (IRA) is the most basic government-approved structure available for retirement savings. Most banks offer IRAs that are easy to set up on your own, as do many asset-management firms. Choosing how much to invest, and in what, is another thing. The choices range from mutual funds, individual stocks, and bonds to complicated real estate investments, such as a real estate investment trust (REIT), and assorted other investment vehicles. Since IRAs are long-term investments, most financial advisers like to park money in one vehicle, a mutual fund, for example, letting it grow over time and rebalancing the portfolio as needed rather than actively trading stocks based on market news and emotional gyrations. The government sets an annual cap, though. The yearly maximum you're allowed to contribute at this writing is $5,000. It's a start on retirement savings, but not nearly enough, especially if you earn more than $35,000 per year or plan to retire soon.

The next step up is a SEP-IRA (Simplified Employee Pension Plan–Individual Retirement Account). These are similar to traditional IRAs but allow you to set aside considerably more money—and therefore reduce your taxable income by a greater amount. At this writing, you can contribute up to 25 percent of your net adjusted self-employment income, with a maximum of $42,000 per year. SEP-IRAs require a formal plan and must be set up by a bank or an investment adviser. Fees can vary widely, so it's a good idea to shop around.

Then there's the Roth IRA. The attraction of the Roth, in the opinion of many investment pundits, is that you pay taxes now and can withdraw the money tax-free in the future. The gamble is that taxes will be higher in the future than they are now and you'll save money in the long run. Basic Roth IRAs have an annual limit of $5,500 (as of 2013), but like regular IRAs, they come in all kinds of variations that can let you put aside more. Check with your investment adviser.

Robert puts as much of his retirement funds as he can in a Roth, choosing it as his preferred retirement vehicle. Anne's accountant advises her to put the maximum into her SEP-IRA and forgo a Roth, unless she has extra money she might otherwise fritter away. This strategy minimizes taxes in the short term.

Emily also saves for retirement with a SEP-IRA, but balances her fund contributions with investments in her home, which she considers her primary retirement investment. It's a good option for Emily because she bought relatively inexpensively into an area with a robust real estate market. It also doesn't hurt that she plans to stay put for a long time—possibly until she dies, but at least until she retires. Using real estate to build up a retirement fund isn't for everyone, however, and comes with its own range of risks and expenses.

There are many different ways of saving for retirement. Ultimately, just like business accounting, it doesn't matter so much how you do it, as long as you do it.

Insurance: Planning for the Worst

Insurance is a form of risk management. You pay an insurance company an agreed-upon amount, called a premium. It, in turn, promises to cover some or all of your expenses under certain conditions. If those conditions don't arise, the insurer makes money on the deal. But if you make a legitimate claim, the insurer pays at the terms specified in the insurance contract.

Health, dental, and disability insurance plans are ways that we manage the risk of finding ourselves needing medical care, or unable to work due

I think health insurance is the single biggest obstacle to freelancing in the United States. It is frustrating to be broke not because you aren't hardworking or good at what you do, but because you are a source of profit for the health insurance industry.

—EMMA MARRIS

to illness or injury. They're another means of investing in and protecting ourselves and our careers.

If you live in a nation where the government provides universal access to health care, you probably don't need to read any further. (Unless, that is, you want to feel a shiver of relief running down your spine.)

If you live in the US, however, your investment in health insurance comes at a high price. Medical spending in the US—including the price of insurance—is about half again as much per capita as that of our peers in other industrialized countries. Because the American system ties health insurance to employment, health insurance can be a major barrier to going freelance. "My individual health insurance cost $128 per month when I started in 2002," says Douglas Fox. "By 2011, my premium had hit $586 per month. I finally dumped my coverage at the end of 2011 and went on my wife's work plan."

Many freelance science writers have similar stories about uncovered medical emergencies or skyrocketing insurance costs, sometimes in return for diminished coverage. As a result, many are forced to make major life decisions based on the availability of health care coverage, rather than on their dreams and ambitions.

The Affordable Care Act

As we wrote this book in 2012, the US Supreme Court upheld the Affordable Care Act (ACA) of 2010—the federal health insurance reform law. Under the law, state-by-state "affordable insurance exchanges" will make it easier for individuals to find and compare private health insurance plans, as well as test eligibility for public health programs and insurance-premium tax credits.

These exchanges should help freelancers at almost any income level find affordable health insurance, although the level of coverage will still vary based on what you pay for. (Note: If your state doesn't create an exchange by 2014, the federal government will operate one on your state's behalf.)

Until then, we're on our own . . . mostly. If you have an existing health issue that insurers are using to deny you coverage—a "preexisting condition" in industry lingo—check into getting a "preexisting-condition insurance plan." This is a new kind of coverage created by the ACA as a bridge to 2014, when the law will make it illegal for insurers to refuse coverage on these grounds.

How to Find Coverage

Health insurance is offered at the state level, which means that plans vary widely by location. If you're under age twenty-six, your parents can add you to their health insurance coverage, as long as it already covers dependents. Most SciLancers get their health insurance in one of the following ways:

- By paying into a spouse's employer-backed plan.
- Directly from insurance companies, also called "the individual market." These plans will be folded into the ACA-mandated health insurance exchanges in or by 2014.
- Through a health insurance agent, who may represent more than one company.
- From an organization that offers group insurance plans to its members. Freelance writers can look into offerings from groups such as Mediabistro, the National Writers Union, Freelancers Union, and the American Society of Journalists and Authors. Chambers of commerce, credit unions, and local business associations may also offer access to group plans.

Dental, life, and disability plans can be easier to find, because such plans can be offered nationally, often by the same groups and organizations. Emily gets her health, dental, and disability coverage through the Freelancers Insurance Company, which was formed by Freelancers Union. She appreciates that FIC makes it simple for members to compare the costs and coverage associated with different plans, and works to keep annual premium increases low, compared to the individual market. She also swears by having a dental insurance plan. Even though her plan's $1,000 annual cap on claims is ridiculously low compared to the cost of a root canal or crown, say, the reimbursements still surpass what she pays in premiums.

Anne joined her local chamber of commerce to get access to health and dental coverage. She was surprised when an insurance agent affiliated with the chamber came out to her home office to discuss the various plans offered by the organization. Having someone who is familiar with the plans walk you through them can help you better decide which plan is right for you.

Picking a Plan

When considering what a health insurance plan will cost you, it's important to look at how your expenses are spread across several plan features:

Premium: The money you pay monthly (or sometimes quarterly) to be a member of the plan.

Copayment: A predetermined fee that you pay each time you visit a doctor.

Deductible: The amount you must pay out of pocket annually, before the insurance company will begin to cover your medical costs.

Coinsurance: A percentage of medical costs that the member must continue to pay even after reaching his or her deductible, up to a yearly maximum amount specified by the insurance company.

Prescription drug coverage: This may come with copayments, deductibles, or cost-sharing terms separate from the rest of the health insurance plan. The list of medications the plan will cover is often called "the formulary."

Annual or lifetime coverage limits: The Affordable Care Act bans maximum lifetime dollar amounts on health insurance benefits and mandates that insurers phase out annual maximums by 2014.

Health insurance usually comes in one of the following flavors:

Major medical: Also called "catastrophic" insurance, this is a safety net that will help pay for major expenses, such as emergency-room treatment and surgery. But it won't cover basic medical needs, such as preventive care. Your payment per month or quarter will be relatively low, but expect to pay many hundreds or thousands of dollars out of pocket before the plan begins to cover your emergency costs.

HMO: Health management organizations typically keep your out-of-pocket costs low by requiring you to see doctors in a particular medical group, and not covering costs for physicians or services outside the group.

POS: Point-of-service plans usually offer modestly priced access to in-network doctors, HMO-style, and not-so-modestly priced access to out-of-network doctors and services.

PPO: Preferred provider organizations offer the most choice, by allowing you to choose between doctors and medical facilities that have contracted with the insurer, and those that have not. However, your total out-of-pocket costs will be much lower if you stay with doctors and facilities "in the plan."

When it comes time to pick a plan, it's easy to become overwhelmed with all the details. But if you can write about complex science, you can figure out which plan is best for you. Just treat it as a reporting project.

Emily and Anne have developed similar methodologies for selecting health insurance. Anne made a spreadsheet of what various plans offered her. Then she narrowed the options based on what she felt her health and finances could tolerate: she eliminated all the plans that had a lifetime maximum and steep coinsurance payments, but decided she was willing to accept a higher annual deductible in exchange for more reasonable monthly premiums. She also asked a neighbor, a retired insurance industry executive, to go over the plans with her. After a session at his kitchen table, she was ready to select a plan.

Emily also creates a spreadsheet every December, when "open enrollment" time arrives. She compares the premiums, deductibles, coinsurance, and copays that the different PPO plans charge. Then she enters her expected medical needs and expenses for the coming year, including prescription drug costs, regular care as well as care from specialists, and tests beyond the basics. While it can't account for the unexpected, comparing these known and anticipated costs helps her rationally select coverage for the coming year.

Managing Medical Expenses

Anne, Emily, and many other SciLancers have found that even though they're shelling out what seem like ridiculously high premiums every month, there will still be bills to pay if they get sick or injured:

> When Anne's family doctor ordered an MRI after Anne got her second hockey-related concussion in ten months, she thought the test would be an interesting science-y experience. And it was, until the bill showed up. Her portion of the nearly $3,000 bill? $1,700. (Anne's brain, by the way, was fine.)

> Despite having what she considers good (for a freelancer) health insurance, Emily found herself in debt for over $10,000 in coinsurance payments one year, when an anticipated knee surgery and physical therapy was followed six months later by a totally unexpected cancer diagnosis, surgery, and weeks of subsequent chemotherapy and radiation treatment. (Emily turned out fine, too.)

If you are confronted with high medical bills that you can't pay at once, here are a few dos and don'ts:

- Do get as much information ahead of time as you can about what a particular examination, test, treatment, or procedure is going to cost you out of pocket.
- Do be sure that your medical care provider is obtaining the needed preapprovals from your insurer; without this approval, the insurer may refuse coverage.
- Do look into whether your insurer offers a "managed care" service, if you are embarking on an extended period of treatment. This can help speed preapprovals and ease other provider-insurer interactions.
- Do talk with your doctor's/facility's billing office about the options for paying over time.
- Do ask your hospital or clinic if it offers a financial assistance program.
- Don't necessarily take no for an answer. If your insurer turns down a claim, find out why. You may have good reason to appeal that decision.

- If you don't have the cash on hand to pay your medical expenses, don't put them on a credit card. Medical billing offices usually don't charge interest and are often much more flexible about payment schedules than credit card lenders are.
- Do update the billing office regularly if you're having trouble paying a bill, to avoid having your account sent to a collection agency.
- If you're losing work time and income because of your illness, do look into joining income-based public programs such as Medicaid. They're called "safety nets" for a reason.

Disability Insurance

"I wish I could knock on every freelancer's door and ask, 'Do you have disability insurance?'" says Ann Boger, chief operating officer of Freelancers Union. "A lot of things can happen that can stop you from working. You can save up, but the 'what if' scenario is so important to plan for, and so few people think of disability insurance as part of that landscape."

Disability insurance can help out during temporary, short-term disabilities or family health crises that prevent you from working.

While access to and costs for disability plans can differ a lot, in our experience there are some common features to consider:

- A choice of how long you have to be unable to work before you can make a claim; typical waiting period options are thirty days and ninety days. Shorter waiting periods mean higher premiums. Longer waiting periods mean lower premiums, but also that you need to have a larger emergency fund to tide you over until payments start rolling in.
- Premiums that increase with both age and income.
- Requirements to produce proof of income.
- Exclusions or waiting periods for preexisting conditions: Health issues that predate your disability insurance coverage may not be covered.

Anne recently applied for disability coverage through her chamber of commerce, and it's proving to be an intensive process, full of detailed questions about her health and finances. But her recent concussion during a charity hockey tournament, which affected her ability to work for six months, gave her some perspective on the importance of disability coverage.

When Emily signed up for her disability insurance through Freelancers Union, she was not asked a lot of detailed questions. (As a member of the group, she was qualified for the plan.) But she did so reactively, after learning she had a serious illness. "I was diagnosed with breast cancer. We caught it early, but even so, the treatments left me with all sorts of aches, pains, fatigue, and scrambled brains."

Since her diagnosis predated her coverage, Emily learned that she might have to wait even longer than her ninety-day exclusion period to receive disability benefits. But she is still lucky, because under New York law, insurance companies can't exclude preexisting conditions forever—only for twelve months. Other states may have different regulations, or even no requirement at all that an insurance company cover a preexisting condition.

Disability insurance isn't part of the Affordable Care Act, which means that previous conditions do indeed count, as Anne discovered. An insurance carrier agreed to cover her for disability but with strings: a trial two-year policy and the exclusion of all hockey-related injuries.

When a freelancer stops working, the checks stop coming. If you have savings, you may be able to weather the financial impact of an illness or injury . . . for a while. Disability insurance can make the freelance life less precarious. Says Boger, "I've seen so many cases of people who have a catastrophic accident, or a baby that ends up sick. It's such an important thing to have insurance in those instances."

In Case of Emergency . . . Don't Break the Bank

Unanticipated expenses are one of the greatest perils of modern life, and the uncertainty in the publishing industry makes science writers substantially more vulnerable. So on top of what you put aside for taxes and retirement (because those are taxes and retirement, not a rainy-day fund), you need to start building up an additional cash reserve to cover your costs if you become injured or sick; if you go through a stretch of unemployment; if the car needs a new transmission or your kid needs braces.

Think of it as your own insurance fund. But instead of sending a premium to an insurance company each month, you're putting the money in your own bank account. Ideally, your goal should be six months' standard expenses in a liquid, money market–type account. And like your retirement account, that money should be sacrosanct.

Saving for an emergency may seem impossible, especially if you're just starting out. Don't freak out. Just do what you can, even if it means deferring the instant gratification of a new smart phone, or curbing dinners out, or living with one roommate too many for another year before striking out on your own. If that rainy day ever comes, you'll be glad you were prepared. And if it doesn't, you'll have peace of mind and a nice chunk of money in the bank.

Growing as a Businessperson

Anne and her dad still discuss business at his kitchen table. Emily still turns to her father to help her untie budgeting knots, or to talk through the pros and cons of different investments. Explaining the problem out loud, answering questions, and getting a fresh perspective help each of them sort things out. Over the years they have also found other treasured advisers: Anne has a gem of a lawyer who never fails to give sound, pragmatic advice, while Emily has a brother-in-law able to parse problems with calm and logic.

Finding people whose opinions and advice you trust can make the business side of freelancing less intimidating. Help is available from family members, accountants and lawyers, local small-business groups, professional organizations, and your own network of colleagues. You just have to be willing to ask for it.

⚜ SciLance says . . .

- Some creative types might not like to hear this, but if you want **to succeed at science writing, you need to treat it as a business**.

- **Make a conscious, educated choice about your business structure**: Sole proprietorship is a convenient way to start

(Continues)

---

out but could leave your assets exposed to lawsuits, whereas creating an LLC or an S Corp provides a "magic shield" to protect you and your life beyond writing.

- Making money is an important part of freelance science writing. **Devote some attention to bookkeeping** to keep more of those dollars in your pocket.

- **Put aside a portion of every payment** that comes in to make paying taxes a lot easier.

- The sooner you **start to save for retirement**, the more dream-come-true and less nightmarish it will be.

- **Comparison shopping for health insurance** is low on our list of favorite activities. But being saddled with huge medical bills because we couldn't be bothered to read the fine print of our policies is at the rock bottom.

- After paying for health insurance premiums, and saving for taxes and retirement, the last thing we want is another expense. But **buying disability insurance is one of the smartest moves a freelancer can make**.

Chapter 20

Networking for the Nervous

By Cameron Walker

After my initial meeting with the director of the science writing program I would eventually attend, I was thrilled. I imagined myself curled up on a couch with lots of books, soaking up knowledge and then scribbling down my deep thoughts. It would be sort of like the fifth-grade report I did on Wisconsin, which relied heavily on the encyclopedia and featured lots of flowery phrases about cheese.

Somehow, the appearance of courses on my schedule like "News Writing," taught by a pleasantly crusty editor at the local paper, didn't clue me in. It was only when we started talking about how to interview sources that I realized I was actually going to have to get up off the couch and talk to people.

It was only later, once I was already working as a freelance journalist, that I realized this need to talk to people went beyond interviews, where I mostly got to listen. No, I would also have to talk to the editors I wanted to work for, and even worse, I would have to talk about myself.

I'd (mostly) gotten over my reporting jitters by realizing that scientists usually love to talk about their research. But a prospective editor was another creature altogether. I had story ideas, and a series of clips from different internships. But I just knew they would immediately notice my bad posture, oversize teeth, and tendency to talk like a Valley girl when excited—not to mention the fact that I didn't know what I was doing.

Starting out, though, gives writers the excuse to be bold. SciLancer Amanda Mascarelli took advantage of this beginner's mind. "For some reason, when I was working on my journalism master's degree, I had the benefit of being fearless about pitching and approaching editors," she says. "I think it's just because I hadn't yet experienced the continual sting of rejection."

I did some of that, too, sending e-mails to editors at places from *National Geographic*'s website to *Psychology Today*. When I didn't hear back, I didn't sweat it—and when I did, I was elated.

And along with getting a few assignments this way, despite my fears, no editor has ever made fun of my voice, or my teeth. If I can learn to network, you can, too.

Start at Home Base

For me, e-mail has taken a lot of the sting out of making connections. I've sent plenty of cold e-mails, which always include my pitch—targeted specifically to that particular magazine—a little bit about my experience, and my contact information. Most editors discourage prospective writers from pitching by phone, but if you're bold, a quick call can help make a connection—and ensure that your query e-mail doesn't go missing.

"For a totally new market, I very often call an editor up and say, 'Hey, I've got a pitch, and while I don't intend to pitch you on the phone, I do just want to make sure you were the right person to send this pitch to,'" says SciLancer Douglas Fox. "I try to send the pitch within two hours after that quick phone chat." The real point, he says, is to have a little human interaction that will make the editor more likely to notice the pitch when you send it, and to respond more quickly.

I've had a few brief stints behind editorial doors, and one of the things I've learned is that editors want to find a great story. Editors take pleasure in discovering a new writer, or stumbling on a story they've never heard of before. And this was a relief to discover, too: editors rarely sit around at a pitch meeting talking about how much a particular writer's teeth resemble a woodchuck's. And if they do, well, you probably don't want to work with them anyway.

To a writer, the reasons for rejection are often mysterious. In reality, the editor could be having a bad hair day when you pitch a story about the science of balding, or maybe the publisher has a personal aversion to reptiles. Or salt. (Read much more about handling rejection in Chapter 13.) That's where getting to know an editor, even virtually, can provide useful insight into both his or her personal tastes and the hidden quirks of the publication. Case in point: The salt thing really happened. I once had to rewrite a long feature lede because it mentioned a chef salting some food, and the publisher didn't want to promote cardiovascular disease—something that I learned later from my editor.

Of course, e-mail is only the beginning of virtual networking. I've experimented with a range of Internet platforms, including a professional website, Facebook, LinkedIn, Twitter, Tumblr, YouTube—and by the time you read this, there will probably be an entirely new list of online opportunities for making connections. (Emily Gertz outlines social-networking strategies in Chapter 24.)

Despite some initial reluctance, I've come to depend on virtual networking, not least to boost my fuzzy memory. Recently an editor friend was looking for help with a book project. I knew I'd worked with a terrific woman a few years ago who would be a good fit, but I couldn't remember her last name. So I just clicked over to LinkedIn, scrolled down through my contacts, and—*voila!*—put the two of them in touch. Networking works both ways, and it's nice to be able to use it to help other people, too.

Play Well with Other Writers

E-mail, online groups, and social networking can also help you stay in touch with other writers. But aren't other writers the competition? If we've learned anything from SciLance, it's that the answer is no, even when it's yes. (Read more about this contradiction in Chapter 14, "Beyond Compare.") Other writers can be your best allies, and a great source of advice, information, and commiseration. And they often have better perspective on particular editors and outlets than the editors themselves.

Besides, if you really want to be mercenary about it, the writer you know today could become an editor at your favorite magazine tomorrow. Being part of a community of writers can bring jobs when a writer friend is overbooked or provide an opening line for an almost-cold pitch ("One of my colleagues suggested I contact you about this story").

One caveat: Be careful when using a contact provided by a friend. If a friend offers the name of an editor but not a personal introduction, don't use your friend's name in your pitch—your friend simply may not know the editor well enough to feel comfortable making an introduction. If you're uncertain, ask your friend if you can use her name. And whether you're contacting an editor about her recent call for pitches or just passing along information about an editor to a friend, always, always, take the time to create a fresh e-mail. Don't just forward the note your writer buddy sent you, complete with its vivid description of how the editor can be a pain in the neck to work with.

Just Show Up

As much as I like the nice safe cave of my office, and as essential as the online world is to my writing life, there's something special about meeting a potential editor, source, or new favorite colleague in person.

At first I did this through internships. I got to know editors and writers at work, saw them interact with one another, and got a better sense of what that particular publication was all about. I left several short-term jobs with freelance assignments in hand. Many of the people I worked with as an intern have gone on to other publications and taken me with them as a freelancer.

Internships helped SciLancer Virginia Gewin make lots of connections, too. Her stint with *Nature* in Washington, D.C., was a prime opportunity to meet editors. When one of them moved over to *PLOS Biology,* she asked Virginia to write a feature for the first issue—a story that led to several years of steady work.

Once your intern days are over, scientific meetings and writers' conferences become the epicenters of science writer networking. Conferences range from the enormous—the American Association for the Advancement of Science (AAAS) annual meeting attracts reporters, editors, researchers, and students from around the world—to a wide range of much more specialized and intimate meetings. Big conferences offer the chance to connect with more people, but smaller ones can allow you to hang out and enjoy extended conversations instead of rushing around to dozens of different sessions.

"I've come to believe that there's no substitute for going to conferences and meeting editors, or at least hearing their talks," says SciLancer Robin Mejia. You'll learn more about their interests and priorities, and perhaps make a personal connection, too. The strategy works so well, she's even taken to re-creating the serendipity of a conference conversation by cold-calling local editors when she travels, to ask for a meeting just to introduce herself and talk about the outlet.

If you've never attended a scientific conference or a writers' conference, you'll probably want to start locally, or with the annual meeting of the National Association of Science Writers (NASW). (Like most of these meetings, it moves location from year to year—you can find information about the next one at www.nasw.org.) The NASW meeting combines sessions on the craft and business of science writing with scientific talks and briefings, and is particularly welcoming to new science writers.

If you want to meet scientists, it can be easier to head to an academic meeting that fewer of your media colleagues will be attending. As Chapter 2 points out, chances are you'll find under-covered stories, and sources eager to share their work with the press. As a bonus, many academic conferences will let in members of the press, including freelancers, for free. Look for the "media registration" section on the conference website; for smaller conferences, you may need to contact the conference organizers and ask about their press policy.

If your work taps into social media (or you would like it to), hit up the Science Online conference, known as a schmoozefest for scientists, journalists, bloggers, and others who are working to communicate, celebrate, and promote science online.

If you cover a particular beat—the environment, for example—look for focused conferences held by professional societies, such as the Society of Environmental Journalists (SEJ). "When I went to my first SEJ conference," says SciLancer Jennifer Cutraro, "I made a point of sitting in on a session on environmental toxins moderated by Beth Daley, the *Boston Globe*'s environmental reporter." Jennifer had lived in Boston for less than a year at that point and really wanted to break into the *Globe*. She introduced herself after the session, "and Beth was beyond friendly and helpful—the first thing she said to me was, 'Oh, do you want to write for us?'"

Back in Boston, Daley introduced Jennifer to section editors, and within a week or two, she had her first assignment at the newspaper. "I was so nervous before introducing myself to Beth," Jennifer recalls. "I didn't want to come off as pushy, or as only wanting to meet her because I wanted to get something out of her. But then I realized, huh, that's half the reason why people go to these meetings. So don't be afraid to just say hello. And don't focus exclusively on meeting editors!"

Navigating the Press Room

So you've got your conference badge and the huge stack of papers that a conference organizer handed you at check-in. What next? You can just strike up a conversation with someone, if that comes naturally. For me, it doesn't.

One science-writing professor of mine urged his class to hang out in the press room to meet other journalists (and the university press officers who are busy trying to network with them). At my first conference, I ducked in and out of the press room, hovered by the coffee, and wondered how I was supposed to be meeting all of these journalists. So I started slowly, trying to commit to sitting for five minutes, then ten, to drink my cup of coffee. I found the few people I did know and talked with them, and introduced myself to their friends. If someone was sitting alone at a table and looked like he was just hanging out, not working, I asked if I could pull up a chair.

Beyond the press room, I use what an art-enthusiast friend once told me about visiting museums: you only have to stand and gaze at paintings *you* really like, not necessarily the Mona Lisa. Over the years, I've gotten better at treating meetings the same way: going to events that actually interest me, from field trips to workshops to poster sessions. So what if everyone seems to be heading to the big-name talk on cancer research? If you want to go to one about the science of chocolate instead, do it. You might meet someone with common interests. This sounds like dating advice from my mother, but she's right—at least some of the time.

Many conferences and events offer sessions and activities specifically for networking, from one-on-one sessions with editors to meet-other-writers lunches. New writers can often sign up to be mentored by a jaded old journalist—I mean, an experienced, seasoned one—who can talk about how he or she approaches a meeting and gets to know people. At these sorts of events, I feel less awkward making contacts, since everyone knows that's the reason we're all there.

You also don't have to travel far to meet people. Local events—from lectures to writing-focused groups—can be a great way to learn more about your community and meet a few new friends. If there's a college or university nearby, check out events on campus, and get in contact with the public information office. Same goes for research institutes and nonprofit groups—if there's a lecture that sounds interesting, why not check it out? As a writer, even one who's just starting out, you have a license to invite yourself to all sorts of interesting events. I even tend to linger in front of bulletin boards, looking for a flyer that might spark an idea or lead to a potential new job. (My husband always thinks I'm spacing out, but there's a method behind my madness.)

As you read in Chapter 2, story ideas are everywhere. So are potential contacts. I met an editor from *Sierra* magazine at the dessert table of my

Recently, at a new-to-me conference where I knew no one, I gave myself the challenge of approaching and engaging a new person at every break. I wasn't allowed to return to my room. I wasn't allowed to spend inordinate amounts of time checking my outfit in the ladies' room. So I sidled up to groups at breakfast. Struck up conversations with people sitting next to me in the conference talks. I even talked to folks on elevators. Some of the interactions were indeed weird and awkward, but most of them turned into really fun conversations.

—ANNE SASSO

childhood best friend's wedding. A few months ago, another parent turned me on to a potential job as we worked in the garden bed at our kids' preschool. The intern you spend a few minutes advising at a conference mixer may one day be an editor at your favorite publication—and may well remember the favor you did for her.

I don't wander around with the intention of networking. (Ugh.) But I do think that showing up, listening to people, and just plain old being nice can get you pretty far. Maybe that's naive, and if you want more of that, the truth is that I really do believe that doing good work, and being pleasant to work with, are the best—maybe the only—ways to successfully sell yourself. Editors will want to come back to you, and other writers will want to hang out with you. That's the payoff of the most genuine strategy of all.

The Introvert's Survival Guide for Conference Cocktail Parties

Imagine everyone is wearing only underwear. Just kidding. This one never works for me—it makes me frightened.

Run, don't walk, toward your social lubricant of choice—but have only enough that you feel social, not sloppy. (Don't drink? Bizarre, conversation-worthy finger foods are usually freely available.)

The high-school-girls-bathroom theory: Bring friends with you. But not too many—you don't want to have so much fun that you'll forget to talk to anyone else.

Find someone who looks even more lost than you, and talk with that person.

Need an icebreaker? Wear an interesting science-themed T-shirt or unusual accessory (making sure you lean toward appealingly quirky rather than so-weird-you're-unapproachable).

Bring business cards. You know, just in case.

Set a small goal of talking with a certain number of people. If you leave and you've talked with only one person, don't worry. People will have seen your face. And besides, you just got free food!

SciLance says . . .

- **Even if you're not a natural self-promoter, you can get yourself out there.**

- Afraid of cold-calling? **Ease yourself into networking by doing it virtually.**

- If you can meet editors in person, do it. **Nothing beats a face-to-face connection.** Looking for editors? Do an internship, head to a meeting, or contact a publication and introduce yourself (politely and professionally).

- At conferences, **meet editors and writers** by going where they gather: the press room, talks and events, and receptions.

- **Networking can happen anywhere.** Follow your nose to what interests you, and you'll likely stumble on a story idea or meet someone who might have work for you—and if nothing else, you'll have fun.

- **Get known for writing well and being easy to work with,** and people will want to help you succeed.

- **Be nice to interns,** and everyone else. The science writing community isn't large, and people tend to move around—and up.

Chapter 21

Paid to Grow

By Robin Mejia

"My documentary." The words felt so strange. *My documentary*—about how problems at crime labs around the country were sending innocent people to prison—was premiering that night. There would be a screening in San Francisco, followed by a panel discussion that included me, the reporter who'd led the project. A few days later, it would air on CNN.

This was January 2005, nearly four years after I'd decided to become a journalist. Mine was not a well-planned career transition: after earning a bachelor's degree in biology in 1997, I'd taken a communications job in the tech industry, but I'd grown increasingly bored editing white papers written by engineers. So in 2001 I quit my job to become a freelance reporter. How hard could that be?

I soon found that as a beginning journalist with no pedigree, the assignments came slowly. I researched internships in my area, eventually landing one at the Center for Investigative Reporting. I joined journalism organizations and went to their conferences, paying my own way for the chance to stake out editors I wanted to meet.

At one of those conferences, the 2002 Investigative Reporters and Editors annual meeting, I attended a panel during which several journalists discussed fellowships that had helped them execute big projects. During the Q & A, a woman in the audience told the panel that she thought journalists often concentrated on the same few famous fellowships—the Nieman at Harvard, for example—and forgot that other programs were also looking for good projects to support. For example, she represented a program at the Open Society Institute that offered a $45,000 fellowship to support reporting on criminal justice issues. $45,000? That was way more than I was making that year as a freelancer. I covered science, not criminal justice, but I made a mental note.

As I grew into my science beat, I stumbled onto a forensics story. I went to a scientific meeting in Orlando, Florida, to learn more about environmental mercury problems. There, I happened to see a presentation on new research that indicated a forensic test the FBI crime lab used to match crime-scene bullets to suspects didn't actually work as advertised. I jumped on that story, writing about it first for *New Scientist* and then for the *Los Angeles Times*. As I reported, I learned about more problems at crime labs. Some were scientific questions about other analytical techniques, but there were also lab-level problems of shoddy work and limited quality assurance, leading to unreliable results and sometimes innocent people being convicted.

I was convinced I'd found an important problem, but I felt overwhelmed. With my background in biology and science reporting, I could handle the scientific papers I was accumulating. But I also had a growing stack of appellate opinions that, with no legal training, I barely knew how to decipher. I was calling defense attorneys around the country. I was learning, but most of the time I was doing this, I wasn't getting paid.

Any freelancer who has wanted to branch out from her established routine—develop a new beat, try a new style of writing, or learn a new form of media—has faced a similar dilemma. We're paid only for stories: words on the page, or minutes on the air. Professional development has to happen on our own time, and usually our own dime.

Clearly, without outside support for the forensics research, I wasn't on a sustainable trajectory. So I looked up that criminal justice fellowship— the Soros Justice Media Fellowship from the Open Society Institute— and put in an application. And to my amazement, they picked me.

I was lucky to stumble on a fellowship that was such a clear fit for a story I was dying to tell. But a surprising number of funding options exist for reporters looking to develop either a particular story or a new area of expertise: journalism "boot camps" sponsored by universities and foundations provide short-term intensive training in a new subject, and a variety of fellowships and grants fund travel, training, or in-depth research.

The benefits of grants and fellowships can go far beyond the money involved. "I firmly believe that it is to any journalist's advantage to have as many experiences as possible and to see as much of the world as they can, both to generate ideas and cultivate an understanding of worldwide issues," says SciLancer Emily Sohn, who won a travel fellowship to attend the 2007 World Conference of Science Journalists in Melbourne, Australia.

In her application for the fellowship, Emily, who was a contributing writer for *Science News for Kids* at the time, made the argument that "going to Australia, which was a trip I did not have resources to do on my own, would open up the world to my young readers," she says. "And while I was there, I couldn't help but notice signs everywhere talking about the epic drought that had gripped the country for years." This observation turned into a feature for *Science News* magazine about the "Big Dry," which was huge news in Australia at the time, but largely unknown outside the continent.

Many scientific and journalism conferences offer travel fellowships to allow journalists to attend their conferences: I've received funding to attend the National Association of Science Writers and Investigative Reporters and Editors meetings. Other organizations support travel for research. The Pulitzer Center for Crisis Reporting, for instance, funds mostly international trips, and its definition of "crisis reporting" includes environmental problems, health crises, and other stories that science writers cover.

Sometimes, however, journalists don't need plane fare. They need time. In 2010 SciLancer Michelle Nijhuis applied for the Alicia Patterson fellowship, which supports journalists as they research a series of related stories.

"I wanted the financial freedom to explore some new ideas and to step up my magazine game—I wanted the time to research and write some really killer pitches," she recalls. The fellowship provided that and more, and she completed several stories examining the fate of rare species in the age of global change.

For those who can uproot for a time, some of the most coveted fellowships pay journalists to study for an academic year at a major research university. The program most familiar to science journalists is the Knight Science Journalism Fellowship at the Massachusetts Institute of Technology. A nine-month residential program, the Knight fellowship is designed to "provide the time for in-depth study—a year away from deadlines to follow your intellectual curiosity."

The Knight fellowship at MIT allows journalists to audit any course taught there, or at neighboring Harvard. The residential fellowships also offer an oasis of financial stability. SciLancer Hillary Rosner found both the financial benefits and the flexibility to be rewarding. Like many fellows, Hillary went in with a concrete study plan, but once she arrived on campus, her plans changed. "I ended up wandering into a lecture on ecology and genetics and it opened up a whole new world of stories that I didn't know were out there," she says. The fellowship allowed her the time to really learn a new beat, and she's still reporting those stories today.

Harvard, Stanford, and the University of Michigan offer similar year-long fellowships that are open to reporters of all stripes: freelancers and staffers, reporters and photojournalists, domestic and international. None specifically target science journalists, but all are open to them. The University of Colorado at Boulder hosts the similar Ted Scripps Fellowship in Environmental Journalism. These programs can be transformational for seasoned journalists, but they all target midcareer journalists, and the competition for the limited number of slots is intense.

Still, that shouldn't dissuade good reporters from trying. And while freelancers can face a challenge in convincing funders that they'll have an outlet for their work, we also bring an important skill to the application process: we know how to write proposals.

"I'd known about the Alicia Patterson fellowship for years, but hearing the executive director of the foundation speak at a conference really motivated me to apply," says Michelle. "She made me realize I'd been making the whole thing too complicated, and waiting for some earth-shattering Big Idea to come along. All I needed was a good story pitch."

A confession: I've applied for more fellowships than I've been awarded. Way more. In 2009 I was a finalist for the Nieman, and in 2010 I was a finalist for the Knight-Wallace program at the University of Michigan. My application to the Knight Science Journalism Fellowship at MIT didn't even make the first cut. The same goes for journalism awards: for every bit of professional recognition listed on my résumé, there are plenty of submissions that went nowhere.

Or perhaps I should say, plenty of submissions that benefited me in less immediately tangible ways. In 2003 I submitted a piece I was exceptionally proud of to the NASW awards contest and lost. Later, after hiring me for a long feature, an editor at *Popular Science* told me that she'd been on the judging committee and had been really impressed by the piece. A different losing contest entry led to an invitation to present on a panel at the Investigative Reporters and Editors organization's annual meeting.

I believe my unsuccessful applications to fellowship programs have helped me as well. Putting together a fellowship application forces me to do a serious assessment of my career: what I've accomplished, where I'm going, where I would like to go. Even when I haven't won, the exercise has always helped me focus.

Similarly, Michelle applied for a Ted Scripps Environmental Journalism Fellowship at the University of Colorado in 2006. She made finalist but not fellow, and later applied the lessons of that near-miss to her successful application for the Alicia Patterson fellowship. "I didn't have a real sense of mission about what I wanted to do with the Scripps fellowship," she says. "I just wanted a ready-made plan for the next year, and I think that came across in my interview."

In 2009 I applied to the Nieman public health reporting fellowship with a proposal to study epidemiological research methods and statistical analysis to better understand the effects of armed conflict on health. Like Michelle, I was chosen as a finalist, but not as a fellow. The process of applying, however, helped me realize how badly I wanted to learn the material. After a bit of soul-searching, I applied to graduate school, and in 2010 I began a master's program in public health at the University of California, Berkeley.

By the time I finish, I'll have completed six graduate-level courses in statistics, far more than I could have crammed into a fellowship year. I've barely had time to read anything besides primary research, let alone write—both challenges for someone addicted to good prose. But I can already tell that my understanding of research—and statistics and data generally—has grown exponentially. And I owe that development, at least in part, to a rejection.

For me, the Open Society Institute fellowship was a similar opportunity to dig deeper. I started it as a young journalist with one important story about a problem at the FBI crime lab, and an inkling that there was a bigger problem that no one was covering. As a Soros fellow I took the time to digest those trial transcripts and appellate opinions. I dove into the history of forensic science. I got to know defense attorneys. During the second half of the fellowship a friend at the Center for Investigative Reporting told me she'd just had a meeting with the head of CNN Presents, the network's documentary unit, and they were looking for proposals. She thought my investigation would be perfect and helped me put together a four-page pitch. CNN bit on the project, bringing me on as a reporter and pairing me with veteran producer Ken Shiffman, who taught me how to make a documentary.

By that night at the premiere in San Francisco, I wasn't just a science journalist with one interesting forensics story. I was the lead reporter on an investigation pointing out serious problems in an important industry, problems that were causing innocent people to go to prison. (More than a year later, an expert panel at the National Academy of Sciences came to the same conclusion.) After the screening that night, I took my seat as a panelist for the post-film Q & A. There were so many questions that the moderator eventually had to shut the evening down.

I remember the wide-ranging questions, which covered innocence cases, crime labs around the country, broader issues of evidence admissibility and accreditation options for labs, and—most important—what kinds of changes were needed to fix a broken system. What I remember most about the evening, though, is that I had answers.

♦ SciLance says . . .

Before you start your fellowship search . . .

- **Evaluate where you are** in your career. Some programs are targeted at beginners; others are geared toward midcareer journalists.

- Ask yourself **what you need now**. Do you want research time for a project you're passionate about? Travel funds? Help developing new skills? An introduction to a new beat? Your specific needs should shape your search. Different fellowships offer very different packages.

- **Consider the downsides**. Being paid to study at MIT for a year may sound like an amazing opportunity—and it is—but uprooting for nine months is not a minor decision, especially for writers with families. If what you really want is a month of research on a specific topic, a more focused research grant might be a better fit.

- **Stretch your imagination**. If you're looking for research funding, consider any beat your project touches. Just as I applied for a criminal justice fellowship to aid my reporting on forensics, a health reporter might benefit from a business reporting fellowship.

- **Attend conferences**. Many journalism and writing organizations' annual conferences feature panels on fellowships or other ways to grow your skills and career.

- **Keep an open mind**. I certainly didn't expect to be a documentary filmmaker, nor did I expect to go back to graduate school, but both turned out to be good choices for me.

Chapter 22

Contract Literacy

By Mark Schrope

To almost every writer who will read this, contracts are boring, and more than a touch confusing. This is because contracts *are* boring and more than a touch confusing, but the resulting lack of attention writers pay to them can be a really, really big problem. Not knowing how to read and improve these contracts is one of the biggest business mistakes writers make. Judging from the examples that most of us see regularly, contracts have grown much less writer-friendly over the past decade, sometimes dangerously so. I'm going to show you the basics of reading and negotiating your contract. These can boost your bottom line, give you an edge over your peers, and help you sleep better at night. I'll also tell you the magic question that can lead to higher rates for your stories, and another one that will in many cases painlessly solve multiple contract woes and possibly get you more cash down the road. Still not convinced? Read on, gentle reader, for I shall also mock lawyers.

First off, I should note that I'm going to talk strictly about contracts for articles, not books. If you are going to write a book of any sort, you are insane not to have a lawyer or agent on your side. Unless you choose very poorly, this adviser will know much more than me—or you. And please—I'm not a lawyer, not even close. The material in this chapter does not constitute legal advice; it's just what I've learned from my own experience and that of other writers, including many of the members of SciLance.

One of the first things to remember is that, with few exceptions, contracts aren't written by your editors. They are written by lawyers hired to protect a company, and to help it make as much money as possible. In most cases, your editor will not have had a say in what the contract contains. Still, while the lawyers are definitely not on your side, the good editors can be. But you need to know how to ask them to help you.

Below, you'll find several key categories of troublesome contract clauses, along with their implications and potential solutions. Oh, one more thing: I'm not a lawyer. I'm just a writer who has watched the contracts deteriorate and has gotten some helpful advice along the way. The information here is based on my own experience, discussions with lawyers, editors, and other writers, and other sources listed in the Resources section.

Liability and Indemnity Clauses

Thankfully, most writers will never be involved in any kind of legal suit tied to something they wrote. But the possibility exists, making this one of the most important topics a writing contract covers. Too often, this involves shifting most or all legal responsibility onto the writer. That usually starts with some guarantees the writer is asked to make. The first part is usually painless:

Lawyerly example:

> Writer warrants that all materials submitted will be original, never before published, and that writer is the sole owner of the work.

What they're really* saying:

> Swear to us you won't pull a scummy fast one by borrowing somebody else's material, or pawning off something you've already published elsewhere.

No problem here. This is absolutely a writer's responsibility. But things can then become a little more complicated.

Lawyerly example:

> Nothing contained in the article will injure, defame, libel, invade the privacy of any person, or violate or infringe on any patent,

_____

*Disclaimer: Okay, so this may not be what they are really, really saying. I've taken some liberties. Don't sue me.

copyright, trademark, trade secret, or other personal or proprietary rights of any party.

What they're really saying:

> This thing had better not piss anyone off for any reason, or otherwise make them uncomfortable enough to complain or sue. And by "anyone" we mean any person or entity with enough money or clout to turn this sort of thing into a real hassle for us. We realize there's no way you can possibly say all these things for sure. Neither can we. But the lawyers work for us, so we figure we might as well shift as much of this your direction as we can.

It is the writer's job to go as far as he or she can to ensure that an article isn't going to say anything erroneous or illegal. That said, the laws governing issues such as trade secrets and libel—writing something false about someone that damages his or her reputation—can vary from state to state and country to country. And remember, even if you're not writing for a foreign publication, the global reach of the Internet means you could be sued over your article in a country you've never even visited. "How on earth do you, the freelancer, know what the particular peculiarities of media law are in all the different jurisdictions where something will be published?" asks Peter Aldhous, an experienced editor at science publications. "It's hard enough for the publishers, who can hire legal teams."

If you can't know all the potentially relevant laws, you really can't say for sure whether you've broken any. You cannot make this guarantee. Ah, if only somebody in the mix had access to lawyers who do know these things, and could review articles to warn against potential libel issues. But wait, somebody does! And it's not the writer.

So what do you do? To shift such language to something he or she actually can guarantee, many writers will request that, at a minimum, the language be changed to say something like, " . . . writer warrants that, *to the best of his/her knowledge,* nothing contained in the article . . . "

We're not done yet, though. The area of greatest concern usually comes next. This is a dreaded little bit of potential devilry called the indemnity clause. Over the past several years these have become ubiquitous. If there is an indemnity clause, it's a key place where the contract determines what happens if an article actually does lead to a lawsuit, and who's going to foot the bill. The very worst ones go something like this:

Lawyerly example:

> In the event that any complaint or claim in relation to the article is made by any third party at any time, whether a formal legal complaint or otherwise, you indemnify and hold harmless the publisher against any and all claims or actions arising out of a breach or alleged breach of the foregoing warranties.

What they're really saying:

> Potential lawsuits make us very nervous. Just read the news—people have gone absolutely bonkers and will sue you for breathing. Here is our plan: In the event of a lawsuit tied to something you write for us, we'd like for you to take responsibility for everything, even aspects of the work and its publishing that are completely out of your control. Also, we'd like you to pay for absolutely everything: legal costs and anything else we end up having to fork over. Yes, we realize this is absurd. But, as previously mentioned, the lawyers work for us.

"Indemnify and hold harmless" is the part that means you're agreeing that whatever happens, it's effectively your fault. And that you'll pay the bill. At a certain level, it may seem reasonable to ask a writer to take the financial responsibility for a lawsuit sparked by his or her article. But here's where the careful reading comes into play. There's nothing in the bad indemnity clause to differentiate a lawsuit tied to actual mistakes or wrongdoing on the part of the writer from something completely baseless.

For instance, a publication, its lawyers, and insurers could decide that it would be easier to just pay off an annoyed person to make a nuisance lawsuit go away. Theoretically you would be on the hook for that, plus legal fees, perhaps without even being consulted in the decision. Even more frightening, under this wording, even if a publisher goes to court and wins a case proving that the writer did nothing wrong, the writer could technically have to pay for the publication's defense.

"Anybody can sue anybody else in this great country of ours for pretty much anything no matter how unmeritorious that lawsuit might be," says Mark Fowler, a freelance writer–turned–publishing lawyer. (Fowler has been kind enough to guide me through the contract world, and is thus exempt from any lawyer-mocking in which I might partake.) Given the real possibility of crazy lawsuits, Fowler says of the scarier indemnity clauses, "I can understand why writers would be intimidated."

He points out that it's unlikely that an indemnity clause will ever come into play. And if it does, and the clause is the type that technically transfers all financial responsibility to the writer, Fowler says, it's even more unlikely that a publisher would go after the writer for everything.

There are numerous practical issues with the whole concept. For example, a lawsuit is likely to name both the writer and the publication as defendants. The publication certainly isn't going to wait to defend itself until the writer coughs up money for lawyers. It would be interesting to see someone try to squeeze a legal fund out of your average science writer.

Fowler says that, at most, a company might settle with a writer for some fraction of the total after the fact, recognizing that getting everything to which the clause technically entitles them would be all but impossible. But Aldhous, who says he fought against such clauses when he was in chief editor positions at *Nature* and *New Scientist,* sums it up: "How many publishers are going to chase a freelancer down and ruin them financially? I don't think most would. But why on earth would you sign a document that has it as even a vague possibility?"

Some contracts will address these issues in ways that most writers consider more reasonable. They might simply ask the writer to guarantee to take "all reasonable care" that the article isn't going to raise legitimate legal issues and that the writer will "fully cooperate with the company to defend the suit," if it does. "I think most reasonable people accept that's about the right balance," Aldhous says. "Publishers do need to be protected against careless and reckless behavior, but freelancers can't be expected to totally indemnify corporations. It's just ridiculous and unjust."

Personally, if there's an unreasonable indemnity clause, I ask the publisher to ditch it. That almost never works, but it makes me feel better to ask. Next, I request an amendment to the clause that says, " . . . provided that such liability is finally established by a court of competent jurisdiction and that such judgment is sustained after all appeals have been exhausted." That kind of amendment will at least free you from responsibility for false claims against your work. If none of that works, you have to decide for yourself whether it's better to walk away or close your eyes and hope for the best. If you choose the latter, you might want to consider avoiding the more incendiary topics, such as autism and vaccines, or chiropractors—yes, chiropractors, the topic of a recent lawsuit against British author Simon Singh.

Fee Clauses

Indemnity clauses are important to consider, but given the odds against an actual suit, they're likely to be more a matter of principle than a financial imperative. But next on the writer's list of top contract consternations is one that has very real effects on our bottom lines: the payment clauses.

The actual rate you'll be getting might be covered in the contract or it could be handled separately. Many writers are afraid to ask their editors for higher rates. Others just don't think to do it. But here's the magic question I promised: "Can you raise my rate?" It's as simple as that. You won't always be able to get a higher fee by asking, but you'll almost never get a raise if you don't ask.

But the trick isn't knowing what to ask. It's knowing when to ask, and for how much. And that's where inside intelligence is important. If possible, find out what other writers are getting at the same publication and what their starting rates were. Obviously these are personal questions, so you have to know a writer well enough for them to trust you with the information. But you can also find relevant numbers in databases maintained by writers' groups, such as the members-only "Words' Worth" database at the National Association of Science Writers website.

If the rate you are initially offered seems low either relative to what others have received or to rates at similar publications, or if you've been writing for a publication successfully for at least a year, it's worth asking for a bump. "When I started out, I took what was offered," says one colleague. "Now I always ask for more money. Whether I get it or not, no editor has ever dropped me because I asked." Others among us are a bit more timid and wait until at least the second assignment.

It should go without saying, but it's especially important to push for higher rates if the rate you've been offered is ridiculous. That happens more and more in an Internet-dominated world where everyone wants content for free. The scales are sliding depending on the work. Personally, I'm willing to take a much lower rate for a story that involves scuba diving in Fiji than for a story about a new inflammation inhibitor.

Many of us might also be willing to work for free to break into a dream publication. But your dream pubs won't be asking you to work for free. The ones that will ask are generally low-tier publications or websites. The "exposure," they may tell you, will be golden. You'll "build your brand." Horse pucky. Hardly anyone is going to see it, and if they do they're not going to then come running to you with high-paying assignments. If a company's business plan involves squeezing free or underpaid writing from eager journalists, then that company should fail. It's that simple.

Another troubling trend is in payment time frames. It was once common for contracts to promise payment within thirty days after *acceptance* of the article, allowing the writer at least a rough idea of when to expect a check. But in recent years, that time frame has in some cases shifted to payment within thirty days after *publication*. With news stories that appear soon after you file them, it's not a big issue. But it can be a huge problem for less time-sensitive features. For monthly magazines, the publication process can take months, with delays often popping up for reasons absolutely beyond your control.

It's not unreasonable to expect payment sooner than publication. To use the analogy SciLancer Emily Sohn offered in Chapter 19: If a plumber fixes one of your toilets, would you tell him you aren't going to pay until you use it—and that you won't use it until the in-laws come for Christmas? Much of what we've come to accept in writing contracts is nearly as ridiculous. It's probably best to leave the plumber out of it, but if you're offered a contract that prescribes payment on publication, and there's any potential for said publication to drag out the process, ask for payment on acceptance. Failing that, ask the publication to pay you a portion of the fee on acceptance and the remainder on publication (paying fees in halves or thirds is a fairly common practice at national magazines). If the publication won't budge, you'll have to decide whether you are financially able and prepared to go without the money for a long time. If not, you might need to walk away.

Rights Clauses

Obviously, the fee you'll be paid for your article is a crucial concern, perhaps *the* crucial concern, for any assignment. But contracts also spell out who owns the resulting work, and that has financial implications, too. Most magazines used to ask for what's called First North American Serial Rights. That means the publication will pay you for the right to be the first one to use your story. But the writer still owns the article under such a contract and is free to sell it elsewhere after a certain amount of time. Even though such resales were relatively rare, it was a nice setup that's hard to find these days.

As online publishing emerged, things got messier. Publishers, not knowing what else to do, wanted to put just about everything from their newspapers and magazines on the Web. And a lot of older material started appearing in web archives. Among other cases, one freelance writer successfully sued the *New York Times* to prevent the paper from putting his past stories into their database without additional payment. It seemed like a victory, but it probably didn't help writers much. Some publications upped their rates a bit to justify asking for additional rights, including online publishing. But most simply rewrote contracts to require that writers give away more rights and for longer—at about the same rates.

From there, everything went further downhill with more and more publications going to all-rights contracts, or what under US law is called "work made for hire." It's a truly lousy form of contract in which the writer agrees that for whatever the publication is paying up front, he or she will relinquish any ownership of the story throughout the universe for all eternity. Technically, that means you can't even post a copy of the article on your personal web page. These contracts tend to go something like this:

Lawyerly example:

> Writer acknowledges that the article shall be [publication's] sole and exclusive property as a work made for hire within the meaning of the United States copyright laws, and that you convey and assign all rights, including copyright, in and to the article to [publication], which may deal with them as [publication] sees fit in its sole discretion. In the event the article is deemed not to be a work made for hire for any reason, writer transfers and assigns the entire copyright throughout the world in any and all media and forms of publication, reproduction, transmission, distribution, performance, adaptation, enhancement, or display now in existence or hereafter developed, in the article, to [publication].

What they're really saying:

> Dear Writer Person: Boy, things are getting confusing out there, eh? Who can keep up with all this crazy online stuff? On top of what we do ourselves, this whole World Wide Web thing means people are coming from all over the friggin' planet asking to reprint

our stuff. It's hard to follow everything. Also, we like to make money. So here's what we've decided: we're going to do a lot more than we used to with your article but we'll pay you the same rate we've been paying for years and call it even. Sure, there's a good chance we'll be reselling your article and may well make more money doing that than we ever paid you, meaning we'll effectively get your article for free. But, well, as previously mentioned, the lawyers work for us.

There are two main schools of thought on these work-made-for-hire contracts. Some are against them as a matter of principle. The American Society of Journalists and Authors (ASJA), for instance, recommends against accepting them under any circumstances. Here's its reasoning: "Should others resell your work for their profit alone? Writers shouldn't let publishers and others profit perpetually from their property while they—the creators of that property—get nothing." Another concern is that if we the writers allow publishers to make this the norm, we are all losing rights and income.

Other writers will accept work made for hire as long as a publication is willing to pay a high enough rate, ideally with a separate amount tied directly to electronic and other additional rights. The person who owns the rights to a story has the potential to make more money from it by reselling it later. Sometimes that won't matter, but sometimes it will. In rare cases, magazine articles even get optioned for movies. Miss a piece of that payday and you'll be very sad.

For the most part, even writers who will accept work-made-for-hire contracts find them detestable. "There has to be a damn good reason for me to sign a work-made-for-hire contract," says one writer, "ideally a lot of money for something I don't care about too deeply." Some writers refuse to work for certain publications with steadfast work-made-for-hire contract policies, especially when a similar magazine offers a much better contract, which is often the case.

It's your business to decide what you want to give away to publications. And it's worth noting that most writers are less concerned or not concerned at all if a company or institution wants non-journalistic work, such as a newsletter article or web copy, to be work made for hire. That's not something you could normally resell anyway. But you need to know what you are or are not giving away.

One alternative to work made for hire is that the writer assigns most or all rights to the publication for a certain amount of time. During that time the publication can publish it however it likes and resell it. Afterward, the writer might get all the resale rights, or the publisher and writer might agree to share any proceeds, or to share the right to resell the article.

If you agree to such an arrangement, know that the details are critical. If the publication has the exclusive right to resell the article for a year without paying you anything, by the time you get rights back, resale is going to be much less likely. Requesting that rights revert to you after sixty or ninety days might be reasonable.

Also, if you maintain or get back rights after a period of time, but the publication can continue reselling without giving you a cut—in legalese the publication is getting "nonexclusive" resale rights—you are in all likelihood being thrown a worthless bone. Anyone looking to reprint an article, say, in a foreign language magazine or on some website, is almost always going to go to the outlet, not you, to get and pay for permission.

With large publications that have foreign editions, pay close attention to how those rights will be handled. Some contracts lay out a set additional fee if your publisher decides to run your story in other countries. Some don't. I recently asked a magazine to convert a contract from work made for hire to something more reasonable. The magazine did, but I got only those nonexclusive rights. I was feeling moderately pleased that I got at least something. Then I got a form letter from the publisher saying that a sister publication in a country I would have trouble spelling was reprinting my article and that I would be paid any additional money according to my contract terms. Yippee! Then came another one. The trouble was, when I checked the contract I realized that those contract terms said the publication didn't have to pay me anything for this reuse. Such a victory.

There are a number of other possibilities worth considering. You might like to post the article on your website, or bundle it with other articles to sell as an e-book. Don't be shy in making reasonable requests.

Other Clauses

Though indemnity, fees, and rights tend to be the greatest contract concerns for writers, they are far from the only clauses worth scrutinizing and, when possible, changing. Look at how kill fees are treated—that's what a publication will pay you if the editors decide to cancel, or "kill," your article. This should rarely if ever come into play, but if it does, many contracts set that rate at 25 percent. That is reasonable enough if the language describing how a publication can do the killing is narrow enough. But if the contract allows the publication to drop your story for anything other than an article that is not up to publishable standards, that's dangerous. Be wary of vague language such as " . . . if the publisher, in its sole discretion, rejects the article."

If you do all the work and turn in an article that meets basic standards but the publication decides not to publish for some reason, you should be paid in full. The contract should not take that right away, but many of them do. You provided the services you were contractually obligated to provide. Not to pick on the plumber again, but if you decide that you're not ever going to use that toilet he installed, it's a good bet that he will still expect full payment.

Early in my career I made the mistake of not understanding kill fees well enough. An editor I'd never worked with at a new publication killed my story even though it was exactly what we had agreed upon. She decided she wanted something different *after* I finished. I made some sheepish arguments but settled far too easily for a 50 percent kill fee. Technically I could have taken the issue to small-claims court and been on very solid ground. Years later I learned the editor had a habit of doing the same thing and when a couple of new victims figured this out, they demanded and received full payment. They identified her pattern because they talked among themselves about the issue, which is almost as important as reading your contracts.

Even contract clauses that seem completely benign might be worth some attention. For instance, most will say legal disputes between the publication and the writer will be dealt with in the "publishers' home jurisdiction," typically New York for large magazines. But asking for your own home court advantage is perfectly reasonable. Which of you is more likely to have the resources to travel to another state to fight a legal battle?

Noncompete clauses, which ask the writer to promise not to write about the same topic for others, can be reasonable. But many writers will cover a given topic or event in various forms after an initial article for other outlets. If the contract language prevents you from doing that for, say, a year, that's way too restrictive, and there's really no justification for it. Thirty or sixty days should be plenty to allow the publication to get the maximum play for an article. And beware language that restricts your right to cover entire topics, rather than more narrowly defined stories. Asking for exclusive access to your reporting on a lab visit or a particular event might be fair, but asking you to refrain from writing for competitors about an entire topic, such as cancer treatments, certainly isn't.

Nice, but Firm

Unless you have a name that will sell magazines on its own, you're not going to get everything you want in a contract. And every writer has different priorities. But even once you figure out what's important to you and have assured yourself that the changes you want are reasonable, actually making the requests can be daunting, especially early in your career as a negotiator. And especially when you're afraid that asking for contract changes will annoy your editor.

I've made a point of asking several editors about this topic, and all told me writers rarely ask for contract changes. When it does happen, they say they aren't bothered by such requests per se. What can be annoying is how the writer asks.

"I do not mind at all when someone says they're uncomfortable with part of the contract and asks whether it would be possible to modify it," says Laura Helmuth, science editor for *Slate*. "I say, 'Sure, send me a short e-mail memo about why you'd like to modify the contract, and I'll forward it with my endorsement to someone who can make that call.'" The only time change requests become annoying, she says, is when the writer gets worked up and indignant before the conversation has even begun and treats the editor like a legal opponent. "It's mostly a tone thing, and a matter of thinking about things from the editor's perspective," she says. "What some writers seem not to realize is that their editor is their advocate—we push for more money for the writer, more expenses, more space, and better photos."

Dawn Stover, a freelance writer and former editor at *Popular Science,* agrees. "I didn't find it annoying, because I sympathized entirely with the writers," she says. "But it did seem that the people who requested changes tended to be naturally testier. I'd strongly recommend that a writer who asks for contract modifications broaches the subject in a friendly, rather than self-righteous, tone."

By all means request reasonable changes, in other words. Just don't be a jerk. Negotiating reasonable contract changes shouldn't be the exclusive domain of the ornery and the obnoxious.

I usually start my contract e-mails with an apology for being a nuisance. That's not some inauthentic attempt to avoid coming off like the kind of writer who has annoyed Stover and Helmuth. It's because I honestly hate bothering editors about contract details. I hate mowing the grass, but I do that, too. Actually, I make my kids do that now, so bad example, but you get the idea. I write those contract messages because they're important.

I also avoid whining about the evils of an indemnity clause or whatever it is I'm hoping to change. At most I'll put in a brief sentence about how such and such is a serious concern that's been red-flagged by organizations such as ASJA and then tell the editor I'd be happy to talk more if she would like. Mostly the editors don't want to or need to discuss the issues further because they're just passing the request on to someone else.

I haven't always gotten all the changes I've requested, but I have often been able to either get offending bits removed, or at least to get language added that converts the offensive to the merely annoying. Most writers I've discussed these issues with describe similar results. In all cases, though, when we don't ask for changes, we don't get any changes.

One More Secret, Revealed

One of the most astonishing things I and other writers have discovered over the years is that some publications have more than one standard contract. So the second magic question I promised is: "Do you have a better contract?" In some cases, this alone will solve many contract worries.

I initially discovered this when asking for some changes to a contract that gave the publication all rights—and at a rate that no one could possibly argue warranted it. The contracts administrator sent me a reasonable contract within about two minutes. I surmised all by myself that that had not been long enough to go to the lawyers for a rewrite.

Later I found that other companies had the good stuff in waiting as well, and I've heard confirmation from other writers. I find this situation a little frightening, but I'll play capitalist and allow that it's the publication's right to try to get the most favorable terms for itself. Who doesn't do that in a negotiation? Just remember to look at it that way: as a negotiation where you need to be thinking about getting favorable terms for yourself.

Only once has someone objected to my requests for changes and argued that I was mistaken in my thinking. It wasn't an editor, it was a contracts administrator. I had written for the online site of a certain very large, very prestigious magazine for a few years. When I started in about 2000, the contract was quite good, and had remained so for several projects. I drifted to other pursuits, but an editor asked me to start writing again for what had become an expanded online site. By this time the contract had devolved into a textbook example of a bad contract.

Despite that, the administrator told me that not one writer had ever had any problem with the provisions of the contract. (Whether that was true at the time I can't say, but I later heard from a number of writers who had major problems with this particular contract.) As I described my concerns, the administrator repeatedly accused me of not wanting to stand behind my work. I tried to explain that that wasn't the case, but with little success. So I took out my contracts file and began reading what I considered more reasonable clauses from well-respected publications with large circulations. In each case the administrator told me the example was moot because said publication was nowhere near as prestigious as hers. I pointed out that an online site might be a great thing, but it was a very different beast from the admittedly prestigious parent magazine.

We couldn't come to an agreement over the phone, but even this example of negotiations gone awry had a happy ending. She told me to send an e-mail describing the changes I felt were needed to make the contract minimally acceptable, and the lawyers agreed to most of them despite the administrator's perspective.

So don't be afraid. Remember, as we've said before, that you have to be a businessperson as much as an artist. Ignore your butterflies and any excuses that may come to mind, and request the changes. Too many writers don't, because they don't know either what to look for or how to solve the problems. One writer put it like this: "I am going to admit that 80 percent of the time, I just sign whatever they send me, because it is boring to look at it, because I am a wuss about asking for changes, because I am too busy writing to be a legal expert, and because the amounts involved seem too small to worry much about."

Many writers feel similarly. But it's a vicious cycle, because when writers don't push back against unreasonable contracts, the publications and lawyers see no reason not to keep shifting the contracts in their favor. If you push back, you'll protect yourself, and you may increase your income. If nothing else, you'll be letting publishers know that more of us are paying attention and that reasonable contracts might be worth considering.

Time and Money: Can I Afford This Project?

By Stephen Ornes

You have to spend time to make money. So how do you minimize the former while maximizing the latter? Some issues to consider before you sign your next contract:

Time: Word rates aren't everything—you need to estimate how long the project will take, including edits and fact-checking. The longer it takes, the more it should pay, no matter the word count.

Money: Will the gig help you meet your monthly income goals, or make you fall behind? Many writers set a minimum per-word threshold, say at $1 or $2, and won't work for less without a good reason.

Hourly rate: Divide your earnings by the hours you work on a project for a more reliable threshold. It's one you can increase over time, as you learn the craft, from perhaps $20 an hour at the start of your science-writing career, to $100 or more for savvy pros. A five hundred–word assignment at 80 cents per word may not seem appealing—until you realize you can knock it out in two hours and earn a cool $200 hourly rate.

The editor: A solid writer-editor relationship can be a joy of its own, while a disconnect can be misery. An editor who offers clear directions and a pleasant disposition can earn a significant discount. Jerks should have to pay a premium.

Exposure: As Mark Schrope cautions in this chapter, don't overestimate the value of "exposure." But if it's a tryout for a new client, or an outlet you've always admired, you might make an exception to your financial expectations—as long as you can make up that income elsewhere.

The topic: New subject areas mean lots of basic research before you even get to the story. If it's interesting to you, that background work can lead to a whole new beat. If it's not, you're probably wasting your time, even if the pay is good.

SciLance says . . .

- With few exceptions, **nobody with your best interests in mind was in the room** when lawyers wrote the writing contract you're about to sign.

- In most cases, **a writer is responsible for making sure a contract is fair** and reasonable.

- **Reading contracts and requesting reasonable changes** is no fun. Do it anyway.

- In most cases, **your editor is your advocate** in a contract negotiation—not your adversary.

- Read the parts of your contract that set out **who will pay for legal challenges** very carefully.

- You'll almost never **get paid a higher rate** if you don't ask for one. So ask.

- **Don't be tempted** by those who tell you that "exposure" is better than a real check.

- It's your article. If at all possible, **avoid signing away all ownership** of it.

- Make sure your contract stipulates that **the publication pays a kill fee** only if your article isn't up to snuff, not if the publisher decides to not run the article based on reasons outside your control.

- If writers don't collectively **pay more attention to the contracts** they're sent, we're all going to keep getting contracts tilted more and more in favor of the publishers.

Chapter 23

The Ethical Science Writer

By Brian Vastag

In science writing, more than many other lines of work, reputation pays the bills. More broadly, "ethics" refers to the rules or guidelines that bind a community. The two concepts are intertwined: ethical behavior enhances your reputation, and ethical breaches can destroy it.

While doctors and lawyers have codified their rules, journalists and the science writing community as a whole have much more informal guidelines, and no hard and fast rules. Unlike in other professions, journalists and science writers are not required to pass tests or take oaths, and any punishment is ad hoc and informal, meted out by a publication, say, or public disapproval. Further, while individual publications and institutions will often have specific ethical guidelines, there is no overall rulebook for journalism or science writing. There are mercenaries and saints, furtive junketeers and self-declared paragons of virtue. There exist ethical *styles*.

Sorting out right from wrong while still making the mortgage leaves many science writers confused, worried, and unsure where to turn for advice. Everyone needs to make a living, and no one wants to feel like a sellout, phony, hack, or shill. Many more than fifty shades of gray exist out there.

Ethical confusion doesn't just strike newbies, either. In the spring of 2012, an accomplished freelance science writer and contributor to *Scientific American* sent this message to her several thousand followers on Twitter: "Was just asked to be included on a bid to write articles for a [National Institutes of Health] publication. As a journalist, would this be unethical? Seems like a [conflict of interest]?"

This chapter is here to offer guidance on such dilemmas; at the end, I hope you will have a better idea of how to make a living while not crashing your career—or blanching when you eye yourself in the mirror.

In my mind, the ethics of science writing can neatly be split into two categories: the ethics of practicing the craft, and the ethics of getting paid for it. Ultimately, listen to your instincts; if any business proposition feels wrong, squidgy, or strange, discuss it with editors and colleagues before proceeding. In ethics, as in many other arenas of life, open communication helps clear the mud.

Ethical Practice

Many guides to the ethics of conducting journalism already exist. Journalism departments offer ethics courses; you can also read the Society of Professional Journalists' code of ethics and its position papers on various ethics topics, posted online at www.spj.org.

Here's my swift recap: Don't lie, cheat, or steal (words). And don't sleep with your sources. (Sleeping with your editors is also probably a bad idea. Sleeping with other science writers is, on the other hand, status quo and has led to long-term relationships and marriages.)

Maintaining ethical relationships with the men and women we report on is vital, but the rules are not black-and-white. Many science writers shift careers after working as scientists, and they maintain connections to researchers with interesting stories: former professors, classmates, lab mates, and so on. While these connections can be fruitful sources of story ideas, they can also be ethically fraught.

SciLancer Jessica Marshall is a chemical engineer by training who married a university researcher. She gets lots of story leads that are "one degree away," meaning they originate with, say, a colleague of her husband's. Jessica often takes a pass on these potential stories for one big reason: she doesn't want to find herself pinched between writing a story the way she sees it and trying to maintain a friendship or a professional relationship. If Jessica feels like she might end up in a situation where she's "going to pull any punches," she passes on the story—or passes it on to a writer friend who isn't so close to it.

When you're reporting a story, even if you spend long stretches of time with a source, remind yourself that it's not your job to build a friendship. Sure, you want to keep things friendly, but it's not your job to look out for the feelings of your sources—in fact, if you're working as a journalist, it's your job to *not* put the feelings of your sources first.

Discerning the line between "friendly" and "friend" can be tricky. SciLancer Michelle Nijhuis often spends days or weeks in the field with her subjects. During these stints, she sometimes reminds her sources that everything is on the record, either by saying so or simply by keeping her notebook in sight. That can help maintain professional distance. Michelle also establishes other boundaries: Sure, she'll have a beer or two with a team after a day of fieldwork. But if the drinking looks serious, she'll leave.

While every reporter has to draw his or her own boundaries when reporting, here are two good rules. Pay your own way (more on that later), and remember that, as we argued in Chapter 1, it's not your job to cheerlead for science or for an individual researcher. Reporters aren't advocates.

Also, keep in mind that if you're writing about the people who pay you (or their employees), you aren't practicing journalism. You're practicing public relations, which is another major branch of science writing, with its own set of considerations. The ethical landscape shifts in that case: you are, explicitly, an advocate. But don't double dip—that is, don't turn around after writing a press release and then pitch the same story to a news outlet as a journalist. That's a big no-no.

Breaking the Rules

An object lesson in the dangers of breaking the rules of journalism arrived in summer 2012 with a spectacular flameout by a young star whose feet apparently lost touch with the ground. In June 2012, thirty-one-year-old Jonah Lehrer was watching his third book, *Imagine,* move up the best-seller charts while beginning a plum job as a staff writer at the *New Yorker.* But then eagle-eyed readers noticed that Lehrer had repackaged several blog posts he had written for *Wired* as new material at the *New Yorker*'s website.

In my mind, this is a minor crime against journalism—writers often repackage and resell their work, although it should be labeled or marked as such in some way—but a terrible start to a relationship with a new employer. Lehrer apparently had not made clear to his *New Yorker* bosses that the blog posts were not original. The publication added a note at the top of each post saying as much.

A month later, though, journalistic felonies emerged. In *Imagine*, Lehrer fabricated quotes from Bob Dylan, of all people. He then lied about making up the quotes to another reporter, Michael Moynihan, who exposed the fake quotes and subsequent deception in a magazine called *Tablet*.

The fallout came quickly. Lehrer resigned from the *New Yorker*, his publisher pulled *Imagine* from physical and virtual shelves, and Lehrer's career was deeply damaged.

Whether a magazine editor or book publisher will someday give Lehrer another chance is an open question. I'm guessing he'll be back in the game after a few years. Very few big-name journalists get excommunicated permanently for such sins. After all, Lehrer has not been accused of wholesale confabulation, which I consider a crime worthy of a journalistic death penalty. (As in, you never get to be a journalist again. Reporters such as Stephen Glass, who confabulated in the *New Republic* in the 1990s, and Jayson Blair, who fabricated quotes and other material in the *New York Times*, fit into this category.) Clearly, though, Lehrer will have to spend some time in the wilderness—and it's safe to say he'll never work for the *New Yorker* again.

Drawing Your Own Lines

Now on to the other matter: Sorting out the ethics of whom to take money from. I'm going to start by saying something that might be seen as controversial: there are no rules but the rules you make. It's possible there was once a time—sepia-toned, no doubt—when journalists, freelancers included, lived by a simple maxim: take money only from respectable journalism outlets. But I doubt it. (For evidence that such a pure past never existed, look up the story of William L. Laurence, a *New York Times* reporter who won a Pulitzer Prize for his coverage of the two atomic attacks on Japan that ended World War II. After his death, it became known that Laurence had also been a paid propagandist for the US War Department, writing press releases that denied the harms of radiation while he was repurposing the same stories in the *Times*. Youch. Don't be a Laurence.)

Today few independent writers can get by peddling their wares only to newspapers, magazines, book publishers, journalistic websites, and the like. The center of gravity for staff positions, meanwhile, has shifted into institutional science writing, which typically includes at least some promotional work. The industry has shrunk and rearranged itself. And the ethical landscape, when it comes to sources of payment, has been shifting with it.

That said, one can still decide to walk the straight-and-narrow path and vow to take money only from well-respected journalism outfits. It's a neat circle: the source of the income defines the occupation ("journalist"). That will clear out a lot of potential quandaries. You can then work within solid, comforting lines. It's a simple and, some say, noble path—but it may be a penurious one, too. Many SciLancers, for instance, derive part of their income from government agencies, universities, nonprofit research institutions, and corporations. (See Chapter 25 for more on these arrangements.)

"I used to think journalists should never get paid for anything other than journalism," says Robin Mejia, who described her investigative work for CNN in Chapter 21. "But how do you pay the basic bills, let alone feed kids on that?"

As an investigative reporter, Robin wanted to be "unassailable." During her first internship, at the Center for Investigative Journalism, this was ingrained. If you're going to take on the big boys—such as the FBI, which Robin publicly flogged for shoddy forensics—you don't want to leave your flank open to a counterattack.

Still, as Robin struggled to make a reasonable living despite landing projects with big-name outlets, she modified her thinking. She began writing for the magazine of the Howard Hughes Medical Institute (HHMI), a nonprofit research funder. It wasn't journalism, but it was interesting science writing that paid well. And Robin was comforted by feeling like she had a free hand in telling the stories she was assigned in the manner she desired.

But Robin took the assignments only after pondering the implications and deciding that working for HHMI would not damage her journalism career. (Several other SciLancers, including myself, have also written for HHMI.) Some factors in her (and my) decision: HHMI does no fund-raising, because it has big cash from its namesake, and it has no profit motive.

So Robin modified her rules and took the HHMI assignments. "I still do think ethics are hugely important and you have to be discriminating about who you take money from," she says. "Ask yourself, 'Is it going to affect my work?'"

To wit: Because Robin, I, and other SciLancers have been paid by HHMI, we are poor candidates for, say, launching a (hypothetical) investigation into any alleged wrongdoing there. (No one has alleged any—I'm just making an example here.) We would have a clear financial conflict of interest. And we may be consciously or unconsciously biased toward giving HHMI a break.

That brings us to the best piece of advice this chapter has to offer: disclose. If a publication approached me and asked for an investigative story about HHMI, I would immediately mention my past business relationship. And then I would turn down the assignment, if the offer hadn't already been revoked.

Think of these choices as closing doors. If you're willing to nudge a door latched via a payment of a few hundred dollars—or slam it shut with many thousands—be aware that you may be squelching future opportunities. Think it through.

Such choices are famously hard to make. Ethical dilemmas can be obvious or subtle, frank or shrouded. And they can tug at deep questions of professional identity.

SciLancer Sarah Webb had carved out a niche writing about the business of stem cells for journals and trade publications. In one piece, she mentioned a company in Germany developing new stem cell therapies. A few months later, a representative of that company contacted Sarah and said he was looking to hire a writer. Further correspondence, however, bore little fruit as to what the job might entail beyond "journalistic support," a baffling term.

Eventually the contact proposed flying Sarah to Germany for a meeting. She worried that if she took the plane ticket, she would be making an irrevocable choice.

"If I'd said yes to him, I would no longer be a journalist who writes about stem cells," Sarah says. "There's a line I can't walk back and forth across."

Wanting to remain a journalist—and not a corporate public-relations agent—Sarah turned down the trip, even though she could have enjoyed Europe for a few days without any of her editors being the wiser. But it would have felt wrong. "I would have had these identity questions," she says. "I wouldn't have felt good about the trip. I have to look myself in the mirror every day."

Over my career, I've been surprised by many situations in which writers engage in what, to me, appear to be clear conflicts of interest. Different writers have different standards.

To wit: In October 2011, some five hundred science writers gathered in Flagstaff, Arizona, for the annual Science Writers conference, cohosted by the National Association of Science Writers and the Council for the Advancement of Science Writing. At a panel session I participated in—"Covering Scientific Controversies"—a big name in the field, Gary Taubes, talked about his work covering nutrition in his book *Why We Get Fat* and various magazine articles.

Taubes then dropped what I considered a small bomb: he's paid to talk to audiences at, among other venues, multinational agribusiness corporations.

Wait a minute, I thought: *Here's this huge figure—Taubes has won many prizes and accolades—and he's admitting to a roomful of colleagues that he takes cash from companies embroiled in the controversies he covers. How is this not a gross conflict of interest?*

At the conference, Taubes made no apologies or justifications. He plainly stated that after years of reporting, he had become an expert in nutrition science. The talks are another means of leveraging this hot work into cold cash.

It turns out the paid lecture circuit—once verboten for journalists—is now lucrative for many big-name writers. In February 2011, in the *New York Observer,* journalist Nick Summers reported:

> Some speak gratis or donate their fees to charity, and straight newspaper reporters know better—or should—than to take cash from groups that they cover. But opinion journalists and ideas-y magazine writers are largely free to collect five- and even six-figure checks for a single afternoon's work.

Bill Leigh, whose Leigh Bureau represents Malcolm Gladwell, Chris Anderson, Atul Gawande, and others, told the *Observer,* "There are journalists at every price point within the lecture field. You can say anything between $5,000 and $100,000 and up. I can assure you that journalists are well represented—and that that is new. That much I can tell you emphatically."

I have a strong hunch that one reason Taubes can "get away" with peddling talks like this without major consequences is that he's such a huge name in the field.

So there's one ugly truth of this business: Name recognition counts. As does a track record of delivering award-winning articles and best-selling books, as Taubes has.

The lesson? A writer just starting out—or a veteran without the same name recognition—might not be able to get away with the same financial conflicts of interest as a big-name writer.

I know what you're thinking: this stinks.

It does. It isn't fair.

But again, this scenario points up the theme of the chapter. There is no rule book, except for the one each of us—editors, publishers, and writers—make. And these rules can shift from year to year, publication to publication, and country to country. If you're unsure how to handle a situation, engage with your editors. Ask what they think. You might be surprised by the answers.

Freelancer Amy Maxmen did just that when drug giant Novartis offered to fly her from New York to Tanzania for an international conference on tuberculosis. The company said it would not tell her what to write about, or for which publications. They just wanted her at the meeting. Maxmen was unsure what to do, in part because she went into science writing after being a scientist, without detouring through a journalism school.

So Maxmen discussed it with three editors. One, at a scientific journal with a news section, told her taking the Novartis money could jeopardize her career. Another was similarly negative. But the third, at a trade publication targeted to life scientists, said he didn't care.

Still, the two strong no's were enough to convince Maxmen not to take the trip—even though it would have positioned her to land stories few other journalists had access to.

Junketeering

Maxmen's case points up a particularly fuzzy ethical area: the ins and outs of paying for travel. When I was hired by the *Washington Post* in 2011, the head of newsroom personnel handed me the *Post*'s ethics guide. The second paragraph reads, "We pay our own way." It continues, "We accept no gifts from news sources. We accept no free trips."

But freelancers don't enjoy the (dwindling) resources of a big newspaper, and many publications have slashed their freelance travel budgets. In fact, in early 2012, the *Post* itself stopped paying expenses for freelancers writing for its Sunday Travel section.

Shrinking travel budgets present a quandary to wanderlustful reporters angling to comb the globe for exotic tales—a description that fits most of us. We want to go get those unique stories, but publications don't want to pay the plane fare. So how do SciLancers respond when a potential source or outside group offers to do so?

SciLancer Cameron Walker, a graduate of the science writing program at the University of California, Santa Cruz, remembers an instructor telling her class to *never* take junkets—they would compromise her writing, her credibility, even her soul. "I got this image of reporters smoking cigars and swilling cocktails on fancy planes," she says.

So she was shocked when she began writing for travel and lifestyle magazines where paid travel was the norm. These glossy magazines rarely foot the travel bills of their writers.

On Cameron's first junket story, which an editor at a travel magazine assigned to her, she was "seriously wined and dined" in Canada. She had a specific assignment covering just one part of the trip, and she knew she would never write about the rest of it. "I don't know if it's Catholic guilt or what, but I never can totally relax and enjoy myself" on such trips, she says, adding that she's never taken free travel for straight news or science stories—only for travel pieces.

Many junkets are organized by foreign governments or their tourist or trade associations. They typically include travel, lodging at swell hotels, and sometimes, fine meals. There's even jargon for these junkets: they're called "fam tours" ("fam" is short for "familiarization").

Despite being the norm in the world of glossy-magazine travel writing, paid travel is forbidden at the *New York Times* and other newspapers. The *Times* stresses that its freelancers must be junket-free. When SciLancer Bryn Nelson landed an assignment with the travel section of the *Times,* he recalls, his editor pointedly asked if he had *ever* taken a junket. (He hadn't.)

The ethics of some types of paid travel are fuzzier to sort out. In 2009, SciLancer Robert Frederick was awarded a trip to an annual conference of Nobel Prize winners in Lindau, Germany. The funding came through the National Association of Science Writers (NASW). Robert, who had a job at *Science* magazine at the time, thought he was in the clear ethically.

But when he arrived in Germany, conference organizers asked him for his receipts. Only then did he learn that the private group putting on the conference had funded the trip via NASW. Robert learned it was common in Europe for science writers to take free travel to such meetings. But he wasn't comfortable with it.

"They literally handed me an envelope with cash in it," Robert says of the organizers. "I felt like I couldn't report a damn thing. I couldn't write for *Science* or freelance from the meeting. I was being paid by the people who put on the conference to cover the conference." There's another term for that: checkbook journalism—news sources paying for stories. It's widely—but, again, not universally—frowned upon.

Given what he saw as a financial conflict of interest, Robert did no reporting from the meeting. Other reporters have felt differently and have, in fact, taken trips to that very conference in Lindau and sold articles from it.

SciLancer Emily Sohn is among the many science writers who find a somewhat different balance than Robert. In 2010 she took a trip to Israel paid for by a university there. She felt as though she had a free hand to report and write what she wanted to from the trip. She sold three stories, and her editors all okayed the arrangement. "Freelancing is tough and travel budgets aren't what they used to be," says Emily. "Sometimes you need to be creative to fund the trips you need to take to write good stories."

So what's the lesson about paid travel? Know where the money is coming from. And, of course, disclose, disclose, disclose—to your editors, at least, if not to your peers.

Managing Conflicts of Interest

Given that it's a messy world out there, conflicts of interest are almost inevitable during a science writing career. To avoid getting tangled up in ethical thickets, feeling lousy about yourself, or crashing your career, think about how to manage potential conflicts. Be conscientious.

Here's one good way to manage conflicts of interest: compartmentalize. Conduct journalism only in fields that don't overlap with the interests of your university, institutional, or corporate clients.

If, say, you take a lucrative opportunity to write newsletters or press materials for a giant drug company, one way to manage potential conflicts is to never write about the drug business journalistically. Confine your journalism to geology or earth science or other fields. That way you'll minimize the number of times you have to ask yourself if your work has been compromised.

As I said at the beginning, every writer needs to make his or her own rules. There will be disagreements. Robert, who declined to write about a conference after the organizers paid for his trip there, owns the rules he made for himself. But he knows they're not for everyone. (That's another good rule.)

"I don't ever want to be in the position where I'm telling someone else what to do and how to do their job," Robert says. "The market being what the market is, if someone is willing to get money for one thing or another, that's fine. But I have a set of rules for myself that I'm comfortable with, and that's what I live by."

The Journalism-Promotion Divide

By Helen Fields

In February 2010, I got an e-mail from a former boss. He was working with an organization that publishes peer-reviewed psychology journals and he needed someone to write occasional press releases. He asked if I was looking for work. As a freelancer, my answer was: *of course*. But I was a little worried—I know some journalism outlets have a problem with freelance reporters who also write press releases or do other so-called institutional science writing.

I called up three editors: one who assigns me short news stories, one who assigns me long features, and one for whom I'd done just a couple of newspaper-style features. I asked each one: If I took this gig, would that limit the kind of work I could do for them?

One said it was fine as long as I didn't write about a study I'd written a press release for. Another said I should stay away from writing about any bigwigs in the organization I would be working for. The third said I couldn't write about any psychology research for her publication. I wasn't particularly interested in covering psychology as a journalist, so I took the gig.

Each press release had a single source: the author of a new study. I didn't dig up critical views of the research or voices of dissent. I didn't investigate researchers' funding sources or step back to ask whether this whole "psychology" thing is bunk. In short, I was not doing journalism. But at the same time, I didn't turn off my brain. I spotted weaknesses in studies. I learned about debates in the field and researchers' criticisms of methodology. I was certainly doing science writing—and in my opinion at least, I didn't become biased toward the studies I wrote the press releases for.

The writer's relationship to sources is different for a press release than it is in journalism, though. The researchers I wrote about approved the text of my press releases, which would never happen in my journalism work. In journalism, sources don't get to decide what reporters write about them. (See "So When Can I Read Your Draft?" in Chapter 4.) To avoid any confusion in case I covered the researchers journalistically in the future, I arranged for someone at the psychology organization to handle that review process instead of me.

I wrote press releases for that organization for two years. Along the way, I learned a great deal about the state of psychology research. And I did develop one bias: a belief that psychology research is cool. But that's pretty normal in journalism. Astronomy writers think astronomy is cool. Political reporters probably even think politics is cool. (Shudder.)

I also decided to keep fitting non-journalism work into my science writing portfolio. By working through the ethical issues around this gig, I've decided—and my journalism editors seem to agree—that I can do both kinds of work. I think the key is to avoid covering the same things in the journalism and non-journalism arenas at the same time. And now that I'm no longer writing psychology press releases, I'm writing more about psychology in my journalism life. I'm glad I had the chance to learn so much about it.

SciLance says . . .

- **Guard your reputation jealously.** Character counts big-time in this business.

- There is **no one set of ethical guidelines** for science writing or journalism. Everyone must find his or her own path.

- **Don't lie, cheat, or steal** (words).

- **Don't double dip** and resell non-journalism work as journalism.

- **Listen to your instincts.** Your gut can help tell you what's right or wrong.

- If a business proposition feels strange, **discuss it with editors and colleagues** before proceeding. Keep the lines of communication open.

- **Be conscious of the choices you make and their implications.** By accepting money from a university or a corporation, for example, you could be closing doors to writing about those institutions journalistically, at least for some time.

- Learn to **responsibly manage conflicts of interest** and disclose any potential conflicts to editors before you agree to take on work.

Chapter 24

Social Networks and the Reputation Economy

By Emily Gertz

Are digital social networks a means to advance our careers, or pathways to professional suicide? Valuable information resources, or bottomless time sinks? In a word: yes. Social networks can greatly enhance a science-writing career. They can build your visibility, promote your work, facilitate your reporting, and more. It's equally possible to use social networks in ways that can damage your credibility, or make it harder to get work. There's an economy on social networks, and its currency is reputation. And our reputation depends on our behavior, the quality of the information we share, and the media we use—words, photos, video, and links being the most common.

What follows are some basic guidelines to working in the digital reputation economy, both getting-started tips for beginners and tune-up suggestions for intermediate users. You can adapt how you use them to fit your own professional needs.

Given the current churn in the social network industry—after all, "would you follow me" today might be as irrelevant as MySpace tomorrow—I'll look at overall best practices for using social networks, rather than techniques specific to particular services.

Journalistic Norms and Social Networks

Social networks may be relatively new. But whether you're a journalist, public relations officer, or educator, the underlying professional norms of traditional science writing should also apply to social media. These include:

- Reporting or writing facts accurately, with verifiable sources to back up those facts
- Forming conclusions based on analysis of the facts, rather than on personal hopes, biases, or opinions
- Attributing quotes, or information reported by others, to the correct sources
- Being an observer rather than a participant in a story (or, in some instances, being transparent about your participation)

Unfortunately, communication on social media routinely violates these norms. Bull-headed opinionizing, ad hominem attacks, and whole-sale invention of information have been features of online community discourse since the days of dial-in bulletin boards. Science writers who want to take advantage of social media's benefits without undercutting themselves, particularly at the outset of their careers, will need to learn to participate in social media without adopting the worst habits of its participants.

How Can Social Networks Help Science Writers?

Two decades into the era of the mainstream Internet, there's still no proof that using online social and sharing networks is crucial to the success of a writing career. Some SciLance members are definitely not true believers. "No one and nothing has convinced me yet that it's worth my time to use social media in my journalism," says Kendall Powell. "I cannot see how it would be anything but a time suck for me."

Others are sold. Hillary Rosner finds social networks "completely invaluable." "It's a way to connect to sources, other journalists, and editors. It's an extra, and really important, tool for circulating your work and your name," Hillary says. "I think it's especially powerful for young writers starting out, because it's a way to get your work in front of editors. It makes the journalism ecosystem a bit more of a meritocracy."

Social networks can connect you with people who are reading, thinking, and doing interesting and important things, and as such they can help you find ideas, meet colleagues and sources, and keep up with fast-breaking news. "I use LinkedIn, Facebook, Twitter, and even Skype to search for information or people in much the same way that I use Google," says Hannah Hoag. "I have, in several cases, found sources through those media that I was unable to track down in other ways."

Other reasons to use social networks: practicing new reporting skills; "following" the information shared at events, such as conferences, that you cannot attend in person; or simply breaking the isolation that free-lance writers often experience while working from home or solo offices. (Read more about loneliness, and how social media can and can't help, in Chapter 12.)

You Are Your Own Words: Creating an Online Persona

In traditional, so-called meatspace office politics, how you look and sound can mean as much as what you do and say (or how you say it). But on social networks there is little if any physical nuance—tone of voice, body language, or facial expression—to what you communicate. On social networks more than anywhere else, you are your own words.* Others will evaluate you based largely on the words and images you share, and how you share them.

Social networks are also characterized by the fast pace, frequency, and brevity of the messages they carry. There's no guarantee that any given person reading your blog entry or status update knows anything about you beyond the words on the screen at that moment. Although the same can be said of your words on the printed page, in that context there are likely to be more of your words in one place, all enhanced by the work of fact-checkers, editors, and graphic designers before they reach anyone's eyeballs.

When readers, editors, and colleagues go looking for more information about you on social networks, you want them to learn things about you that will enhance your credibility. You can prepare for this ahead of time by developing a digital "persona": a public personality similar but not identical to who you really are.

Consciously building a social media persona might strike some as disingenuous. But we do something very similar when engaging in the in-person networking that SciLancer Cameron Walker described in Chapter 20. When schmoozing at conferences, public readings, editorial meetings, and happy hours with colleagues, we emphasize the upbeat

---

*Credit and my appreciation to the online community The WELL and its longtime copyright policy, "You own your own words," which I ripped off to make this point.

developments in our work and downplay the problems. Most of us avoid sensitive subjects, such as religion, politics, or our bank accounts, and instead "curate" the facts about ourselves that we share in public, even among close colleagues, to put our best selves forward. We try to be thoughtful about the boundary between professional and personal in what we say and how we behave.

Professionally oriented commentary, sharing, and reciprocity are all part of the online reputation economy. Some suggestions for professional messaging on social networks:

- Link to your own latest stories or other works.
- Congratulate colleagues on professional accomplishments.
- Link to news related to your beat, such as the potential impact of a new medical study or environmental regulation, that you find informative, well-written, or otherwise worthwhile to the people who follow you online. Pointing out what you found interesting is a good "value-add" that subtly emphasizes your expertise.
- Support your markets. I make a point of "following" publications I write for, and reposting links to their articles and features. This kind of mutual support is intrinsic to community building on social networks.
- Create live "coverage" of events related to your beat. Since I cover a lot of environmental stories, I like "live-tweeting" related events now and then, such as congressional hearings, even if I'm not on assignment.

A Careful Blend of Personal and Professional

You can choose to keep your social-media activity strictly professional, and some of us do. Blending personal updates with professional messaging is a bit riskier, but it can also build the depth of the connections you make on social networks.

Think about how you would do this in a face-to-face setting—at the aforementioned happy hour, for example—and use that experience as a guide. People have varied levels of interest and comfort with different subjects. You're probably not going to offend anyone by sharing anecdotes about your adorable kid's latest exploit, the tasty taco you just ate, or the latest win by your favorite sports team. But by the same token, people who read your social network postings because you're a great science journalist may not be interested in your opinions about sports, food, or your saintly offspring. They may even find them irritating.

Achieving your optimum personal-professional balance on social networks may take some trial and error. If you're really feeling at a loss for how to get started or continue, try picking out a few people on your networks you find the most fun, readable, or informative, and consciously observe their behavior and use of the media. Why do you like their updates? How would you describe their digital personas: Upbeat? Sardonic? Low-key? Excited? How often do they post, and how much do they talk about their own work in comparison to external events or the work of others?

You may divide your professional and personal personas by platform: Some journalists use Twitter for professional purposes, for instance, and reserve Facebook for sharing more personal information. Others organize their lists of social-media contacts so that only certain people can see their more personal updates. But keep in mind that these measures aren't foolproof. Any information posted online, even to a restricted circle, can become public with a stray click or two. So whether your post is personal or professional, be sure it's something you could live with if it roamed far from its intended audience.

What Not to Share

No matter how you shape your online persona, there are certain professional and personal matters that you should never share on social networks:

- Negative opinions about editors, colleagues, or anyone you've worked for. Those opinions will become part of your permanent reputation and possibly close doors to future work.
- Anything about personal finances.
- Gripes about your family.
- Details about assignments in progress, including travel updates.

If you feel you must post on a political issue, one tactic is to comment only on the policies or behavior involved, not on the particular people or political parties. Just remember that not everyone reading your message will detect this nuanced approach. "I'm much more cautious about linking to anything that's partisan or political," says SciLancer Bryn Nelson.

"Even on Facebook, I limit my very occasional politically oriented posts to friends-only instead of to acquaintances." It's good advice: remember that not everyone in your network shares your assumptions or sense of humor, any more than everyone in your extended family does. If in doubt, leave it out.

Time Management and Social Networking

Writers are great at finding ways to put off working. (See Chapter 11 on procrastination.) But now, with the Internet just a click away, the opportunities to kill time really do seem infinite. Along with all the online videos, recipe collections, and celebrity news, it's easy to spend hours on social networks, catching up on news posted by friends, family, or colleagues, following updates from live events, or sharing jokes. The key word here is "spend." Unless you happen to have a gig that pays you to be on social media all day (and I can personally attest that these do exist), there's a fine line between making a reasonable time investment in your digital network—and squandering your most productive hours.

I can't really define where that line is for you. Nor can I provide you with the willpower you'll sometimes need to tune out, turn off, and get back to work. But here are some ideas for managing your time and attention:

Make appointments. If you are the sort of person who can get online and then off again at an appointed time, you already know who you are. One way to use this talent with social networks, where the online audience and topics can shift quickly, is to schedule two or three brief sessions each day.

Sort your stream. For most of us, social networking is most satisfying and efficient when we break down the mass of people and entities we're following into different categories. Different networking platforms conceptualize sorting in different ways: lists, circles, and groups are some of the current modes. Use these tools to help you focus on one type or source of information at a time—say, personal friends or energy news.

Use integration and scheduling tools. Many social networks make their application programming interfaces, or APIs, available to outside programmers, who create tools that enhance use of the network. These tools are typically web browser add-ons, stand-alone computer applications/

programs, or smart-phone/tablet apps. They range from improved visual interfaces, to applications that manage multiple networks at once, to programs that analyze activity. Some are free, while others charge a license or subscription fee. Useful time savers include tools that schedule updates ahead of time, and automatically forward messages that you post on one network to others.

Be selective. You don't need to be on every social network, or even half of them. Instead, think about what you want to accomplish, and decide which network is best suited to the task. "I use LinkedIn to see who's looking at me, like editors," says SciLance member Anne Sasso. "I also use it to monitor activity at clients. If someone starts to increase activity and build up their network, they're often worried about losing their job or about to jump to another job. That's often an opportunity for me to expand my client base."

Finding networks that fit your goals may take some research and experimentation. Pick a few networks to focus on, and downplay or close your other accounts. You can use the time you save to socialize the old-fashioned way.

Blogging: My Digital Calling Card

By Sarah Webb

As a former scientist, I viewed blogging as an experiment. Would writing for free be a useful career move? I gave it a year. I launched a simple Wordpress blog and named it *Webb of Science*. I write about anything, as long as it had some connection to science.

Blogging quickly became a way to share the bits of stories that didn't fit into my finished articles. I posted extra anecdotes and reflected on my personal connection to stories, my experiences as a working scientist, and the challenges women face in male-dominated fields. Blogging helped keep my writing muscles limber and gave me a venue to develop kernels of ideas into something more substantial.

(Continues)

Blogging: My Digital Calling Card *(Continued)*

Over time, the traffic to my blog outpaced the page views on my professional website, and *Webb of Science* became an important part of my online presence. I merged my writing portfolio, bio, and other website information with the blog, making it a one-stop shop for people interested in me and my work. Traffic quickly grew, and though it remains a relatively small blog, I occasionally meet people who say, "Oh, you're *Webb of Science*."

Oh, that single year I envisioned? I've been blogging since 2009.

I find it incredibly gratifying to be recognized for work that doesn't involve an editor or a large corporate media operation. I built the blog, and I write the blog. I make no money directly from it, but *Webb of Science* is both my creative outlet and my digital calling card, and it has become part of the digital engine that powers my business.

SciLance says . . .

- On social networks, **people evaluate you** based on the information you share, and how you share it.

- Apply **the same ethics and self-editing** on social media that you do in your other work.

- Social media are great for promoting your own work, but you'll **build your community** by linking to work by others.

- Don't share details **about assignments-in-progress**, not even travel updates.

- **Manage your social media time**: Find tools and strategies that help you get the most out of digital networks without losing hours from your work day.

Chapter 25

The Diversity of Science Writing

By Sarah Webb

Many science writers start their careers intending to work only as journalists. Journalism alone can be diverse: news, features, blogging, editing, and book projects. But it's also difficult to make a sustainable living solely from journalism, especially for freelancers. Fortunately, journalism outlets represent just one of many possible sources of income for science writers.

Universities and research institutions, corporations, public relations firms, and even individuals hire science writers as editors, and to write news articles and press releases, scientific papers and technical documents, newsletters, and even books. Such work, done on a staff or freelance basis, often pays better than journalism. Is this work right for you? Can you do it and continue to follow your journalism ambitions? Let's look closely at the smorgasbord of science writing opportunities.

The Shapes and Sizes of Science Writing

I started my science-writing career in New York City, and moved from journalism internships to part-time or project-based work combined with freelance journalism. For more than a year, those part-time gigs and projects brought in regular paychecks, and I wrote magazine articles on the side. But by the time I finished up work on a major project in February 2006, my goals had shifted: I wanted to try real, work-from-home-type freelancing. When July hit, however, I had a rather cruel awakening: I brought in exactly $0 that month. Nothing. Not a penny. My future husband had decided to go back to school to get his doctorate. I either needed to make more consistent money as a freelancer, or I needed to look for a full-time job.

As I took stock of my fledgling business, I realized that I couldn't rely on paying the bills solely with hard-to-get popular magazine assignments. I needed to build relationships with a set of clients who required less time to pitch and offered consistent assignments and quick pay. It took months, but I built a foundation of steady science-writing work, and after several years of effort and experimentation, achieved the income security I was looking for. It still takes constant adjustment, but now I'm able to maintain a mix that works for me.

Steady Gigs to Pay the Bills

Depending on your lifestyle, family situation, and cost of living, you have to decide what combination of work will both help you pay the bills and keep you creative and sane. The pressure of basic bills can send writers looking for a full-time job and benefits, and that can be a fine solution. But science writers can also find financial stability by taking on part-time editing or fact-checking work, or relying on a small group of regular clients.

During that July in which I made no money, I noticed that the thing I needed to do most—pitch story ideas and projects to new clients—weighed me down. My idea well felt completely dry, and I realized that I needed a certain baseline level of income to feel free to pursue more ambitious projects. Soon after that I landed a regular fact-checking gig that brought in steady money and helped me fill in gaps between projects. It didn't nurture my writing directly, but it led to related writing work with editors and gave me the income floor I needed to pursue my ambitions.

These days I have several clients who either come to me at the end of one year with several projects for the next year or offer consistent assignments that I can pencil in as likely income. It's an interesting mix of projects: I write features for a life sciences journal and news articles for a trade magazine. I also take on technical editing work for another journal and occasionally for individual researchers.

Freelancing does have a reputation for being a thrill-seeker's game, an "only the strong survive" entrepreneurial situation. For some, it is. But the experience of several SciLancers shows it doesn't have to be. When Virginia Gewin first had her two children, she maintained a regular gig with a science journal, writing profiles of scientists and dissections of new scientific papers. She knew the work was coming, knew the expected formats, and knew how much time each project would take. As her children got older and her work hours expanded, this setup also allowed her the time and financial security to develop news and feature ideas to pitch.

Sampling New Cuisines

So how do you find these higher-paying, non-journalism projects? They usually don't involve the pitch process outlined in Chapter 3. These clients are typically looking for someone who can carry out an already well-defined project, not propose a new idea.

Science writers often hear about these jobs through connections we've made in other contexts—yes, these jobs are another possible outcome of the networking Cameron Walker described in Chapter 20. Sometimes the editors are people we've worked with before, or they've seen our work elsewhere. We might get a referral for a project from a colleague, or get a tip from an online ad on the National Association of Science Writers (NASW) website. And you can always pitch yourself and your science-writing abilities (rather than a story idea) to universities and other institutions. Over the years, I've contacted organizations that might use science writers with a brief e-mail, introducing myself and pointing to my website for samples of my work. Sometimes you can start valuable relationships with a cold call.

Alison Fromme found the NASW job announcements particularly helpful when she was looking for science-writing projects. "Often, I didn't get the original job," she says. "But I did end up in 'the system,' and in some cases people called me with work years later—sometimes even from a different company." Anne Sasso found a favorite client in a similar way. "A cold call led me to a graphic designer, and we got together for lunch," she says. That led to a connection with one of the designer's clients, "and that one introduction led to work with divisions of the company in North America, Europe, and Asia, a fantastic relationship that is still going strong eight years later." Anne works regularly with the graphic designer, too.

Some science-writing projects might involve writing corporate press releases or articles for a sponsored website or publication. Perhaps a non-profit organization needs a science writer to summarize a scientific meeting or write a newsletter for its members. Some of us have written curriculum materials for educational publishers. We've helped small businesses develop the copy for their websites, and we've written and edited white papers and other reports. Sometimes scientists hire us to edit their scientific papers or grant proposals, or universities and research organizations hire us to write press releases, or contribute to annual reports and institutional websites.

In our collective SciLance experience, these types of projects pay at least twice as much per hour as our journalism work. "I did not take very many non-journalism projects the first year or two that I freelanced," says Kendall Powell. "But after realizing how many hours I'd have to work to make the kind of salary I wanted doing just journalism, I started to pick up more PR clients." Sometimes the work also gives us a needed change of pace from the intensity of reporting and writing a complicated journalism story. And as Helen Fields related in Chapter 23, we might also learn about topics that we never would have thought about otherwise, opening up new stories in the future.

Jennifer Cutraro spends part of her work time developing classroom lessons based on science and health news. "Curriculum writing lets me tap into the latent teacher inside me, and think about ways to present science to kids," she says. She still relishes the original reporting she does, too, and loves getting a source on the phone.

"I find that the two approaches complement one another," Jennifer says. "Keeping a foot in science journalism keeps me tuned in to the dynamic nature of science, the little 'aha!' moments that can really hook someone on the topic, and I try to use that in the curriculum work I do." When it comes to getting kids interested in science, she says, "it's the newness of it, the adventure in it, and the people behind it that gets them excited. What better way to stay on top of that than to stay connected to science journalism?"

Wise Work Pairings

Working for both journalism and non-journalism clients can present real or apparent conflicts of interest. Those of us who have a mix of clients draw various lines that separate that corporate or institutional work from our work as journalists. On the occasions that our non-journalism work butts up against a journalism story, we might need to turn down a project or discuss the situation with our editors. See Chapter 23, "The Ethical Science Writer," for more on this topic.

Just because your cash flow is steady doesn't mean you've achieved the perfect mix of work. Maybe you have a great idea for an ambitious feature or a book proposal, but your schedule is too booked with the projects you rely on to stretch and branch out.

Sometimes our careers outgrow the steady gigs that launched us, and we need to recognize when a work situation no longer fits our business needs or our lives. I try to take stock at least once each year to consider which projects I enjoyed, which paid well, and what I'd like to be working on in the next year. Sometimes that leads me to pursue new clients, drop a client that isn't working for me, or even to ask for more money.

It can be difficult to let a steady gig go. But sometimes the results are exhilarating. When her family relocated, SciLancer Emma Marris left her staff reporter position at *Nature* and went on retainer at the journal—an arrangement in which the writer isn't employed by the publication but is guaranteed a certain amount of work each year. At first, Emma says, it seemed like the perfect steady gig to support her new freelance career. But the arrangement also left her with a nagging fear that she wasn't meeting the magazine's unspoken expectations, even though the editors reassured her multiple times.

As a result, Emma took more *Nature* work than she could handle, she says, and "worked like a maniac, shortchanged my book and my family, and started snapping at people." Finally, she decided the retainer deal wasn't worth the stress it caused, and she quit. "Even though I still write for *Nature* a lot, I am so much less stressed, it is unbelievable," she says.

SciLancer Thomas Hayden says that the balance between easy, high-paying work and more personally meaningful, less lucrative work has been "the secret of my financial and emotional happiness." That sweet spot between feeling creatively challenged and financially secure is often elusive. In almost any month, I can look at the work on my plate and find something to feel dissatisfied about. But increasingly, I'm looking for financial and creative balance over the long haul instead of the short term: an individual week or month might not include the perfect mix, but a year might. And because I'm free to steer my own business, I can keep adjusting my course, getting ever closer to a satisfying and sustainable journey.

- When **looking for work outside journalism**, make a list of your skills and interests outside writing. Companies, universities, or nonprofit organizations in those areas could represent future clients.

- **Answer job ads that look interesting**. Even if you don't get the job, you have made contact with a new potential client.

- **Stay in contact with people you've worked with** over the years and make sure they know what you do. You never know when they might need a writer, and you might be the first person who comes to mind.

- Your online presence helps. **Make sure that your website and your social media profiles showcase the full range of your work** and the topics you cover.

- Do research on **organizations that might need science writers**. Find the appropriate e-mail address or phone number for an editor or marketing contact. Introduce yourself and how you might be able to help the organization.

- **Take stock regularly of your projects** and consider factors such as pay rate, ease of working with the client, and your interest in the work. Then you can make adjustments to increase your income or your work satisfaction.

Chapter 26

Sustainable Science Writing

By Jill U Adams

Many science writers get into the business because they love to learn new things about how the world works. They may dig deep into a new interest, play the dilettante, or both over the course of a career. However, as Sarah Webb described in Chapter 25, making a living from science writing may mean taking on the occasional less-than-inspiring project, or doing once-exciting regular work that has become routine. It's not uncommon to lose sight of the reasons you're doing this work, especially during slow stretches or shifts in the media landscape.

In other words, the arc of a science-writing career can take on quite different shapes. Still, we've noticed in SciLance that when you look at enough examples, some general outlines emerge. The key is not just to survive the early, steep part of the curve, but also to find a more comfortable but still challenging plateau that makes science writing sustainable, both financially and creatively, in the long run.

The Climb

Science writing has a steep learning curve. So does freelancing. I took on both, simultaneously, after leaving my academic-scientist career behind. I wrote profiles featuring scientists' hobbies, I wrote about the culture of laboratory work, I wrote about trends in biomedical research. I loved all that, both the process and the results. I was lucky to have a couple of early editors who gave me good feedback, taking the time to explain why this bit I wrote didn't work and—equally important—why that bit did. I also took on some things that didn't fit me so well, such as helping scientists write papers and grants.

My workflow evolved rather organically. I continued with jobs that challenged me in good ways. I quit jobs that had me swearing under my breath. So one lesson I learned in terms of sustaining my own career was to make sure I assessed what the payoffs of different jobs were in terms of enjoyment and accomplishment.

Money plays a role too, of course. And yet, for me, even a big, fat hourly rate couldn't sweeten the scientific-paper writing gigs. I know other science writers make careers out of this, and I admire their business savvy. I had the skill—indeed, I'd been exquisitely trained in this kind of writing—but I couldn't stomach the work.

The Summit—or "Am I There Yet?"

When I was finally making a living wage as a freelance science writer, I examined my numbers. I calculated how much each client contributed to my overall income, as Anne Sasso and Emily Gertz advised in Chapter 19, which was interesting. But I was looking for something more.

So I wrote notes next to my list of clients, describing my quick impressions about pay and payoffs from each:

Good hourly—getting formulaic, but nice product, good relationship. I was no longer challenged by these assignments, but I was happy with the clips and was getting paid well. That's a keeper.

Excellent hourly—plodding work. I was bored to tears writing for this client, but they paid well enough to keep on my docket in small doses.

So-so hourly—I like this market, makes me want to work hard. That last bit, I've learned over the years, is pretty important to me.

Poor hourly—love it, new genres, quick interviewing and writing practice, great relationship. Tricky, right? But once I framed this work as developing skills, I decided I could continue, again within limits.

These little judgments—and let me emphasize "little"; I jotted those notes down in less than ten minutes—helped me see what I had done with my year and helped me make some decisions about the next year. I hadn't done anything as exhaustive as the annual reports Alison Fromme described in Chapter 14, but by analyzing whether and why I wanted to keep working for a particular client, I was learning what kind of work I liked to do. Now I use this kind of information as I seek out new clients.

My point is that career planning need not be all about money and formulaic business plans. You're the boss, even if you work for someone else. You get to decide what work you do, and you should have a rubric for those decisions beyond "I need rent money!"

SciLancer Bryn Nelson says that until recently, he just grabbed at anything that came his way. "I'm now beginning to shape my career a bit more," he says. "One big choice was to drop a regular column that didn't fit with my career goals. That felt like a big step forward to me, because it means I'm taking more control over what I write about and for whom."

Freelancers and staffers alike can benefit from thinking about what you offer to those who hire you, putting a value on that, and communicating that value to your clients or bosses. This can really lift you to the next level, even if you used to be so thrilled to find your byline on the newsstand that you barely cared what you got paid.

Thinking about where you would like to be down the road can also guide work decisions that help you shape your career arc in a more purposeful way. Long-term goals might include more pay, more prestige, or just truly engaging the world around you.

SciLancer Emma Marris, who regularly contributes to *Nature,* says she would like to write for the "Big Sexys"—*Harper's, The Atlantic,* the *New Yorker*—at some point in her career. "But my real goal is to enjoy myself and have interesting conversations," she says.

Oh, That Was a Plateau . . .

By the time I started jotting down those quick-and-dirty business-planny notes, I had gained experience with science writing and freelancing. My learning curve was leveling off. So one key motivator—the challenge posed by "Can I do this science-writing thing?"—was falling away. I was feeling more blasé about my work and I fell into some pretty pathetic work habits.

It's a common story. First you learn, scramble, network. Soon, or not so soon, you have a steady stable of clients. You feel you've arrived, you've done it, you're a successful freelancer.

Then slowly, perhaps inevitably, you begin to feel less and less satisfied. You're bored with the work coming in. You see other writers you know getting plum assignments, and writing features that get selected for *The Best American Science Writing* anthology series, while you continue doing the same-old same-old in relative obscurity.

It happened to me. I would read an article in the *New York Times Magazine* and think, could I do that? I knew it would mean working harder and climbing onto much shakier ground. Perhaps I needed to be happy where I was, making a reasonable income and having lots of quality time for myself and my family, not to mentioning vegetable gardening and running the school science fair.

I stumbled along in that vein for nearly a year. I recognized feelings of wanting to strive higher, but I didn't know if those feelings were coming from outside expectations or from within. Just because I saw other writers doing more ambitious things didn't necessarily mean that model was right for me. Indeed, I had plenty of nonwork things in my life that felt fully worthwhile. Perhaps, I thought, I should just be happy with what I have.

I was sure about one thing: I wanted to make freelance writing work. It was my second career, and I had little interest in starting a third.

Other writers may think more broadly about what else they could do that will earn a living or satisfy a need to make a difference. "I've considered changing my career to something that is more applied and has more of an impact on people," says SciLancer Hannah Hoag, "such as medical school, nursing, or public health." Hannah is sticking with science writing for now, but SciLancer Robin Mejia has made the leap to academia, a transition she described in Chapter 21.

SciLancer Hillary Rosner finds that all she has to do is toy with the idea of doing something else, and she deepens her commitment to her career exactly as it is. "Whenever I hit a slump on the career front, I always try to imagine what else I want to do," she says. "I say, 'Okay, I'm quitting as of now. What's next?' And I can never come up with anything. Five minutes after I mentally quit, I'm already crafting story pitches in my head. I think it's just a question of liberating myself—once I imagine cutting the cord, it becomes fun again, a privilege to be able to make a living this way."

Keeping the Climb Alive

When I told my SciLance colleagues that I'd fallen into a career funk, I got some great advice.

There was the practical, from Emma: "What do I do when I fall into a funk? Run out of money, panic, and start writing again."

The empathetic, from Monya Baker: "I think I have a funk with every story—I hate every single one at some stage and convince myself I'm in the wrong career. Then the deadline comes and the story is out of my life, and somehow the next story seems full of possibility."

A key insight, from Hannah: "A lot of it is recognizing that I'm in a funk and that it is better to go and do other things instead of dwelling on the issue."

My soul-searching resonated with my writer friends, yet I knew I had to answer my questions for myself. So I contacted a life coach for writers—someone I'd heard good things about—and signed on for eight coaching sessions. We started with the surface stuff, such as how (poorly) I spent my time, what burdens ("tolerations," as these coaches say) I carried around, and what I liked and didn't like about my work.

Over time our conversations dug deeper: What stopped me from doing the things I said I wanted? We broke down the long process from idea to story proposal, identifying the one or two steps that routinely tripped me up. Then we went still deeper, reaching the stuff that's much harder to verbalize.

That's where I hit pay dirt. I had an utter epiphany, which went something like this: I have a creative drive, and my general malaise about life and work came from not exercising that drive.

For me, this realization has been enough to challenge me for the foreseeable future. It has also brought tremendous relief. Now I schedule time into my workweek for what I call "Jill projects," instead of vaguely telling myself that I'll tackle dream projects on the weekends. Those breaks have helped me plow through the workaday, pay-the-bills stuff with much less foot-dragging.

Mine is only one path. And it's not as if I'll never fall into a funk again. But I do believe there's much to be learned from looking inward. So I suggest you go ahead and listen, really listen to others' stories; do engage with the world, and report the heck out of it. But make sure you find time to listen to your own stories, too. And as you move through your career, pause to examine what drew you into science writing in the first place. Does that still have meaning for you? Or do you need to find a new motivation?

Finally, believe that while your interests may change, what interests you will always interest others, too. Find those people, and write for them.

- **Take stock of your career and plan ahead**, by making either a formal business plan or informal notes.

- Keep an eye on the bottom line, **but consider your personal satisfaction, too**.

- Contemplate **alternatives within and beyond the writing life**.

- Find **new writing challenges**—maybe change up your beat or try a new storytelling mode, take on editing or teaching, write haiku.

- Create **a support network** of like-minded peers.

- **Seek outside help** in answering the big questions; a writing/career/life coach can work wonders.

- Meditate, dig in the garden, do yoga, go on long hikes, draw in your sketchbook, practice tai chi, take up distance running—**whatever it takes to know thyself**.

AFTERWORD

Finding, or Founding, Your Own Tribe

By Kendall Powell

With more than a decade of science writing under my belt, my career still captivates me every day. I've tramped the foothills of northern Colorado with researchers hunting for ancient pack-rat middens, which, when held intact by crystallized pee, can reveal the types of vegetation the animals hoarded in past millennia. I've watched the premiere of an anti-creationist comedy in a Kansas City movie theater. Even in my phone reporting, I get to learn about the outer frontiers of medical research from some of the world's most passionate intellectuals.

Like the scientists I interview, I'm driven by curiosity, and crafting stories of discovery never fails to satisfy my mind. It also satiates my desire to leave the world a little bit better than I found it. I hope I'm making science not just accessible, but also enjoyable and meaningful for others. And the challenges of running my own business, balancing deadlines with playdates, and pulling just the right words out of my keyboard mean I'm rarely bored or idle.

But the writing life can be an insular one, too. The work of processing and stitching stories together happens largely inside my own head—and for me, inside my own home. My home office can quickly become fraught with ego, insecurities, the crossfire between self-doubt and overconfidence, and procrastination (disguised as domestic chores). As a freelancer, I also often feel like an emotional and physical outsider, without the keys to a publication's culture—or even its accounts payable system. With the wisdom and wit they share, my SciLance colleagues save me from myself every single day.

The good news is, there's a fascinating science story waiting to be told almost anywhere you look. Whether you've been a science writer for years, or you're just now thinking of trying it out, we encourage you to find or form your own version of a writing community. Community has been vital to our development as writers, and we think you'll find it hones your business skills, improves your reporting and writing, and saves your own sanity.

Building your own writing community doesn't take any magic (see "I Started My Own Group and So Can You" on p. 281), but it does take some clear guidelines. To distinguish SciLance from more public and therefore more anonymous listservs, I invited only people I personally knew, or who were recommended by someone I knew. We capped our numbers to keep the group intimate and manageable, and we pledged to be like Vegas: whatever discussion happened on the list, stayed on the list (for a complete list of our ground rules, see our website, www.pitchpublishprosper.com).

But virtual connections will carry you, your mental health, and your career only so far. You need face time, too, with both your colleagues and your editors. Those connections will always be your window to new endeavors and opportunities. We've made sure SciLance doesn't exist only online: we make every attempt to get together in person to imbibe, sing karaoke, hike, and kayak. "SciLance helps all of us keep expanding our professional circles, because we're always meeting each other's acquaintances and colleagues. It's a group that looks outward rather than inward, and that's a big part of its strength," says SciLancer Michelle Nijhuis.

As we've matured as a group, many of us have contributed to the broader online community of science writers: we nurture new online groups, create content and participate in craft discussions at The Open Notebook (www.theopennotebook.com), and blog at the popular science blog *The Last Word on Nothing* (www.lastwordonnothing.com).

I would like to leave you with my own pithy words of encouragement about how much I've gained from my fellow writers. But not surprisingly, I find that another SciLancer said it far better than I ever could. "It's enormously helpful to know that people who I view as far more accomplished than I am have dealt with the same insecurities, frustrations, and occasional heartbreaks that come with this particular career choice," says Jennifer Cutraro. "Seeing many of you break into new markets, land book deals, and take on heavyweight interviews reminds me that it is possible for any of us to have great success in this field—if we put in a hell of a lot of work."

I Started My Own Group and So Can You

By Helen Fields

In 2009, my friend and fellow science writer Naomi Lubick was living in Zurich. I was in Washington, D.C., trying to sort out my new freelance career. Whenever I had a question about how to run my new business or handle a story, I instant-messaged Naomi. She did the same, and it was great.

It was also inconvenient, because she was six hours ahead of me, and it was distracting, since once we'd started, we would get to chatting about her adventures in the Alps and my adventures in health insurance. I liked having a connection with someone else who was working at home, but I wanted more than one person to share my worries with.

Naomi and I had both heard about SciLance through a mutual friend. Great idea, we thought. Any idiot can start an e-mail list! We opened a group, gave it an uncreative name—the Very Small Group, or VSG—and started inviting friends. We adopted SciLance's guidelines, and at first invited only people one of the two of us knew and liked; later we invited trusted friends of other VSG members.

Starting VSG is probably the smartest thing I've ever done for my freelance career. I've shared pitches with the group for comments. I've complained about editors. I've entrusted them with an embarrassingly entitled rant about a prize I didn't win. We reach out to each other when we're excited about a new gig, or when we're wondering how to phrase an e-mail asking for more money. We share everything from jokes to tips on eyebrow shaping, and laugh together at idiotic press releases. We try to meet up with other VSGers when we travel, which has meant some lovely meals in D.C. and, since a third of our members are in Europe, several meetups abroad.

Some of us even use VSG to help us work: when someone is feeling unmotivated, he or she suggests a "sprint." We join an online video chat

(Continues)

I Started My Own Group and
So Can You (Continued)

at a specified time, tell each other what we're going to work on, then buckle down for a set amount of time. We mute the microphones on our computers but leave the video on. I'm still working in my living room, but instead of staring at my screen wondering if anything new has happened on Facebook, I can look at the chat screen and see my colleagues, each hard at work on his or her annoying task of the day. It brings a bit of the newsroom into my life and makes me feel accountable—after all, I can't come back at the end of the sprint and tell everyone I spent the whole time goofing off. (I've been called out for going to make a cup of tea during a sprint.)

The success of any writing community depends on trust, which takes time to build. For us, it has been important to keep our group small. Every now and then we hear from someone who would like to join, but we've held firm at a baker's dozen. In fact, one member of VSG has confided that she felt more comfortable sharing when we had only five people, and thirteen is too many for her.

Fortunately, writing communities can be built in all sizes and configurations. Remember, any idiot can start an e-mail list.

ACKNOWLEDGMENTS

The Science Writers' Handbook started, strictly speaking, with a string of enthusiastic e-mails in 2008. But it is rooted much further back, in the expansive, chaotic, ongoing conversation of a group of science writers called SciLance. All members contributed to this project, but some individuals deserve special thanks for their extraordinary roles.

As business manager, Anne Sasso helped keep us solvent and sane; as project manager, Alison Fromme helped keep us on track and on schedule. Emily Gertz and Sarah Webb coordinated outreach efforts with Da Capo Press and, with the quirktastic help of designer Ron Doyle, developed our web page at www.pitchpublishprosper.com. Cameron Walker kept track of other marketing efforts, Robert Frederick produced our video trailers, and Kendall Powell, as SciLance founder and "list mom," served as driving force, benevolent taskmistress, and court of final appeal for all disputes.

It says something about the value and importance of the National Association of Science Writers that nearly all thirty-five current SciLancers are also NASW members. We gratefully acknowledge the NASW for providing the generous grant that helped start this book on its long road from concept to reality, and thank the members of the NASW Idea Grants Committee for their careful reading of and valuable feedback on our initial proposal.

Our agent, Andrew Paulson of Zachary Shuster Harmsworth, led us through the genteel turbulence of a book auction and has been our irreplaceable guide in putting our "pitch, publish, and prosper" motto into action.

Andrew led us to Da Capo Press, and our editor there, Renée Sedliar. Renée practically became the thirty-sixth SciLancer during the writing and editing of this book, and she coached, guided, and goaded our thoughts into the finished form you see now. To her, and the dedicated team of designers, editors, and marketers at Da Capo, we express our gratitude and admiration.

Five professional colleagues read and commented on early drafts of this book in detail and, by being our first readers, helped make the book much more useful to all those who follow. Our thanks go to Robert Irion of the University of California, Santa Cruz, Science Writing Program, Ann Finkbeiner of the Johns Hopkins University Science Writing Program, Usha Lee McFarling of the University of Washington Department of Communication, San Francisco–based freelancer Tienlon Ho, and Gen Y representative Danielle Venton, science reporter at North Bay Public Media–KRCB.

For the most part, we drew on the experience and expertise within SciLance for the stories and advice in this book. But each of us in turn has been inspired and guided by countless other practitioners, editors, and mentors along the way. Some are named or quoted in the text. Many others are not, but their influence is pervasive throughout, and we're grateful for it; with this book, we hope to pass on some of the many lessons they gave to us. For many of us now working as science writers, the *NASW Field Guide for Science Writers* was also an important early influence, and we thank its editors, Deborah Blum, Mary Knudson, and Robin Marantz Henig.

As the editors of this book, we've had the unique joy and challenge of editing our own friends and peers—and have benefited immeasurably from their insights, hard work, and good company. The authors of this book met every deadline, responded with creativity and grace to every edit, and exceeded expectations with every revision. Writing is a solo pursuit, but SciLance proves it doesn't have to be lonely. Our partners and young children, meanwhile, have withstood even more crankiness and distraction than usual during the birthing of this book. Without the support of Jack and Sylvia, and Erika, Seamus, and Eleonora, both the book and its editors would be greatly diminished things. We thank our families, our communities, and last but not least, each other for the extra and continued helpings of patience, generosity, and fine companionship.

Thomas Hayden and Michelle Nijhuis
October 2012

CONTRIBUTORS

Jill U Adams writes about health, medicine, and nature for such publications as the *Los Angeles Times, Audubon, Nature,* WebMD, and *Discover.* www.jilluadams.com

Monya Baker writes about biotechnology for Nature Publishing Group. Her work has appeared in *The Economist, Nature, New Scientist, Wired,* and elsewhere.

Jennifer Cutraro specializes in writing for kids and educators. She contributes to *Science News for Kids* and publishes a weekly science lesson in the *New York Times* Learning Network.

Helen Fields lives, writes, and knits in Washington, D.C. She used to have staff jobs at magazines but has been working for herself since 2008. www.heyhelen.com

Douglas Fox has written for *Discover, Scientific American, Popular Mechanics, Esquire,* and the *Christian Science Monitor.* His work has appeared in *The Best American Science and Nature Writing.* www.douglasfox.org

Journalist, artist, vocalist, and producer **Robert Frederick** is a multimedia freelancer with a background in mathematics, philosophy, art, and voice. He specializes in physical sciences. www.robertfrederick.co

Alison Fromme has tracked rattlesnakes, witnessed dynamite blasts, and eaten goat stew—all in search of a good story. She lives in Ithaca, New

York, and writes for magazines, educational organizations, and research foundations. www.alisonfromme.com

Emily Gertz covers environment, science, and technology for outlets including *Popular Science, Popular Mechanics,* O'Reilly Media, and TalkingPointsMemo.com. Her handle is "ejgertz" on most social networks. www.emilygertz.com

Virginia Gewin writes about science broadly, but she's partial to ecology. She has written for the *Oregonian, Nature, PLOS Biology, Portland Monthly,* and *Consumers Digest.* www.virginiagewin.com

Liza Gross writes about wildlife, ecology, and environmental health, focusing on science and society. She's an *Environmental Health News* contributor, KQED QUEST blogger, and *PLOS Biology* staff editor. www.lizagross.com

Thomas Hayden teaches science writing, environmental journalism, and sustainability science at Stanford University. His cover stories have appeared in *National Geographic, Wired, Smithsonian,* and many other publications. www.thomas-hayden.com

Adam Hinterthuer has written about everything from estrogen mimics to electric fish barriers. His work has appeared in *Scientific American, BioScience,* and Audubon.org.

Hannah Hoag trained as a molecular biologist before becoming a journalist. She writes for *Nature, Wired,* the *Globe and Mail,* and others, covering science, medical research, and environmental issues. www.hannahhoag.net

Emma Marris writes mostly about the environment. Her first book is *Rambunctious Garden: Saving Nature in a Post-Wild World.* www.emmamarris.com

Jessica Marshall earned her PhD in chemical engineering before becoming a science writer via the University of California, Santa Cruz, science communication program. She lives in St. Paul, Minnesota. www.jmarshall.us

Amanda Mascarelli enjoys covering a wide range of topics, from the neuroscience of magic to the ecology of Arctic songbirds. She lives in Denver with her husband and three children. www.amandamascarelli.com

When she's not applying to fellowships or graduate programs, **Robin Mejia** writes award-winning stories and dances salsa.

Susan Moran lives in Colorado and covers energy development, environmental health, climate change, and business for the *New York Times, The Economist,* and *Nature.* She also cohosts a science show on KGNU Community Radio in Denver and Boulder. www.susankmoran.com

Bryn Nelson is a Seattle-based freelance writer and editor with a particular affinity for stories about science, medicine, the environment, and unconventional travel destinations. www.brynnelson.com

Michelle Nijhuis's award-winning reporting appears in *National Geographic* and other publications. She is a longtime contributing editor of *High Country News* and was a 2011 Alicia Patterson fellow. www.michellenijhuis.com

Stephen Ornes writes about physics, math, and cancer research from a cozy shed in his backyard in Nashville. www.stephenornes.com

Kendall Powell covers biology, from molecules to maternity, in such places as *Nature* and the *Los Angeles Times.* Based near Denver, she founded SciLance in 2005. www.kendallpowellsciwriting.com

Hillary Rosner was a 2012 Alicia Patterson fellow and a 2010 Knight Science Journalism Fellow at MIT. She writes about the environment for many national publications. www.hillaryr.net

Vermont-based writer **Anne Sasso** is a geologist and accomplished freelancer, equally at home in the pages of popular magazines and the boardrooms of corporate clients. www.annesasso.com

Mark Schrope writes for publications such as *Nature* and the *Washington Post.* Assignments have taken him around the world, from Colombia to Egypt to Fiji. www.markschrope.com

Emily Sohn covers health, food, news analysis, and more from Minneapolis. Publications include *Discovery News,* the *Los Angeles Times, Health,* and dozens of books for young people. www.tidepoolsinc.com

Gisela Telis has written for the *Christian Science Monitor, Science,* and other national publications. In 2011–2012, she was a Rosalynn Carter Mental Health Journalism Fellow.

Brian Vastag, a science reporter at the *Washington Post,* freelanced for seven years. He is a cowinner of the 2012 American Geophysical Union David Perlman Award for breaking news. www.brianvastag.net

Andreas von Bubnoff, PhD, mostly covers science for American and European publications. His work has also appeared in *The Best American Science and Nature Writing.* He lives in Brooklyn.

Cameron Walker is a California-based writer. She covers science, travel, and the quirks of the Pacific coast, and blogs at *The Last Word On Nothing.* www.cameronwalker.net

Trained as a PhD chemist, **Sarah Webb** has written for *Discover, Science News, Science News for Kids, Science, Nature Biotechnology,* and many other publications. www.webbofscience.com

SELECTED RESOURCES

Writing about writing means standing on the shoulders of giants. Here, we list some of our sources of inspiration—and some places to dig more deeply into the topics covered in this book.

Part I: The Skilled Science Writer

Chapter 1: What Makes a Science Writer? by Alison Fromme

The National Association of Science Writers, www.nasw.org, is the nerve center of the science writing community. New science writers can find information, advice, mentors, and colleagues through the NASW website and at the organization's annual meetings.

ScienceOnline, www.scienceonline.com and www.scienceonlinenow.org, organizes a popular annual gathering (and other events throughout the year) for science bloggers, journalists, students, educators, and others interested in communicating science online.

Other organizations that may be of interest to science writers include the Society of Environmental Journalists, www.sej.org; the Association of Health Care Journalists, www.healthjournalism.org; Investigative Reporters and Editors, www.ire.org; and the American Society of Journalists and Authors, www.asja.org.

Find a directory of US courses and programs in science journalism and science communication at dsc.journalism.wisc.edu.

The Poynter Institute, www.poynter.org, a nonprofit organization dedicated to professional education for journalists of all types, offers a wide range of courses at its St. Petersburg, Florida, campus, at selected locations nationwide, and online through its News University, www.newsu.org.

The *Columbia Journalism Review,* www.cjr.org, has been reporting on the state of journalism in the US and beyond for more than fifty years, and the perspectives in its pages are well worth the price of a subscription. The Observatory, an online *CJR* column, takes a close look at science journalism. Similarly, the Knight Science Journalism Tracker, ksj.mit.edu, posts a daily critique of recent science reporting.

Chapter 2: Finding Ideas by Emily Sohn

In "Progression," a 2011 article for the *New Yorker,* master nonfiction writer John McPhee suggests taking a deeper look at subjects that interest you, even if you don't have a clear idea yet where they'll lead. "For nonfiction projects, ideas are everywhere," he writes. "They just go by in a ceaseless stream."

For inspiration of a more general sort, I often turn to Annie Dillard's *Pilgrim at Tinker Creek.* It reads like a long ode to nature. At its heart, it is simply about the details the author notices in the world around her. It goes to show that anything can become a story if you look at it closely and write about it well.

Chapter 3: Making the Pitch by Thomas Hayden

The weird art of pitching is not well codified. Though general references for freelancers, such as *Writer's Market,* list the basic ingredients of a good pitch, magazines and individual editors often have their own preferences. The best way to learn is to study examples of successful pitches: an excellent selection of science-oriented magazine pitches is available at The Open Notebook, www.theopennotebook.com. The American Society of Journalists and Authors, www.asja.org, also maintains a database of successful pitches by members. The detailed submission and writing guidelines at *ScienceNOW,* news.sciencemag.org/pitching-sciencenow.html, are essential before pitching this online news arm of *Science* magazine. They also serve as a reliable guide to pitching science news stories anywhere.

Chapter 4: Getting the Story, and Getting It Right
by Andreas von Bubnoff

Reporting and Writing: Basics for the 21st Century by Christopher Scanlan is a great resource for beginners.

Writing to Deadline: The Journalist at Work by Donald Murray covers the newswriting process from beginning to end. Written in an accessible, lively style, it includes case studies and interviews with working journalists.

The Investigative Reporter's Handbook: A Guide to Documents, Databases and Techniques by Brant Houston and Investigative Reporters and Editors, is an invaluable guide to investigative work, and useful to reporters of any stripe.

The Craft of Interviewing by John Brady discusses the interviewing process in great detail.

The Fact Checker's Bible: A Guide to Getting It Right by Sarah Harrison Smith outlines the typical fact-checking process at major magazines. Useful for learning to fact-check your own work, or for smoothing your relationships with fact-checkers.

Chapter 5: By the Numbers: Essential Statistics for Science Writers by Stephen Ornes

Read the *Health News Review,* www.healthnewsreview.org, for a critical look at current coverage of health research, including the use and interpretation of statistics by the media.

STATS, www.stats.org, a group of statisticians based at George Mason University, can provide an expert voice for your news story or help you with background statistics questions. Click on the "Are you a journalist?" link at the top of their web page.

For a deeper look at the misuse of numbers in public discourse, read *Proofiness: The Dark Arts of Mathematical Deception,* by New York University journalism professor Charles Seife.

Chapter 6: Excavating the Evidence: Reporting for Narrative by Douglas Fox

A good starting point for improving, expanding, or polishing your narrative skills is *Telling True Stories: A Nonfiction Writers' Guide from the Nieman Foundation at Harvard University*, an anthology of short essays on craft by well-known narrative writers. *You Can't Make This Stuff Up,* by Lee Gutkind, provides strategies, insights, and examples to help readers understand and create powerful nonfiction writing.

The Open Notebook, www.theopennotebook.com, mentioned above, publishes interviews with the authors of outstanding science stories, with an emphasis on narrative.

Find wonderful examples of new and old long-form journalism and great discussions about narrative craft on the Nieman Storyboard, a project of the Nieman Foundation for Journalism at Harvard: www.niemanstoryboard.org.

Chapter 7: Sculpting the Story by Michelle Nijhuis

I'm a habitual collector of how-to-write books, and a few that I regularly pull down from my shelf are: *Telling True Stories,* mentioned above; *A Writer's Coach: An Editor's Guide to Words That Work* by Jack Hart; and *The Elements of Story: Field Notes on Nonfiction Writing* by Francis Flaherty.

Follow the Story by James Stewart is a good in-depth look at what's often referred to as the *Wall Street Journal* feature structure. *The Sound on the Page* by Ben Yagoda is a terrific exploration of writers' personal voices. I also like to check out the annual *Best American Magazine Writing, Best American Science and Nature Writing,* and *Best American Science Writing* anthologies for inspiring examples.

John McPhee, also mentioned above, is a past master of structure. You can read his books, read his many articles in the *New Yorker,* or read about his process in a lengthy 2010 *Paris Review* interview with journalist and former student Peter Hessler, available in full at www.theparisreview.org.

Chapter 8: Working with Editors—and Their Edits by Monya Baker and Jessica Marshall

In the classic writing guide *On Writing Well,* William Zinsser publishes a couple of pages from a draft of the book, showing how he was able to trim and improve his own writing. Zinsser's book is a great place to hone your self-editing skills. Also read "Why William Zinsser's Writing Book Is Still Number One," an ode to the book and its advice on editing, at www.poynter.org.

Other insights into the writer-editor relationship and the editor's world can be found in *The Art of Making Magazines: On Being an Editor and Other Views from the Industry,* edited by Victor S. Navasky and Evan Cornog; *Coaching Writers: Editors and Writers Working Together Across Media Platforms* by Roy Peter Clark and Don Fry; and *The Elements of Editing: A Modern Guide for Editors and Journalists* by Arthur Plotnik.

And finally, "The Manifesto for the Simple Scribe," a collection of mantras by Tim Radford, former science editor at *The Guardian,* will make you smile—and help you turn in the best possible product to your editor. Available at www.guardian.co.uk.

Chapter 9: Going Long: How to Sell a Book by Emma Marris

Ready to write a book? First try reading *The Forest for the Trees: An Editor's Advice to Writers* by Betsy Lerner and *Thinking Like Your Editor: How to*

Write Great Serious Nonfiction—and Get It Published by Susan Rabiner and Alfred Fortunato.

The Open Notebook, www.theopennotebook.com, mentioned above, often features interviews with authors of science books. In a 2011 interview, Rebecca Skloot discusses the structure of *The Immortal Life of Henrietta Lacks*. And in a 2012 piece, "From News to Books," six science authors talk about how they began writing books.

To find an agent, look for names in the acknowledgments section of your favorite books. Then use the Association of Authors' Representatives database, www.aaronline.org, to search for their details.

Chapter 10: Multilancing by Robert Frederick

Transom.org has been and continues to be the go-to place for people who really love thinking about and making better radio, with links on everything from story structure to equipment reviews. Videomaker, www.videomaker.com, is a venerable and wide-ranging site about creating good videos.

Journalist and journalism educator Mindy McAdams follows the trends and literature in the online journalism field, and blogs at mindymcadams.com/tojou. Her tutorials and teaching materials are freely available at Journalists' Toolkit, www.jtoolkit.com.

The Knight Digital Media Center, www.knightdigitalmediacenter.org, offers trainings and maintains a well-organized list of new media resources. The BBC Academy, www.bbcacademy.com, also offers classes on multimedia story production and related topics.

Chapter 11: Just Write the Friggin' Thing Already! by Anne Sasso

Two go-to books help propel me out of an entrenched procrastination eddies: *Thunder and Lightning: Cracking Open the Writer's Craft* by Natalie Goldberg and *Writing Tools: 50 Essential Strategies for Every Writer* by Roy Peter Clark.

Roy Peter Clark also has an app, available on iTunes and elsewhere, that addresses many of the procrastination-triggering steps in the writing process.

Other SciLancers recommend the classic but still very relevant *The Now Habit: A Strategic Program for Overcoming Procrastination and Enjoying Guilt-Free Play* by Neil Fiore.

Part II: The Sane Science Writer

Chapter 12: The Loneliness of the Science Writer
by Stephen Ornes

To start shaking off the chill of loneliness: Get thee to a group. It doesn't really matter what kind. Meetup.com offers a variety of groups, including writing groups, in almost any city in the US.

The NASW freelancer listserv, as others have mentioned, is a widely read and often lively discussion board that covers all aspects of science writing.

Why not get to know your enemy? Psychologist John Cacioppo at the University of Chicago has been studying loneliness—and its impact on other aspects of life—for twenty years. Check out his book *Loneliness: Human Nature and the Need for Social Connection.*

Chapter 13: Good Luck Placing This Elsewhere: How to Cope with Rejection by Hillary Rosner

While there are any number of self-help books about healing a bruised ego, my best antidotes to rejection are exercise, good company, and the following:

2 parts fresh squeezed lemon juice or a mix of fresh orange and lemon
2 parts whiskey or rye
1 part simple syrup
Mix and serve over ice. Repeat as necessary.

Chapter 14: Beyond Compare by Michelle Nijhuis

Status Anxiety by Alain de Botton is a fascinating and very accessible exploration of the roots of envy and comparative thinking.

The classic writing guide *Bird by Bird* by Anne Lamott is terrific for all sorts of reasons, but it has an especially funny and memorable chapter about jealousy.

A 2003 *Granta* essay by Kathryn Chetkovich, "Envy," is admirable for its honest account of life as the partner of uber-successful novelist Jonathan Franzen.

In "How 'Iris Chang' Became a Verb," by Paula Kamen, published by Salon.com in 2004, a friend of Iris Chang's eulogizes the brilliant journalist, and honestly examines her own envy of Chang's success.

Chapter 15: An Experimental Guide to Achieving Balance by Virginia Gewin

Parents magazine, www.parents.com, has a whole section devoted to articles on work-life balance.

The American Medical Women's Association report "Creating a Work-Life Balance Plan" is available at www.amwa-doc.org.

David Roberts's essay "The Medium Chill," at www.grist.org, describes one writer's approach to balance.

And as always, there's an app for that: check out the "10 Apps for Achieving Work-Life Balance" at www.businessnewsdaily.com.

Chapter 16: Creating Creative Spaces by Hannah Hoag

David Pogue reviews just about every camera, computer, operating system, and app that comes across his desk in his column for the *New York Times*. Follow *Pogue's Posts* at pogue.blogs.nytimes.com.

Transom.org, mentioned above, is about making public radio, but its Gear Guides are essential for anyone interested in preserving audio interviews or setting up a small recording studio for radio or podcast productions.

The blog *Lifehacker*, lifehacker.com, is full of nifty tech tips for improving your efficiency at work and elsewhere.

Finally, a great overview of coworking and directory of coworking locations is available at wiki.coworking.com.

Chapter 17: Avoiding Domestic Disasters by Bryn Nelson

The *FreelanceSwitch* blog, freelanceswitch.com, has published some thoughtful entries on maintaining a proper work-life balance and on defining yourself as a professional. See especially "How to Manage Your Work Life Balance and Reduce Stress" and a wry post about earning respect called "Mixed Marriages: When One Spouse Goes Freelance."

Also see an excellent 2009 article from the *New York Times*, www.nytimes.com, "When Home Turns Office for Two."

You can relieve your stress anytime with this hilariously accurate cartoon observation by The Oatmeal, "Why Working from Home Is Both Awesome and Horrible," www.theoatmeal.com.

Chapter 18: Children and Deadlines: A Messy Rodeo
by Amanda Mascarelli

Beyond One: Growing a Family and Getting a Life by Jennifer Bingham Hall is my favorite work-related parenting book. It helped prepare me for the realities of life with multiple kids, and showed me how a fellow journalist is managing them.

"Confessions from a Former Parenting Editor" is one of many charming essays about parenting available at www.babble.com.

Brain, Child: The Magazine for Thinking Mothers, recently rebooted, is a thought-provoking magazine filled with rich, honest essays on tough parenting topics.

Part III: The Solvent Science Writer

Chapter 19: Minding the Business by Anne Sasso
and Emily Gertz

The IRS, www.irs.gov, has many informative publications for small-business owners, including #334, "Tax Guide for Small Business," and #587, "Business Use of Your Home."

The US Small Business Administration also offers a wealth of online resources at www.sba.gov.

To learn more about your health insurance options and the national Affordable Care Act, start with www.healthcare.gov. The Commonwealth Fund Health Reform Resource Center, www.commonwealthfund.org, offers good information on consumer rights under the act.

Anne's go-to reference for business-related dilemmas is *The Business Side of Creativity: The Complete Guide to Running a Small Graphic Design or Communications Business* by Cameron Foote. Emily often digs into the pages of *Running a One-Person Business, Revised Second Edition,* by Claude Whitmeyer and Salli Rasberry. Although this book is out of print (and thus its technology suggestions are dated), copies are often available via online resellers.

Other good business books include *What to Charge: Pricing Strategies for Freelancers and Consultants* by Laurie Lewis and *The Money Book for Freelancers, Part-Timers, and the Self-Employed: The Only Personal Finance System for People with Not-So-Permanent Jobs* by Joseph D'Agnese and Denise Kiernan.

Chapter 20: Networking for the Nervous by Cameron Walker

Peter Bowerman's *The Well-Fed Writer* focuses on copywriting rather than journalism, but it includes solid tips on marketing. Other useful books on marketing and business relationships are *The Creative Business Guide to Marketing: Selling and Branding Design, Advertising, Interactive and Editorial Services* by Cameron Foote; *Fierce Conversations* by Susan Scott; and *Getting Naked: A Business Fable About Shedding the Three Fears That Sabotage Client Loyalty* by Patrick Lencioni.

The Marketing Mentor website, www.marketing-mentor.com, offers free marketing tips as well as marketing calendars, planners, and coaching. The site is primarily for graphic designers, but many of the tips are equally useful for writers.

Chapter 21: Paid to Grow by Robin Mejia

JournalismJobs.com is a good place to start looking for fellowships. However, not all their listings are up to date, so if a program interests you, double-check to make sure it still exists.

Here's a sampling of fellowships for science writers.

Residential Fellowships
Nieman Fellowship at Harvard, nieman.harvard.edu
Knight Science Journalism Fellowship at MIT, ksj.mit.edu
Knight-Wallace Fellowship at the University of Michigan,
    mjfellows.org
Ted Scripps Fellowship in Environmental Journalism at the
    University of Colorado, Boulder, www.colorado.edu
Kavli Journalist-in-Residence Program at UC Santa Barbara:
    www.kitp.ucsb.edu

Reporting Fellowships and Grants
Alicia Patterson Foundation Fellowship, aliciapatterson.org
Rosalynn Carter Fellowships for Mental Health Journalism,
    www.cartercenter.org
Kaiser Media Fellowships in Health, www.kff.org
Pulitzer Center on Crisis Reporting, pulitzercenter.org
Fund for Investigative Journalism, fij.org
Fund for Environmental Journalism, www.sej.org
NASW Idea Grants, www.nasw.org

Boot Camps and Other Short-Term Programs
Knight Science Journalism boot camps at MIT, mit.edu
Knight Digital Media trainings, www.knightdigitalmediacenter.org
Logan Science Journalism Fellowships at the Marine Biological
    Laboratory in Woods Hole, hermes.mbl.edu
Ocean Science Journalism Fellowships at Woods Hole
    Oceanographic Institute, www.whoi.edu

Chapter 22: Contract Literacy by Mark Schrope

Most writing organizations, including the National Association of Science Writers and the American Society of Journalists and Authors, offer some form of personalized help to members, and many have freely available advice on their websites.

SciLancer Kendall Powell's excellent article "Liability: How to Limit Yours," is available at www.nasw.org. It includes detailed language that can be used to improve indemnity clauses.

Former writer and media lawyer Mark Fowler writes a helpful and at times even entertaining blog called *Rights of Writers,* www.rightsofwriters.com. It's a great place to learn about contract issues and a range of related topics such as plagiarism, liability, and what happens if you, say, write something incorrect that gets somebody killed.

Chapter 23: The Ethical Science Writer by Brian Vastag

The Society of Professional Journalists' ethics page includes essays on various ethics topics and the group's own code of ethics. See www.spj.org/ethics.asp.

Journalism.org, home of the Pew Research Center's Project for Excellence in Journalism, maintains links to ethics guides from the *New York Times,* NPR, and dozens of other news outlets and professional groups.

Still stumped about doing the right thing? Staff at the Poynter Institute will address ethics questions on deadline if you reach them during East Coast business hours at (727) 821-9494 (and if you call after business hours, maintenance and security staff will do their best to contact an ethics expert for you). The institute also maintains resources on ethics at www.poynter.org.

The 2003 movie *Shattered Glass,* based on the case of disgraced *New Republic* reporter Stephen Glass, dramatizes his attempt to replace journalism with fabulism.

The Journalist and the Murderer, Janet Malcom's absorbing and controversial 1990 study of the relationship between a journalist and his subject, is still discussed today.

Chapter 24: Social Networks and the Reputation Economy
by Emily Gertz

Social media guru Sree Sreenivasan, chief digital officer and journalism professor at Columbia University, updates his tips, resource pointers, and workshop schedule at bit.ly/sreesoc. He blogs on social media at news.cnet.com/sree-tips.

Science Online, scienceonline.com, mentioned above, typically has a robust online presence, letting you follow along from afar if you can't make it to North Carolina in January for the conference.

The Online News Association, journalists.org, also has an annual conference as well as active local groups.

Poynter News University, newsu.org, mentioned above, offers all sorts of digital skill-building classes online, including how to use social media as a journalist.

MuckRack, muckrack.com, helps you find journalists to follow on Twitter by beat, news affiliation, and more.

To track the uses, impacts, and business of social media (and other things tech+media), read *All Things D,* allthingsd.com; *Mashable,* mashable.com; *O'Reilly Radar,* radar.oreilly.com; *ReadWrite,* readwrite.com; and *PaidContent,* paidcontent.com.

Chapter 25: The Diversity of Science Writing by Sarah Webb

Freelance Success, www.freelancesuccess.com, is an online subscription-only organization, but its discussion boards are a great resource for information about all types of freelance writing work. Through Freelance Success, I found an extremely useful online business planning class taught by Erik Sherman, www.eriksherman.com.

The National Association of Science Writers maintains a jobs list available to NASW members.

Chapter 26: Sustainable Science Writing by Jill U Adams

Stephen Johnson's TED talk "Where Good Ideas Come From" convinced me that my ideas are worth working on, no matter how big or little, and even if I never sell a story I've worked on, doing the work will prepare me for success with a future one.

The writers, actors, and artists interviewed by Terry Gross on the NPR program *Fresh Air* often talk about where they got their ideas, what kept them going, and how they keep motivation alive in the face of likely futility.

Marla Beck, www.marla.typepad.com, offers small doses of helpful tips for writers in her blog *The Relaxed Writer.*

INDEX

"AB/BC" rule, 81–82

Absolute risk, 58

Academic journal system
embargoes and, 12–13, 22
major journal examples, 12
obscure/international journals,
14, 22
online news services, 13
press releases, 13–15

Accountants, 202

Adams, Jill U, 15, 45, 88, 128, 140,
162

Affordable Care Act, 206, 207, 208,
212

Albany Times Union, 15

Aldhous, Peter, 30, 48, 87, 91, 92,
93, 94, 95–96, 232, 234

Alicia Patterson fellowship, 225,
226, 227

Allen, Frank, 49

Alvin research submarine, 189

American Society of Journalists and
Authors (ASJA), 207, 238, 242

Angier, Natalie, 150

Annual Reviews, 41

Atlantic, The, 145, 275

Audubon, 20

Backpacker, 19

Baker, Monya, 42, 127, 144, 154,
177, 180, 277

Balancing work/life
breaks, 162
freelancing while working full
time, 165–166
office location, 158–159
smart phones and, 160–161
time boundaries, 159–160
turning down work, 161–162
vacations, 162, 163–164
See also Children and writing

Banaszynski, Jacqui, 79

Barton, Hazel, 16

Beekeeper's Lament, The
(Nordhaus), 145

Belden, Kathy, 105

*Best American Science and Nature
Writing*, 20, 21, 111

Best American Science Writing,
111

Billboard/nut graf, 79, 84–85, 89

Bird by Bird (Lamott), 151

Blair, Jayson, 249

Blogs, 6, 265–266, 280

Boger, Ann, 211, 212

Book tours, 109

Book writing
agents, 102–104
benefits, 99–100, 105
coauthoring, 109–110
compilations, 111–112
contract, 105–106, 230

Book writing (*continued*)
  editing, 108
  "Fear, The," and 106–107
  length, 109
  money and, 99, 100, 110,
    111–112, 115
  process overview, 100–109
  proposal, 102–105
  publicizing, 108–109
  query letter sample, 112–113
  recognizing book idea, 114
  research, 101–102
  self-publishing, 100, 105
  selling to editor, 104–105
  social media and, 109
  tips summary, 115
  trade book vs. text book,
    105–106, 111
  writing process, 106–108
Booker, Christopher, 77
Bookkeeping
  basics, 199–202
  cash vs. accrual accounting,
    200–201
  single vs. double entry, 200
  written vs. computerized
    methods, 200–201
Boston Globe, 139, 219
Burdick, Alan, 143
Business cards, 172, 221
Business issues
  advisers, 213
  professional attitude, 8,
    147–148
  project time/payment
    calculations, 244
  tips summary, 213–214
  See also specific components
Business structures, 195–199

Calendars, 170
Cancer Chronicles, The (Johnson),
  81
Cancer Research, 119

Cancer Today (*CR* magazine),
  19–20
Career sustainability, 273–278
Causation vs. correlation, 55
Center for Investigative Reporting,
  223, 227, 250
Checkbook journalism, 255
Chetkovich, Kathryn, 149
Chicago Tribune, 21
Children and writing
  child care options, 187
  managing, 163, 183–191
Christian Science Monitor, 35, 63
Clark, Roy Peter, 128
CNN, 14, 16, 223, 227, 250
Communication equipment
  overview, 169
Competition. *See* Envy
Computer recommendations,
  167–169
Confidence interval, 55, 57
Contracts (articles)
  fee clauses, 235–236
  indemnity clause, 232–235
  kill fees, 239–240
  lawsuits and, 231, 232–235
  liability clause, 231–232
  other restrictions, 240–241
  requesting changes, 241–243
  rights clauses, 236–239
  tips summary, 245
  "work made for hire," 237–239
Corcoran, David, 92
Corporation (S Corp) business
  structure, 196–198, 199
Correlation vs. causation, 55
Council for the Advancement of
  Science Writing, 251–252
Crichton, Michael, 35
Cutraro, Jennifer, 51, 139, 187,
  219, 270, 280

Daley, Beth, 219
Dallas Morning News, 118–119

Davis, Joshua, 64–65, 71
De Botton, Alain, 152
Dek/standfirst, 76
Dental insurance, 205, 207
Disability insurance, 205, 211–212
Discover, 15, 34, 35, 69, 72
Discovery News, 13
Diversity of science writing
  non-journalism projects,
    267–271
  tips summary, 272
Dobbs, David, 6, 145
Documentary on crime labs, 223,
  227–228
Dodd, Scott, 96–97
Domestic peace
  office and, 175, 177–178
  overview, 175–182
  setting expectations, 176–177
  tips summary, 182
  working vacation, 175, 180–182
Dylan, Bob, 249

Editors and writers
  contact during assignment,
    88–91
  deadlines and, 91
  edits and, 93–96
  filing the story, 91–93
  tips summary, 97–98
  understanding, 87–88
  word count and, 91–92
Embargoes, 12–13, 22
Envy
  examples/coping, 149–155
  tips summary, 156
Equinox, 26, 27
Esquire, 83
Ethics
  of conducting journalism,
    247–248
  conflicts of interest management,
    255–256
  description, 246

Jonah Lehrer example, 248–249
lecture circuit, 252–253
money and, 248, 249–255
press-releases and, 256–257
reputation and, 246
tips summary, 258
travel funding and, 72, 248,
  253–255

"Fam tours," 254
Fellowships
  benefits, 72, 224–228
  examples, 223–224, 225–226
  tips summary, 228–229
Fields, Helen, 78, 82, 128, 270
Finkbeiner, Ann, 81–82
Foley, Jim, Jr., 196, 197, 198, 199
Fowler, Mark, 233–234
Fox, Douglas, 8, 14, 18, 20, 47, 77,
  78, 111, 116, 121, 126–127,
  138, 140, 153, 159, 163, 189,
  206, 216
Frederick, Robert, 12, 16, 42, 127,
  148, 157, 160, 162, 179, 203,
  205, 254–255, 256
Freedom of Information Act
  requests, 24, 41
Freelancers Union/insurance, 202,
  207, 211, 212
Fromme, Alison, 18, 19, 82–83,
  269, 274–275
*Frontiers in Ecology and
  Environment*, 15

Galen, Russell, 100
Gertz, Emily, 195, 202, 203, 205,
  207, 209, 210, 212, 213, 217,
  274
Gewin, Virginia, 14–15, 21, 97,
  127, 186, 188, 218, 268–269
Glass, Stephen, 249
Goldberg, Natalie, 125, 128
Google Scholar, 41
Graduate school/degrees, 5

Grimm, David, 90–91, 92
Gross, Liza, 43–44

Hayden, Thomas, 12, 20–21, 43, 47, 75–76, 107–108, 110, 124, 127, 139, 162, 163, 186, 271
Health insurance
    Affordable Care Act, 206, 207, 208, 212
    finding coverage, 207
    medical expenses management, 210–211
    overview, 205, 206–211
    plan selection, 208–209
    terminology, 208–209
Helmuth, Laura, 90, 93, 94, 96, 97, 241, 242
High Country News, 61
Hinterthuer, Adam, 186, 188
Hoag, Hannah, 42, 43, 127, 161, 188, 260, 276, 277
Howard Hughes Medical Institute (HHMI), 250–251

Idea theft, 30
Ideas
    finding, 9–10, 12–22
    scientific conferences, 15–16, 22
    travel/hobbies and, 17–19, 22
Imagine (Lehrer), 248–249
Immortal Life of Henrietta Lacks, The (Skloot), 99
Institutes for Journalism and Natural Resources, 49
Insurance, 205–212
    See also specific types
Internships, 5–6, 218, 223, 250
Interviews
    anonymity and, 44, 50
    conducting, 43–44
    fact-checking during, 45
    number needed, 46
    "on/off record" terminology, 50

preparation for, 42–43
    questions list, 42–43, 49
    quotes and, 44
    recording, 45–46
Investigative Reporters and Editors meetings, 223, 225
Ioannidis, John, 21
IRA (Individual Retirement Account), 204
Irion, Robert, 11, 46
Isolation. *See* Loneliness

James, Clive, 151
Johnson, George, 81
Journals. *See* Academic journal system; *specific journals*

Kicker, 79–80, 85
Knight Science Journalism Fellowship, 225–226

Lamott, Anne, 151
Last Word on Nothing, The, 6, 280
Laurence, William L., 249
Lawsuits, 196, 231, 232–235
Layer cake style, 85
Lede, 28, 76, 79–80, 84, 85
Lede example, 83
Lehrer, Jonah, 248–249
Leigh, Bill, 252
Life insurance, 207
LLC (limited liability company), 196–197, 198–199
Loneliness
    café culture and, 138
    community examples and, 140, 279–280, 281–282
    coping with, 137–141
    social media and, 140–141
    tips summary, 141
Los Angeles Times, 16, 21, 84, 91, 224
Lubick, Naomi, 281

Marris, Emma, 140, 171, 181, 205, 271, 275, 276

Marshall, Jessica, 17, 18–19, 44, 79–80, 138, 189, 247

Mascarelli, Amanda, 20, 90, 120, 124, 152, 161, 181, 215–216

Mason, Betsy, 92, 93, 94

Maxmen, Amy, 253

Medicare taxes, 197, 198

Mejia, Robin, 16, 153, 218, 250, 276

Men's Journal, 34, 35

Mestel, Rosie, 91, 92

Moran, Susan, 7, 90, 177

Moynihan, Michael, 249

Multilancing
  benefits, 116, 120, 121
  challenges, 120–121
  description, 116–118
  selling your content, 118–120
  starting out, 117–119
  tips summary, 122

Narrative style, 85

National Association of Science Writers (NASW), 218–219, 225, 226, 235, 251–252, 254, 269

National Geographic, 34, 70, 145

National Geographic Adventure, 34, 35

National Public Radio (NPR), 117, 118, 119, 189

Nature, 13, 20, 25, 41, 63, 76, 90, 218, 234, 271, 275

Nelson, Bryn, 15, 65–66, 89–90, 95, 121, 128, 159, 160, 254, 263–264, 275

Networking
  conferences, 218–220
  overview, 215–221
  in person, 218–221
  press room, 219–220
  tips for introverts, 221

  tips summary, 222
  virtual networking, 216–218
  See also Social media

New Republic, 249

New Scientist, 16, 19, 30, 48, 72, 87, 224, 234

New York Observer, 252

New York Times, 81, 92, 150, 237, 249, 254

New Yorker, 143, 248, 249, 275

Nieman fellowship, 223, 226, 227

Nijhuis, Michelle, 7, 16–17, 30, 60–61, 68, 97, 141, 158, 179–180, 188–189, 225, 226, 227, 248, 280

Nordhaus, Hannah, 145–146

"Not for attribution," 50

Notes storage, 77–78, 170

Nut graf/billboard, 79, 84–85, 89

Obama, Barack, 17

Odds ratio, 57

"Off the record," 50

Office equipment
  chair/desk recommendations, 169
  overview, 167–174

Office location
  overview, 158–159, 170, 172–173
  spouse/partner and, 175, 177–178

"On background," 50

On Call in Hell (Hayden), 107

"On/off record" terminology, 50

OnEarth.org, 96

Online community groups
  examples, 140, 279–280, 281–282
  starting a group, 281–282

Open Notebook, The, 36, 280

Open Society Institute, 223, 224, 227

Oprah, 99

Ornes, Stephen, 7, 19–20, 79, 80, 158, 200, 202
Outside, 71

P-value, 56–57
Parenting, 165
Pearson, Helen, 25, 90, 91, 92, 93, 95
Percent vs. percentage points, 54–55
PIO (public information officer), 41–42, 220
Pitch
    conversation and, 26, 30–31
    disclosure and, 36, 38
    elements of, 23–24
    email attachments and, 29
    endurance/Antarctica expedition example, 33–35, 69
    feature pitch example, 37–38
    finding target, 27–29
    frequency, 31
    guidelines, 27
    low-risk proposition and, 25
    mistakes to avoid, 32–33
    news pitch example, 36–37
    outlet numbers, 31
    pay rates and, 28–29
    query letters, 23–24, 36–38
    research and, 25
    response and, 25–26, 29–30
    timing and, 29–30
    tips summary, 39
    writing process and, 75–76
PLOS Biology, 165, 218
Popular Science, 14, 226, 241
Portland Monthly, 21
Potts, Malcolm, 110
Powell, Kendall, 63, 76, 88, 95, 160, 184, 260, 270
Principal investigator, 40
Procrastination
    books that inspire, 128–129
    coping with, 125–130

creative procrastination, 124, 125, 129, 130
    deadlines and, 126–127
    distractive procrastination, 123, 124, 125, 126, 129–130
    friends/writing friends and, 128
    getting in the zone, 125–126
    list making and, 127
    no deadlines and, 129
    rewards and, 127–128
    tips summary, 132–133
    too much work vs., 130–132
Proposal. *See* Pitch
Public information officer (PIO), 41–42, 220
PubMed, 33, 41

Reconstructing stories, 64–66
Redford, Robert, 143
Rejection
    coping with, 142–143, 144–148
    reasons for, 143–144
Relative risk, 57
Reporting plan, 48
Reporting process
    controversies and, 46
    drafts and, 47, 51
    fact-checking, 47–48
    "Fear, The" and, 40
    investigative reporting, 46
    sources, 40–42, 48
    tips summary, 52
    See also Interviews
Research
    access, 63–64
    backup data, 62
    "big story," 70–71, 74
    diabetes in Tohono O'odham people example, 59–60
    digital recorders, 61–62
    downtime and, 61
    equipment and climate, 62
    historical roots and, 67–68
    note taking, 60–61

notes storage/sorting, 77–78, 170

personal history and, 68

photos/videos, 62, 65

reconstructing stories, 64–66

time investment, 68–70

tips summary, 73–74

visiting sources, 66–67

See also Travel funding

Retirement savings, 203–205

Rogers, Adam, 25, 87–88, 89, 90, 91–92

Rosner, Hillary, 19, 51, 78, 82, 104, 111, 151, 152–153, 179, 225–226, 260, 276

Roth IRA, 205

S Corp (corporation) business structure, 196–198, 199

Sasso, Anne, 45, 139, 159, 162, 180, 195, 202–203, 204, 205, 207, 209, 210, 211–212, 213, 220, 265, 269, 274

Savings

for emergencies, 212–213

retirement savings, 203–205

Schrope, Mark, 14, 17, 106–107, 184, 204, 244

Science, 13, 41, 90, 92, 119, 121, 254, 255

Science News for Kids, 225

Science Online conference, 219

Science writers

associations of, 8

backgrounds, 4–7

mission, 4

overview, 3–4

questions/answers, 5–6

recommendations for beginners, 6–8

Science Writers conference (2011), 251–252

ScienceNOW, 119

Scientific American, 67–68, 71, 246

Scientist, The, 15

SciLance community, 279–280

Seife, Charles, 100

SEP-IRA (Simplified Employee Pension Plan-Individual Retirement Account), 204–205

Seven Basic Plots, The (Booker), 77

Sex and War (Hayden and Potts), 107–108, 110

Shiffman, Ken, 227

Sierra magazine, 165, 220–221

Singh, Simon, 234

Skloot, Rebecca, 99

Skype, 169

Slate, 90, 93, 241

Smithsonian, 16, 34, 35, 60

Social media

benefits, 260–261

blogging, 6, 265–266, 280

norms, 259–260

online persona, 261–262

professional/personal balance, 262–263

reputation and, 259, 261–262

time management, 264–265

tips summary, 266

what not to share, 263–264

Social Security taxes, 197, 198

Sohn, Emily, 43, 62, 80, 84, 159, 160, 162, 181, 186, 190, 199–200, 224–225, 236, 255

Sole proprietor structure, 196

Soros Justice Media Fellowship, 224, 227

Sources

finding, 40–42

online databases, 41

statisticians, 55, 56

Standfirst/dek, 76

Statistical significance, 56

Statistics

explaining uncertainties, 53–54

overview, 53–58

Statistics (*continued*)
    terminology, 56–58
    tips summary, 58
Stories
    anatomy, 84–85
    elements of, 22
    topics vs., 10–11
Story styles
    magazine feature, 84–85
    newspaper, 84
Stover, Dawn, 241, 242
Success measuring, 154–155
Summers, Nick, 252

Tablet magazine, 249
Taubes, Gary, 252
Taxes
    business structure and, 195–196,
        197–199
    Medicare/Social Security taxes,
        197, 198
    quarterly payments, 196, 197,
        198, 202–203
Ted Scripps Fellowship, 226, 227
Telis, Gisela, 121, 160
*Thunder and Lightning: Cracking
    Open the Writer's Craft*
    (Goldberg), 128–129
Tolstoy, Leo, 76–77
Travel funding
    ethics and, 72, 248, 253–255
    nonprofit fellowships/grants, 72
    publication travel budgets,
        71–72, 254–255

Vacations
    balancing work/life, 162, 163–
        164
    working vacations with
        spouse/partner, 175, 180–182
Very Small Group (VSG), 281–282
Vidal, Gore, 152

VoIP applications, 169
Von Bubnoff, Andreas, 21

Walker, Cameron, 78, 80, 116,
    127–128, 150–151, 184, 254,
    261, 269
Wall Street Journal, 49
Washington Post, 253
Webb of Science, 265–266
Webb, Sarah, 17, 95, 96, 128, 139,
    159, 162, 176–177, 178, 251,
    273
Website, 172
Why We Get Fat (Taubes), 252
Wilde, Oscar, 175
Wine Spectator, 165
Wired/Wired.com, 25, 34, 64, 71,
    87, 92, 93, 146, 248
Workshops for science writing, 5
Writing Down the Bones (Goldberg),
    125
Writing process
    blueprint, 77–78
    drafts, 47, 51, 82–83
    hero, 77
    pitch and, 75–76
    publication's style and, 77,
        92–93
    skeleton, 79–80
    story type, 76–77
    tips summary, 86
    transitions, 81–82
    writing, 80–82
    See also Editors and writers
*Writing Tools: 50 Essential Strategies
    for Every Writer* (Clark),
    128–129

Yo-Yo Ma, 17

Zimmer, Carl, 83, 102, 104, 107,
    111